ROBIN EGGAR

DARING DAYS OUT

GW00691903

metro

First published in Great Britain in 1997
by Metro Books (an imprint of Metro Publishing Limited),
19 Gerrard Street, London W1V 7LA

© Robin Eggar

Robin Eggar is hereby identified as the author of this work
in accordance with Section 77 of the Copyright, Designs
and Patents Act 1988.

British Library Cataloguing in Publication Data. A CIP
record of this book is available on request from the British
Library.

ISBN 1 900512 09 2

10 9 8 7 6 5 4 3 2 1

Typeset by SX Composing DTP,
Rayleigh, Essex

Printed in Britain by Clays Ltd.
St. Ives plc

For Jordan and Rowan, may they continue to grow up adventurous.
As ever, to Jacqui.

ACKNOWLEDGEMENTS

Sophie Walker, who thought researching this was going to be easy but persevered nonetheless. Sebastian Woods-Walker who ably assisted her.

Photographers Michael Hoppen and Matthew Ford, who delighted in taking pictures of me in extemis.

Writing this book would not have been possible without the assistance of a great number of organisations, instructors and companies who gave their advice, time and expertise freely. If I have inadvertently missed anybody out (and forgotten, or misspelled surnames), my apologies, but special thanks are due to:
Guy Malpas and Matt at Bray Watersports; Philip Clark at The Balloon Company; Andy Shaw and Jeremy Maddox at Green Dragons; Baz and Sean at the National Surfing Centre, Fistral Beach; Laura Beglan at Thorpe Ski; Andy Archer at Jet Ski UK; Pat Ainge at Team Powerboating; George Atkins and Julian Clapham at the National Watersports Centre; Fort Bovisand Underwater Centre; Iain Jennings and John Thomas at Rocklea Activity Centre; Robert Hollings at Mayhem Sporting Events; Geoff Mayes; John Gorst and Alan at Wild Tracks; Paul Wilson at the Ford Motor Company; Prism Marketing; the staff at Silverstone Driving Centre; the staff at South Bank Bicycles for constantly repairing my bike; Mark Debenham and the staff of Adrenalin Village, London; Phil Philipps at Lasham Gliding Club; Pete Allum and the instructors at Headcorn Parachute School; Glenda Wild at Heli Air, Denham; Ian Callaghan and Ian Stokes at Moorland Flying Club; Alec Greening of the Brigsteer Bridgeswingers Club. Rockport for making brilliant boots.

Special thanks to: Julian Alexander and Kirstan Romano at Lucas Alexander Whitley. Susanne McDadd, Kate Todd, Cheryl Lanyon and David Furse-Roberts at Metro Publishing.

Cover photographs: front cover © Tony Stone Images; back cover © Matthew Ford.
Plate section photographs: ballooning © British School of Ballooning; bungee jumping © Michael Hoppen; zipwire © Matthew Ford; motocross and mountain biking © Robin Eggar; white-water rafting © Canolfan Tryweryn; 4x4 off-road driving and motor racing © The Ford Motor Company; gliding © Terry Joint; scuba diving © Benny Sutton; climbing © British Mountaineering Council; skydiving © Dougie Young; microlight flying © Ian Callaghan.

CONTENTS

INTRODUCTION 7

PART ONE: WIND 13

Windsurfing 13

Hang-gliding 28

Ballooning 41

PART 2: WATER 52

Jet skiing 52

Powerboat race training 61

Diving 70

Surfing 82

Water-skiing 94

White-water rafting 106

PART 3: EARTH 117

Caving and potholing 117

Climbing 127

Motocross 142

Motor racing 153

Mountain biking 164

Off-road driving 169

Paintball 179

PART FOUR: SKY 190

Bungee jumping 190

Gliding 199

Helicopters 211

Microlight flying 222

Skydiving 234

PART FIVE: EXTREME 245

Bridgeswinging 245

**MULTI-ACTIVITY
LISTINGS** 252

VOUCHERS 253

INTRODUCTION

Last summer I did a lot of flying, cycling, driving, swimming, sinking and climbing. I played with different elements: in wind, water, earth and sky. I spent a large proportion of my days in stomach-knotting apprehension, scared out of my wits, drenched to the skin, suffering motion sickness or having to get up while the rooster was still out cold. I came home bruised, scratched, bleeding from cuts, aching all over and too tired to focus on the telly. There are still times when my palms go sweaty, my eyes glaze over and my mind goes on a trip. Most of all, I remember falling and the fear of falling. I had a great time.

Daring Days Out – like many things – was born out of other people's dreams. Down the pub one lunchtime we were talking, as one does, about dreams, about the things we had always wanted to do. I had, still have, a burning ambition to go helicopter powder skiing in the Canadian Rockies; one man wanted to learn to climb; another who commutes up and down the M4 saw the jet skiers having fun every day and yearned to have a go; someone else wanted to windsurf; another to skydive. Nobody wanted to go caving, but it was recalled with a shudder how a very pretty office junior had said she thought it sounded brilliant. As the conversation rolled on to expose other more personal fantasies – yes, OK, we started to talk about sex – I realised that I didn't want to do just one of the adventure sports that had been discussed, I wanted to try them all. Even caving. So I did.

There are a lot of books available that cover individual adventure sports but they are written by experts, from their specialist points of view. And most experts cannot remember what it felt like when a 'v. diff' gritstone face looked unclimbable, or how keeping a hang-glider in the air for 5 seconds can be as exhilarating as cruising aloft for 5 hours at a time. It takes a lot of dedication, time and, frequently, money to become really good. Often, however, the most difficult thing of all is that very first step. We all have dreams, fantasies of flying, of surfing, of running a marathon, of kissing the girl next door. Going out to try the reality of that dream can be the hardest thing of all.

It doesn't have to be. One of the advantages of living on this small island is that almost everything is available within a 2-hour drive. One of the disadvantages is the weather – but more of that later. We are spoilt for choice. So stop fantasising and start acting. You never know what it is like until you have tried it.

What exactly is an adventure sport? Everyone has their own definition. To me, it is an activity, carried out by a relatively small number of people, which does not involve a ball, is only possible because of modern technological innovations, and would not have been conceivable before the late 20th century. And one that is considered dangerous.

It is the last category, the danger, that is most important. In general, adventure sports are perceived to be more dangerous than they actually are – driving a car, as everyone pointed out to me, is statistically far more dangerous. However, people do die skydiving, they fall off mountains, and gliders collide when they are circling in the same thermal. In the early days of microlighting, when the machines were little more than a hang-glider wing, a deck chair and a lawnmower engine with a propeller attached, there were a number of high-profile accidents that still haunt the image of the sport today (in fact, a modern microlight can withstand higher G-forces than a commercial jet liner). It's a rule of media life – when adventure sports go wrong, it's news.

After taking part in twenty-three of these activities I can state, hand on pounding heart, that my life was never in danger. My legs may have all but failed me, my stomach hatched more butterflies than a summer garden, my adrenal glands worked overtime, but my closest encounter with the Grim Reaper was a mouthful of polluted river water. Throughout I have been extremely impressed not only with the quality of instruction I have received but the tremendous stress all the instructors have placed on safety procedures.

There are a few 'adventure sports' that aren't included here for a variety of reasons. Early on, I decided to exclude sailing and horse riding. Both have been around for thousands of years and are very well catered for by other publications and facilities. I was going to go canoeing until I discovered that it would take a minimum of two days before I would be allowed anywhere near white water and that any adrenaline rush could be duplicated on a rubber raft. I chose flying a helicopter over a fixed-wing light aircraft, and hang-gliding over paragliding, from a combination of personal prejudice and the feeling that to do them all would duplicate experiences and make boring reading.

Ballooning, scuba diving and skydiving were the only three sports I had prior experience of, but I have written up those accounts from the notes I took at the time and updated the information. I have always intended to do another sky dive because it is one of my lasting regrets that I did not complete a full Accelerated Freefall Course. But, as time and deadlines have conspired against me, I am still waiting to do it again. Which reminds me, I don't do enough diving either. There's obviously a lesson here...

BE PREPARED

I do not wish to moan about the weather on this beautiful island of ours but most adventurous activities do rely on good weather. This can be most frustrating in Britain even, or rather especially, in that season we call summer. While researching this book, I've been becalmed by flat seas and grounded by heavy winds, it's been too wet to hang-glide and water-skiing in a thunderstorm is downright pointless.

Most of the activities I've covered take place in the late spring and summer months but you need to be aware that different sports flourish in different conditions. The first time I tried to go surfing it was a baking hot day and unfortunately the waves were non-existent. So I rushed off to go microlighting instead, whereupon the flight was cut short because of sharp, gusting winds. I could have saved myself a very long drive by making a couple of phone calls. Always call the night before, or first thing in the morning, to check it's actually going to happen before turning up.

All the activities I cover provide the necessary equipment for the first-time participant but you do need to take some basics. My all-eventuality bag included a swimming costume, a towel, a change of clothes and socks, a pair of walking boots, a pair of trainers that could get wet if necessary, a windproof/waterproof jacket, a fleece top and a good book. A quality pair of sunglasses is essential for flying, looking cool and hiding behind. Also take a cheque book as many centres don't take credit cards.

INSURANCE

The majority of adventure sports are now established enough to have either governing bodies or associations that oversee and, if necessary, enforce the requisite safety standards. In the listings I have omitted places not recognised by these central bodies and anywhere which does not have public liability insurance. This is required by law, though the amounts of cover can vary. What public liability means is that, if there is an accident as a result of the activity that could and should have been avoided by the instructor and/or the centre, the accident victim is covered. If, however, the accident occurs as a direct result of the victim ignoring safety procedures and instructions, or misleading the centre (for example by forgetting to mention a pre-existing medical condition), they can make no claim. In some cases the accident blame may be apportioned – for example, 70 per cent victim's fault, 30 per cent centre – and any subsequent payout divided accordingly.

Alec Greening, a qualified mountain guide and the man behind the Brigsteer Bridgeswingers Club (see page 245), also works for Allied Dunbar Assurance plc. I asked him to clarify the life insurance position. 'In general,' he explains, 'the official line is that if there was no intention on your part to take up a dangerous sport at the time you took out the policy and then subsequently you do so, the major life insurance companies will continue to cover you. If you take up an activity within a year, it is deemed that there was prior intention to do so.'

It is important to note that Alec is referring to the major life insurance companies. Fifty years ago climbers were often considered to be social outcasts, yet now rock climbing is no longer considered a dangerous sport. However, mountaineering, private aviation (flying anything), motor car and motor cycle racing and scuba diving (below 10m) are. According to the statistics, the most dangerous sport of all is horse eventing. It is possible to get life insurance coverage whatever activity you undertake but, the more dangerous it is perceived to be, the higher the premium will be.

Getting personal accident insurance is harder than getting life insurance. If you have private health insurance, make sure to check the fine print and look for the exclusions – while they may be very hard to find, rest assured they will be there. If in doubt, consult a broker. To arrange personal accident insurance, the best step, according to Alec Greening, is to call the governing body or umbrella organisation for your chosen activity. 'They should be able to steer you in the direction of a specific broker,' he says. 'The rule of thumb is that the more people do a sport, the easier it is to get cover.' The BMC (British Mountaineering Council) and the BHPA (British Hang-Gliding and Parachuting Association), for example, can put you directly in touch with brokers who specialise in personal accident policies for climbers and hang-gliders. The policies are out there but, the more arcane the sport, the more expensive they will be.

In the activity listings in this book (see the explanation below) insurance is mentioned only if special conditions apply, or there is some useful information to give, such as who can supply Personal Accident insurance for a particular sport, or if insurance is included in the cost of an activity. In the interests of brevity, the following initials are used for types of insurance: TPL – Third Party Liability; PA – Personal Accident; PL – Public Liability.

LISTINGS

At the end of each account of my personal experience of each activity are listings to help you find a place where you can try it out. For some activities – bungee jumping, white-water rafting, motor-racing schools, for instance – this was relatively easy as there aren't very many. For others, like climbing, scuba diving or windsurfing, there are literally hundreds of places to choose from. I have concentrated on a few of the biggest centres which are geared up to encouraging and teaching novices. The prices quoted, while correct at the time of going to press, may have changed. The booking details give an indication of how much advance warning the centre requires.

If there isn't somewhere nearby, call the national organisation I have listed and explain your needs to them. That is what they are there for. I do not list places that are not endorsed by their national organisations. If you call a place and don't like their attitude, don't let yourself be bullied or snowed-under by technical mumbo-jumbo. Always go to a place where you feel comfortable – that instinct is seldom wrong. In some cases I have also listed other avenues to explore, whether they be World Wide Web sites or dedicated magazines, which I have found particularly useful. There is also a separate listing for multi-activity centres (see page 252) that offer a variety of experiences for a weekend or a whole week. This is an ideal way to try several things out to see whether you like them.

AND FINALLY...

It is my intention and hope that *Daring Days Out* should regularly be updated and that I will be revising, rewriting my experiences and, above all, trying out new things in the years to come. I certainly want to try paragliding – with or without a motor attached to my back – while sand yachting on the beaches of Perranporth sounds both terrifying and exhilarating. I might even go down a cave again. Now I've started I don't want to finish.

I don't expect anyone to be crazy enough to do everything I've covered but I hope you will try at least one Daring Day Out. If you do and you have a good or bad experience at any adventure sports facility – not just the ones listed here – please fill in the form you will find at the back of the book and send it to the publisher. It is our intention to make this guide even better and more comprehensive in years to come, but to do that we need your help.

So now it's time to stop dreaming, stop talking about it, go out and do it. Go have a Daring Day Out.

PART ONE
WIND

WINDSURFING

Fortunately I was right down one end of Bray Lake – the wrong end, which was half the problem – so my screams of frustration, accompanied by a stream of obscenities, only disturbed a family of ducks. After 20 minutes in which I had travelled precisely nowhere except underwater, my arms were drained from hauling the mast out of the lake and my temper had snapped. Beating a windsurfing board with your fists and stamping on it is, I have to admit, very childish. I know it's not the board's fault I'm stuck again, but it made me feel better. Screaming was both release and relief and, after losing my self-control so absolutely, I knew that now I had to get it right or keep trying until either I or the wind cracked.

On my first session two days earlier it had all been so much easier. The wind had been a gentle 1 on the Beaufort Scale (1-3 knots) so sailing across that wind had not been too difficult – especially on the Hifly Revo, a large training board that is closer to a life raft than a speed machine. Today the wind was up to scale 4 (11-16 knots), ideal for the experienced board sailor but not for the tyro. My life was further complicated by being in the lee of a small island so the wind was not consistent, coming in gusts and eddies that were difficult to judge. Time after time, I hauled the mast up, got ready to sail and then a sudden gust wrenched the sail out of my hand and back into the water. Matt, my instructor, soon realised that I wasn't going anywhere – except incandescent – and sailed off back to the Bray Watersports Club House to get a smaller sail.

It would be just about possible to complete a Royal Yachting Association (RYA) Level 1 course in one day of private tuition – but only if the weather is kind. If the wind is too strong, no matter how fit you may be, hauling the mast out of the water is exhausting and tired people do not make good sailors. To spread the course over two days, preferably with a rest day in-between, makes sense. There is a lot of both practical and theoretical information to absorb. Learning to windsurf is not just about getting on a board and setting sail.

All beginners (at Bray they start as young as eight) wear a wetsuit, either wetsuit shoes or trainers, and a buoyancy aid. Getting into a soggy wetsuit is not much fun but it is better than freezing. Boards vary in length from 240 to 390cm but more important than length is the volume. A beginner or intermediate should look for a board with a reserve volume equal to their own weight. Reserve volume is the amount of buoyancy a board has left with you standing on it. For example, the sailor weighs 75kg, the rig, board and clothing add a further 28kg, giving a total of 103kg. Add the reserve of 75kg to give a total of 178 kg. The sailor should be looking at a board with at least 180 litres of volume.

The sail you use on the beginners' course is a soft type, without any battens, which lacks power and control in stronger winds and is around 5.5 square metres in size. For stronger winds you drop to 4.5 square metres.

– IT'S MUCH EASIER ON DRY LAND –

The first thing Matt shows me is how to rig the board which, given today's technology, is a simple enough process. Everything has technical terms, which will be familiar to sailors and alien to landlubbers. When rigging the sail, always keep your back to the wind. It may be useful to know how to tie lots of different knots but the 'Easyrig' cleats on the mast and the boom are extremely effective at holding the rope steady. A universal joint (which rotates through 360°) is attached to the bottom of the mast, which is then pushed in and clipped on to the mast foot.

Before I am allowed to enter the water Matt demonstrates everything on the simulator. He runs through all the positions and then lets me have a go. It's much easier on dry land. The first lesson on water is to get the feel of the board under foot, so I just paddle out (without the rig) and try to stand up. The object is always to keep your weight on the centre of the board, parallel with the dagger board (the keel). I've got a reasonable sense of balance so this doesn't appear to be too difficult – until I try to attach and pull up the rig.

I climb on to the centre of the board, knees either side of the mast, then it's up on to my feet and, leaning back slightly and bending my knees, I use my body weight and leg muscles (not my arms or back) to haul the rig up out of the water, using the uphaul rope. I transfer my hands to the mast and hold the sail at 90° to the board. My feet are shoulder-width apart on either side of the mast foot and I am now in the 'secure position'. Well, that's what they call it.

The next step is to try to sail on a 'beam reach' across the wind, at 90° to the wind direction. So with the wind on my back I release my back hand from the mast and place my rear foot behind the dagger board, pointing out. My front foot is just behind the mast, foot pointing forward. I grab the boom with my rear hand and then transfer my front hand to the front of the boom. Amazingly enough it works and I start to travel sedately across the water. When I have reached my destination I simply return the sail to the secure position, rotate the board through 180° and reverse the process. It sounds simple, but then the wind starts to make its presence felt.

It is not possible for any sailing craft to sail directly into the wind. It is possible to sail at an angle of approximately 45° on either tack. When sailing at 45° to the wind, the board is said to be close-hauled. So to make your way upwind a sailor has to zigzag, first sailing close-hauled on the port then on the starboard tack. The area in between the two close-hauled courses is the No Go Zone; if you end up in that – and I did many a time – the board will stop, the sail will start to flap and you will fall in.

In fact I'd been on the board for a full 30 minutes before I made my first splash. This was entirely due to my getting muddled up with the steering. To turn the front of the board towards the wind, you incline the rig towards the back of the board; to turn it away from the wind, you lean the sail forward. A windsurfer is not a motor boat, it takes time for the adjustments to take effect, so to begin with you are never quite sure whether you are doing the right thing. I was, but I panicked and did the opposite, so the board slowed to a halt and I got my first mouthful of the blue-green algae that inhabit Bray Lake.

After 80 minutes on the water the wind dropped to scarcely a breath, so my first session ended in a 'Full Self Rescue'. This involves sitting down on the board, detaching the mast and the boom clip, then releasing the ropes, rolling up the sail, sitting on the whole shebang and paddling in to shore. I don't doubt that it would be much more difficult in choppy sea conditions but I was surprised how easy it was, which can only help to increase confidence. Back on land, Matt goes through some more basic sailing theory, rules of the road (who gives way to whom) and I go home cock-of-the-board.

——— GYBING WITHOUT STYLE ———

The object of the second session, two days later, is to complete a simple triangular course which will involve tacking in both directions, sailing downwind (with the wind behind me) and gybing (swinging the sail across the front of the board). My feelings of confidence lasted all of 30 seconds, when a strong gust pulled the sail out of my hands. 'It's not your fault,' reassured Matt, 'the gusts are really strong and unpredictable here.' So began an hour of frustration: getting stuck in a bush, falling in, hauling the rig out of the water, being becalmed, turning the board into, rather than out of, the wind and being blown off the board backwards, running aground, hauling the rig out of the water, falling in again, hauling the rig out of the water again, having the rig wrenched out of my hands by a strong gust for the seventh time, losing my temper, upsetting the local wildlife, falling in again, beating the board with my fists, and sitting on the board sulking until Matt went and fetched the smaller sail.

While having a smaller sail made a lot of difference, it was the initial fighting with the bigger one that made it easier in the long run. After a couple of abortive goes and splashes, I got the rhythm right: tacking back and forth, preparing for big gusts by leaning further out and not being frightened of making my turns faster. The spit of land which had proved my nemesis for the past hour was soon passed and I got more and more confident, gritting my teeth and refusing to let the wind rip the sail from my grasp. I was moving at quite a lick, aiming to just miss a moored motorboat, when I was rammed from behind by a teenager fooling about. Matt was furious, snapping, 'Keep away from us'.

Eventually, while I tacked back and forth, Matt went off to set up the triangular course, which I completed without much style, and I did gybe the wrong way around the barrel after my downward reach. On the downward reach you have to have both feet back, on either side of the dagger board, and keep the mast vertical using the sail like a giant V in front of your face. You get to see where you are going by looking through the clear bit in the sail. By now I felt in control, my turns were sharper and I was leaning back into the wind. Once I even managed to go faster than the brat on the board who had rammed me. Stick that in your wetsuit, buster!

Today's theory was all about the tides, the wind and the weather. Ultimately, windsurfing is about going on the sea and in Britain, because we have such high and low tides, it is very important to be aware of all the safety aspects. Accidents can happen, but there is no excuse for not being prepared or letting other people know your sailing plans and intended time of return. I was impressed by the care the course places on that element as, at sea, risks must be minimised.

For me, the sea was still a way away. What I needed to do was practise more on the lake and then step up a gear. One final word of advice from the pros: if you want to learn to windsurf, keep hiring your gear until you are ready to buy. It'll be cheaper in the long run. That is what I aim to be doing next summer.

WHO TO CONTACT

Royal Yachting Association (RYA)
RYA House
Romsey Road
Eastleigh
Hampshire SO50 9YA

Tel: 01703 627400
Fax: 01703 629924

▶ The RYA is a massive organisation dating back to 1875 – right at the beginning of organised racing. Despite its name, its role is to develop boating under sail and power, in all its recreational and competitive forms.

▶ The RYA has 78,000 personal members, 1,340 member clubs, 160 affiliated classes and 1,500 recognised teaching establishments. It has a 55-strong council and a series of expert committees, all of which are operated by volunteers. RYA House has 70 full time staff, handles 800 calls and 900 pieces of mail each day and is subdivided into different categories. So if you are inquiring about sailing don't speak to the guy in charge of powerboating.

▶ The RYA sets minimum safety standards and runs high-quality training schemes for beginners through to instructors, as well as programmes designed specifically for schools. Every year over 120,000 people complete RYA training courses in sail cruising, dinghy sailing, motor cruising, sports boats or windsurfing.

▶ The RYA annual membership fee of £19 includes free third party insurance cover, free allocation of sail numbers, an RYA Visa card (with no annual fee) as well as special discounts on insurance, hospital and medical care and car rental. There are currently over 9,000 windsurfing members – nearly 12 per cent of the total.

▶ At present, there are 264 RYA recognised windsurfing centres offering the RYA National and Junior Windsurfing schemes. These centres operate to standards set by the RYA and are inspected annually. The Junior scheme is a national scheme for 8-14 year-olds: three levels of award take youngsters from beginners to a planing competence; and 250 RYA approved centres operate the National Windsurfing scheme, which takes you through five levels of competence.

WHERE TO GO

Company:	**Bray Watersports**
Address:	Monkey Island Lane, Windsor Road, Maidenhead, Berks SL6 2EB
Tel:	01628 38860
Fax:	01628 771441
Facilities:	Shop, hot and cold snacks, hot drinks. Hot showers; changing facilities; toilets. Company days; gift vouchers.
Price Range:	RYA level 1 £69. Private tuition £20 per hour.
Payment Methods:	Cash, cheque, Visa, Access
Booking Details:	In summer, and at weekends, books some weeks in advance due to heavy demand from children
Capacity:	No more than six per course
Insurance:	TPL
Other Notes:	Open 09.00-dusk, seven days a week. Closed Christmas and New Year and during the week of the Boat Show in January. Also: dinghy sailing, junior courses

Company:	**Loch Insh Watersports Centre**
Address:	Loch Insh, Kincraig, Inverness-shire PH21 1NU
Tel:	01540 651272
Fax:	01540 651208
Price Range:	Introductory 2-hour course (min 4) adult £19, child (under 13) £15.50; private instruction (min 3) £15 per hour, 2-day course. Low season £49, £84 (inc B&B, packed lunch), £97 (full board). High season £55/91/103. Call for prices on 5-day course.
Payment Methods:	Cash, cheque, major credit cards
Booking Details:	As far in advance as possible

Capacity: 80 beds and chalets

Insurance: First £10 of any loss or damage to equipment is responsibility of the hirer.

Facilities: Insh Hall lodge and Loch Insh chalets available for accommodation. Licensed restaurant; changing rooms; showers and toilets; gift/equipment shop; disabled access arrangements; corporate events organised.

Other Notes: Also: sailing, canoeing, mountain biking, salmon fishing, dry slope skiing, skiing (winter only!). Sport-a-day holidays by arrangement.

Company: **Lochore Meadows Windsurfing School**

Address: Lochore Meadows Country Park, Crosshill, By Lochgelly, Fife, KY5 8BA

Tel: 01592 860264

Price Range: Beginner lesson (2 hours) £25; RYA Level 1 (12 hours) £70; juniors (age 6-16) £6 for 90 mins. Group discounts.

Payment Methods: Cheque, cash

Booking Details: 2 days

Capacity: 20 maximum

Facilities: Local B&B; café; changing rooms, showers and toilets on-site; equipment shop; gift vouchers and corporate events organised.

Other Notes: Bring own shoes. Open Apr-Oct, weather permitting.

Company: **Rossendale Waterpark**

Address: Clowbridge Reservoir, Burnley Rd., Clowbridge, Burnley, Lancs

Tel: 01282 412965

Price Range: Taster £30; RYA Level 1 £70 (over 2 days)

Payment Methods: Cash, cheque, Visa, Mastercard

Booking Details: 2 weeks in advance

Capacity: 10-12 per course

Facilities: On-site catering in summer, in winter on demand only. Changing rooms, showers, toilets and rest room. Equipment sold at Moby Dick's shop. Corporate events organised and gift vouchers available.

Other Notes: Open all year round for lessons and courses.

Company: Surface Watersports
Address: Whitwell Watersport Centre, Rutland Water, Whitwell, Empingham, Leics LE15 8QS
Tel: 01780 460632
Fax: 01780 460632
Price Range: Taster £18; RYA Level 1 £75; private tuition £15 + equipment hire (£8.50)
Payment Methods: Cash, cheque, Visa, Access, Switch, Delta
Booking Details: 1 week in advance
Capacity: 6-12 per course
Facilities: Shop, café/restaurant, bar, changing rooms, showers, toilets. Gift certificates.
Other Notes: Also: sailing, powerboat to RYA certification, canoeing to BCU certification. Lessons Mar-Oct.

Company: Tallington Lakes
Address: Tallington Lakes, Barolm Road, Tallington, Tamford, Lincs PE9 4RJ
Tel: 01778 346573
Price Range: Water ski (cable tow) from £13.50 per 20 mins; coaching tow £18.
Jet ski from £10.25 for 20 mins. Windsurfing from £8 per 20 mins. Membership and launch fee details on request.
Payment Methods: Cash, cheque, Access, Visa
Booking Details: Apr-Oct, 7 days a week, 10.00 till dusk
Capacity: Water size: 8 lakes, 160 acres
Facilities: Local accommodation, camping. Changing rooms, showers, toilets. Hot and cold food, club house, bar, gear shop. Corporate entertaining and gift vouchers.
Other Notes: Offers: Jet ski, water-skiing, windsurfing, sailing, canoeing, sail boards, dry ski slope, wake boarding, knee boarding, aqua sausage rides.

Company: The Outdoor Trust
Address: Windy Gyle, 30 West St, Belford, Northumberland NE70 7QE
Tel: 01668 213289 / 01665 721241
Price Range: Beginners £12 half-day, £24 full day; multi-activity £24 per day
Payment Methods: Cash, cheque
Booking Details: 4 weeks

Capacity:	15 windsurfing; 40 accommodation; 60 multi-activity
Facilities:	Accommodation available (40). Catering facilities, changing rooms, showers and toilets all on-site. Corporate events and gift vouchers can be arranged.
Other Notes:	Formerly the Bearsports Outdoor Centres. Also: sea and river kayaking, climbing, abseiling, cliff jumping, gorge walking, management training; windsurfing, both inland and coastal.

Company:	**Waterfront Sports**
Address:	The Seafront, Exmouth, Devon EX8 2AY
Tel:	01395 276599
Fax:	01395 225335
Price Range:	Taster £20; RYA level 1 (2 days) £50
Payment Methods:	Cash, cheque, Access, Visa, Switch, Delta
Booking Details:	2-3 days
Capacity:	2-6 per class
Facilities:	Locally available accommodation from camping to hotels. Café nearby. Changing rooms, showers and toilets at estuary site. Easy on-site parking. Corporate water activity sessions organised.
Other Notes:	Also: boogie boards, surf skis and banana rides.

Company:	**West Wales Windsurfing and Sailing**
Address:	Dale, Nr Haverfordwest, Pembrokeshire SA62 3RB
Tel:	01646 636642
Fax:	01646 636642
Price Range:	Half-day £39; day £55 (non-residential); weekends £99 (non-res), £149 (res), full-board residential course £439
Payment Methods:	Cash, cheque, Visa, Access
Booking Details:	As far in advance as possible, 7-10 days usually possible
Capacity:	Up to 40
Insurance:	Optional on booking form, call for details
Facilities:	Local B&B and hotels. Gift vouchers.
Other Notes:	Also: dinghy, catamaran sailing, canoeing, water-skiing, mountain biking, juggling, kites, surfing.

Company:	**Wight Water Adventure Sports**
Address:	19 Orchardleigh, Shanklin, Isle of Wight, PO37 7NP
Tel:	01983 866269
Fax:	01983 866269
Price Range:	Surfing and windsurfing £12 per 90-min lesson, 5 lessons for £55
Payment Methods:	Cash, cheque
Booking Details:	1 week in high summer, groups 4-6 weeks in advance
Capacity:	1 instructor to 8 students; up to 20 surfers; 50 body boarders
Facilities:	Local accommodation. Café and changing rooms on-site, toilets nearby. Cliff-top public car park. Disabled catered for by arrangement.
Other Notes:	Season: Apr-Sept, 7 days a week, evenings by arrangement. Lessons 10.00-13.00; 14.00-17.00. Also: sailing, canoeing, archery, rifle shooting, orienteering, mountain biking (groups only).

Company:	**Aquasports Company**
Address:	Mercers Country Park, Nutfield Marsh Road, Nutfield, Nr Redhill, Surrey RH144E
Tel:	01737 644288
Fax:	01737 645869
Price Range:	RYA level 1 £65; children £50
Payment Methods:	Cash, cheque, Visa, Access, Mastercard
Booking Details:	2 weeks adult; 3 weeks children
Capacity:	150 students per day (all activities)
Facilities:	Corporate entertaining; gift vouchers; local B&B; catering and shower/toilet facilities; disabled toilet facilities; retail shop; parking.
Other Notes:	Also: dinghy, canoe courses.

Company:	**Ardclinis Activity Centre**
Address:	High Street, Cushendell, Co Antrim, Northern Ireland BT44 0NB
Tel:	012667 71340
E-mail:	ardclinis@aol.com
Price Range:	£30 per day
Payment Methods:	Cash, cheque
Booking Details:	Essential to book in advance, 2-4 months ahead

Capacity:	Groups of 4-12; high instructor/student ratio promised
Insurance:	PA insurance included in course fee
Facilities:	Team development groups, varied local accommodation, limited parking.
Other Notes:	Also: mountain climbing; powerboat handling two day courses; mountain biking, rafting, gorge walking, Canadian canoeing. Open all year. Ardclinis is the first commercial centre in NI and is situated in the Glens of Antrim, close to Belfast.

Company:	**Plas Menai Watersports Centre**
Address:	Llansfairisgaer, Caernarfon, Gwynedd LL55 1UE
Tel/Fax:	01248 670964
Price Range:	14 different courses ranging from 2-day courses £87 (non-residential), £128 (residential), to 5 days £216/308
Payment Methods:	Cash, cheque, may have credit card facilities in summer 1997
Booking Details:	Last-minute bookings considered but book as early as possible for popular courses
Capacity:	80 people maximum residential
Facilities:	Management courses, team-building courses, company days out etc. Facilities include fitness room; swimming pool; climbing wall; bar; TV lounge; recreation room and pleasant grounds.
Other Notes:	Also: dinghy sailing, canoeing, powerboating, climbing and walking

Company:	**Calshot Activities Centre**
Address:	Calshot Spit, Fawley, Southampton, SO45 1BR
Tel:	01703 892077
Fax:	01703 233063
Price Range:	Windsurfing £45 taster; introductory weekend £105 (non-res), £120 (res)
Payment Methods:	Cash, cheque, Visa, Access
Booking Details:	2-3 weeks
Capacity:	6 students per course
Facilities:	Accommodation, catering facilities, changing rooms, showers and toilets; shop; parking. Adequate access for disabled (on level). Corporate events organised.
Other Notes:	Also: dinghy sailing, canoeing, dry slope skiing,

mountain biking, climbing, archery, rifle shooting. Climbing courses available on indoor walls and Dorset sea cliffs (prices on application). Children from 10 years.

Company:	**Coverack Windsurfing Centre**
Address:	Cliff Cottage, Coverack, Helston, Cornwall TR12 6SX
Tel:	01326 280939
Price Range:	Day £3; taster weekend £95 (accommodation inc), £60 (accom non-inc); week course £250/175
Payment Methods:	Cash, cheque
Booking Details:	2-4 weeks but always worth a call
Capacity:	Max 12 per course, instructor ratio 1:6
Insurance:	Accident/cancellation may be available through centre
Facilities:	Youth Hostel (res and non-res). Changing rooms, shower, toilets. Disabled: contact to discuss. Corporate events organised.
Other Notes:	Open sea and inland reservoir for when sea is too rough; both locations with lifesaving facilities. Also free use of surf skis and RYA-approved powerboat handling courses. Courses beginning Apr-end Oct. Robin Hobson has been teaching windsurfing courses for 16 years and insists on 'keeping it small and personal so that in a week's course we can get a complete beginner close to Level 3'.

Company:	**Grafham Water Centre**
Address:	Perry, Huntingdon, Cambridgeshire PE18 0BX
Tel:	01480 810521
Fax:	01480 812739
Price Range:	RYA Level 1: full weekend £107.50 (inc all meals and accommodation). Shorter weekend £75.
Payment Methods:	Cash, cheque, major credit cards
Booking Details:	Early bookings recommended
Capacity:	Up to 60 beds – check for non-residents
Insurance:	Cancellation insurance available for £5
Facilities:	Residential centre with dormitory-style single and double rooms; changing rooms; showers and toilets; catering facilities and bar; gift/equipment shop; parking. Disabled access. Corporate events, conference centre, development training.

Other Notes: Also: dinghy sailing, national powerboat certificate courses, canoeing, RYA instructor training, archery.

Company: **Haven Sports**
Address: Marine Road, Broad Haven, Haverfordwest, Pembrokeshire SA62 3JR
Tel/Fax: 01437 781354
E-mail: havensports@netwales.co.uk
See page 91 (surfing) for details

Company: **National Water Sports Centre**
Address: Adbolton Lane, Holme Pierrepont, Nottingham, NG12 2LU
Tel: 0115 982 1212
Fax: 0115 945 5213
See page 116 (white water rafting) for details

Company: **Outdoor Adventure**
Address: Atlantic Court, Widemouth Bay, Nr Bude, Cornwall EX39 1NG
Tel: 01288 361312
Fax: 01288 361153
Price Range: Weekend £143; day £45
Payment Methods: Visa, Access
Booking Details: Gets fully booked July and August, so book 1-2 months in advance
Capacity: 20
Facilities: Accommodation for up to 27, bar, entertainment.
Other Notes: Season: end Mar-end Oct. Open: 09.30-17.00.

Company: **Poole Harbour Boardsailing**
Address: 284 Sandbanks Road, Lilliput, Poole, Dorset BH14 8HH
Tel: 01202 700503
Price Range: Taster: prices on application; RYA Level 1 £49; private tuition £20 per hour. Also, group tuition and instructor courses.
Payment Methods: Cash, cheque, Visa, Mastercard, Switch, Delta
Booking Details: 7-10 days in advance
Capacity: 6 per course, min 2 courses per day in high season

Facilities: Teaching facility includes changing rooms, showers and simulator. Café, hotels and B&B nearby.

Company: **Rickmansworth Windsurfing and Canoeing Centre**
Address: The Aquadrome, Frogmore Lane, Rickmansworth, Herts WD3 2DH
Tel: 01923 771120
Fax: 01923 771120
Price Range: Taster sessions from £5; £91 for junior multi-activity weeks; £67 for Level 1 (can be done in 1 day or over weekend).
Payment Methods: Cash, cheque, Visa, Access
Booking Details: 1 week+ in summer; 2-3 days in winter
Capacity: Up to 70 on multi-activity days; 60 boards, 100 rigs
Facilities: Corporate days out and team-building. Equipment shop, changing rooms, showers. Local accommodation available: 2 hotels and various B&Bs. 35-acre lake, 250 acres of land.
Other Notes: Also: canoeing, climbing and abseiling.

Company: **Dacre Windsurfing**
Address: Dacre Lakeside Park, Brandesburton, Driffield, Yorkshire, YO25 8SA
Tel: 01964 543704 / 01964 542372 (close season)
Price Range: Introductory course (daily at 11.00 and 14.00) £22; RYA level 1 (2 x 4 hours) £50; RYA level 2 (4 hours) £50
Payment Methods: Cash, cheque
Booking Details: 2-3 weeks in advance
Facilities: Corporate entertaining; gift vouchers. Local B&B; bar snacks; toilet and shower facilities, and for the disabled; parking; camping; windsurfing accessory shop.
Other notes: Open 1 Mar-31 Oct. RYA level 1 and 2 instruction only.

HANG-GLIDING

Thank God the Stubby has wheels. Tim and I are absolutely shattered from lugging the damn thing up the hill, taking it in turns to push and pull up beyond the windsock, trying to sneak an extra 10m each time just so we can squeeze a few more precious seconds in the air. It isn't like this in the movies when hang-glider pilots launch themselves from mountain tops to soar like giant eagles through the sky. That is what our instructor, Jeremy Maddox, can do and when he languidly tells you of five-hour flights, while you are gasping to get your breath back it is, frankly, rather irksome.

Tim and I have managed to steal an extra 100m uphill from the second windsock without Jeremy noticing, so we've made it a third of the way up the hill. Right on the top are two other 'wannabes' who are close to completing their Club Pilot Course as well as half a dozen paragliders who all spend a lot more time aloft than either Tim or I. Enough griping, I think, as I slip into the harness, pull on the helmet and prepare to take off for the fifth time this morning. Tim lifts the Stubby's nose, I clip the carabiner into both the main and back-up harnesses hanging from the keel. I lie prone, suspended two hand-widths above the crossbar, the harness is secure so I'm not going to fall to my death from 4m up. Tim holds the nose up a bit higher; feet behind the crossbar I place both my shoulders inside the tube triangle, arms straight down, hands gripping the tube, palm towards me.

It feels very uncomfortable and I know I look like a farmyard rooster trying to take off. I still don't really believe that this thing will fly. Jeremy tells me to fix my gaze on my target – the tree on the other side of the field. I start to run, take two or three steps and I can feel the weight of the glider lift off my shoulders. 'Change to

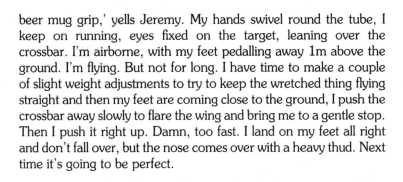

beer mug grip,' yells Jeremy. My hands swivel round the tube, I keep on running, eyes fixed on the target, leaning over the crossbar. I'm airborne, with my feet pedalling away 1m above the ground. I'm flying. But not for long. I have time to make a couple of slight weight adjustments to try to keep the wretched thing flying straight and then my feet are coming close to the ground, I push the crossbar away slowly to flare the wing and bring me to a gentle stop. Then I push it right up. Damn, too fast. I land on my feet all right and don't fall over, but the nose comes over with a heavy thud. Next time it's going to be perfect.

PERFECT CONDITIONS

The conditions, Jeremy had assured us, were ideal for our first day. Which made a change. I was getting tired of dragging myself out of bed before 7am to call Green Dragons to find out whether we were flying today. Rain and thunderstorms had kiboshed yesterday but now we had virtually no wind blowing up the natural bowl in the lee of the North Downs, within walking distance of their office. The Green Dragons operates from a farm just 10 miles south of Croydon. It was initially set up in 1974 as an army cadet force by former Para Les Shaw. Along with his two sons, Mike and Andy, he had spent time with the Red Devils Free Fall team. Originally, the Green Dragons concentrated on the emerging sport of paragliding – chief instructor Andy Shaw is the current British and former World, European and Army Paragliding Accuracy Champion – and in 1994 it amalgamated with the Skywings Sports Hang-Gliding Centre.

Paragliding is easier to learn than hang-gliding, you can launch from higher up earlier on, fly for longer much sooner and the equipment is much less heavy to carry. But experienced hang-glider pilots can operate in much higher winds and have more scope. Tim and I agreed we'd rather do it the hard way. He's a bathroom fitter from Billericay in Essex who has yearned to hang-glide for years. 'I did a couple of days of a course a few years back, Rob,' he admits, 'but then I bought a house and it just drifted away. This time I'm going to complete the EPC (Elementary Pilot's Course) and eventually get my own glider.'

—— TOGETHER ON A STUBBY ——

Since I first saw it back in the 1970s, the idea of hang-gliding has appealed to me but somehow circumstances had always conspired to prevent me realising that dream. The first two generations of gliders seemed prone to disaster – or maybe what accidents there were always got reported. Then a friend of a friend, who was an ace pilot, was 200 feet up when his glider disintegrated; he survived but spent nine months in hospital, so I put if off again. These days, the technology has been developed and refined to the extent that 99 per cent of accidents are due to pilot error.

The Stubby on which we are learning is a third-generation glider. It is a safe, tough training machine. It is also heavy and we are grateful that it has wheels fitted. (The latest fifth-generation machines are much lighter and more sophisticated, with wing tips and sails that can give a maximum forward speed of 70mph.)

Before we set out to fly, Jeremy takes us into the classroom and gives us a briefing about what to expect. He talks about the principles of flying, of lift, ridge soaring and thermals, and what to expect from the day, how we need to attain forward speed of 12-15mph to take-off; how we always take off and land into the wind. 'The object is to get a smooth take-off, glide in a straight line and land safely,' he says, firmly ending my premature delusions of soaring turns and long glides. Then he takes us to the store room. The Stubby comes in a bag about 4m long which is strapped atop the roof rack on Jeremy's ageing Metro. We drive to the launch site and set about assembling the glider.

Within 10 minutes, not helped by my faffing about trying to insert the wrong length batten into the wing, we have a machine made of steel tubing and wires, resting on two dinky wheels, that is supposed to be able to fly. Were the wings made of paper not of nylon, we could be with the Wright Brothers at Kittyhawk – except that the sail wing used on a hang-glider was originally developed by Frances Rogallo as a means of recovering space vehicles. Before going any further, we must check the whole glider over using the mnemonic SWANK (Sail, Wires, Airframe, Nuts and bolts, Kingpin).

The sail is checked for any large tears; the wires and their connections must not be worn; the tubing that makes up the airframe must not be bent – particularly at the leading edge (the front of the wing) – the nuts and bolts all tight; while the kingpin (which protrudes above the sail over the A frame and control bar) must be secure. Then it's time to climb the hill for the first time.

—————— UP AND DOWN ——————

Standing at the launch point looking down the hill, it looks very easy. Wearing the harness and helmet and attached to the glider, it looks very steep and very frightening. Those first few steps are a leap of faith and, if you look down, your faith will not be rewarded. The natural reaction once the weight of the glider leaves your shoulders is to stop running; it is a false take off and you have to keep on running especially as there is very little wind. On our first goes, both Tim and I make that mistake – as a result our flights are mercifully brief.

Soon, however, we have gained confidence, so much so that Jeremy attaches two ropes to the glider. One is to the top of the kingpin, the other to the nose. This enables him to help us take off – pulling the kingpin rope pulls the wing up – or stop quickly by pulling the nose down. This also means he has to run down the slope after us, and for some reason he doesn't seem to want to help us to push the Stubby back up again. I'm getting good take-offs while Tim is getting better landings; a couple of times I actually get 8m in the air and have time to make a couple of quick corrections to my direction but, inevitably, I end up turning too far right and landing at an angle. However, I am landing on my feet and, cockily, I decide to put on my shorts.

For the first day we are holding on to the uprights on the A frame (not the crossbar, which allows you to lie in the prone position more easily). You change direction by weight shifting: shift weight left and you turn left, but the glider does not respond instantly and, with only a few seconds in the air, this can be a bit scary. The slower your air speed, the less control you have.

My sixth flight starts badly and gets worse. When changing my grip, my right hand slips off the frame, I keep on running but my body is too far over the crossbar, with the result that I don't get airborne for a long time. Jeremy pulls the rope back and I get airborne but I've lost confidence; I'm flying too slowly to control my direction of turn. Coming in to land, I flare too soon, gain height and come in to land on my stomach. That doesn't hurt but my landing site does. I cruise to a gentle halt travelling all the way through a large bed of extremely virulent stinging nettles. My legs were still stinging and itching two days later. That's hubris for you.

THE TURNING-POINT

With hindsight, that is the turning-point of my day. I never get my landings right again, while Tim is taking off well, getting good roll control and travelling in a straight line for much further. As the afternoon wears on, the wind speed increases and the direction changes. After waiting for 20 minutes wearing the harness and helmet, we have to pull the glider to a different launch site. Somewhere in the transfer my bottle goes. My first take off is OK but, once flying, instead of pulling the bar in towards me, I push it away. Now I am going too slowly to initiate turns quickly enough; I come in to land but as my feet brush the ground, I realise that the ground is dropping away; I gain a bit more altitude but take too much of a right turn, over-compensate and land safely on my knees.

Jeremy tells me to pull the crossbar in more once I have taken off. I go for it, but the wind has dropped this time and so I maintain a forward speed 3ft off the ground and narrowly avoid a forest of nettles 6ft high. I claim an extra flight for an aborted take off. Unfortunately, if my last flight was a farce, this one is a débâcle.

I gain height quickly and easily, the glider is winging round to the right. I shift weight to my left and hear Jeremy shouting, 'Left, left'. I hear him and, for a reason I still cannot account for, I panic and shift my weight right. The glider turns sharp right and I crash wing tip first into the hill. I am fine – fine and furious – hurling my helmet to the ground and screaming obscenities. Once he realises I am OK and only my pride is injured, Jeremy shows much more concern for the glider. The end tube on the leading edge of the right wing is bent out of shape. There will be no more flying today.

It's 5pm and starting to drizzle. Tim tries to console me. 'Bad luck mate, you should end today on a high.' Instead it's a low. Jeremy tells me we have both done very well and not to worry. My legs are still stinging like crazy. I am really pissed off.

This is how I spent my first day hang-gliding. I got up before 7am and drove through rush-hour traffic. Tim and I spent 6 hours or 360 minutes on the ground, pushing and pulling this superannuated kite up a hill, or sitting down to recover. In total, we each spent approximately 120 seconds in the air. My ego was severely dented and my legs were in agony.

Would I do it again? In a flash. Not maybe, *definitely*. I really enjoyed it. I'd do it again tomorrow. Except this time I'll keep my trousers on.

WHO TO CONTACT

The British Hang-Gliding and Paragliding Association
The Old Schoolroom
Loughborough Road
Leicester LE4 5PJ

Tel: 0116 261 1322
Fax: 0116 261 1323

► **The BHPA is the national organisation that governs, promotes, represents and co-ordinates this type of flying in the UK. It also licenses flying schools and coaching clubs to ensure that newcomers to the sport receive the safest, most professional training possible, monitoring all registered schools for the safety and quality of the training they offer and the equipment they hold.**

► **The BHPA will provide you, for £3, with a full information pack, a directory of clubs and schools, a membership application form and a copy of *Skywings*. The directory of schools is reasonably comprehensive and differentiates clearly between paragliding (the more popular branch of the sport now) and hang-gliding, and between full- and part-time schools. Full-time schools are the most likely to** be able to accommodate your needs, but make sure that any school you join is currently BHPA registered.

▶ Membership (Training Member £29, Annual Member £59) provides a subscription to the monthly *Skywings* magazine, third party liability insurance cover to protect you, and they can put you directly in touch with brokers to arrange personal accident cover, kit and travel insurance. Or contact directly, Yvonne Jukes, Airports Insurance Bureau, 48 Alexandra Rd, Cowes, Isle of Wight, PO31 7JT Tel: 0983 298480 (24 hours).

——————— WHERE TO GO ———————

Company:	**Green Dragons**
Address:	Warren Barn Farm, Slines Oak Road, Woldingham, Surrey CR3 7HN
Tel:	01883 652666
Fax:	01883 652600
Price Range:	Hill Fun Day £69; Elementary Pilot Course £270; Club Pilot £230 + £10 per day glider hire
Payment Methods:	Cash, cheque, Visa, Access, Switch
Booking Details:	2-4 weeks in advance
Insurance:	£8 per day for £1 million TPL; PA cover available but contact office 2 weeks in advance
Facilities:	Camping and B&B on farm. Tea, coffee, juices, sweets and snacks. Toilets and showers – campers have washroom block; shop; classroom. Corporate events and large groups organised (part of multi-activity). Gift vouchers – 'surprise one-day fun-day'.
Other Notes:	Green Dragons is best known for Paragliding, as it was started by former Red Devils back in 1974. In 1994 it amalgamated with Skywing Sports Centre. Chief hang-gliding instructor Russ Crowley has been teaching the sport since 1980.

Company:	**Sheffield Hanggliding and Paragliding**
Address:	Cliffside, Church St, Tideswell, Derbyshire SK17 8PE
Tel/Fax:	01298 872313
E-mail:	101333.3065@compuserve.com

Facilities:	Local B&Bs; classrooms; equipment store; toilets; tea, coffee and snacks available. Corporate entertaining; gift vouchers
Price Range:	2 day £85; EPC £195 (5 days); CPC £195
Payment Methods:	Cash, cheque
Booking Details:	2 weeks
Capacity:	15 maximum; 4 gliders
Insurance:	PA can be arranged through BHPA
Other Notes:	Paragliding (£100 for 2-day taster; £200 for Student Pilot Course). Taster courses are run Mon, Tues and some weekends. 60 per cent of courses are hang gliding as 'The Peak District is the Centre of the Universe for British hang-gliding – Scotland and Wales may have better hills but they have worse weather'. Winch towing for hang-gliders will be available from the spring but only for CPC students.

Company:	**High Adventure Hang Gliding and Paragliding Centre**
Address:	Yarborough House, Nettlecombe Lane, Whitwell, Isle of Wight, PO38 2QA
Tel:	01983 730075
Fax:	01983 731441
E-mail:	phil@highad2.demon.co.uk
Facilities:	8 bedrooms; restaurant; bar; equipment shop; corporate entertaining; gift vouchers.
Price Range:	£60 per day; weekend £115; Elementary Pilot Course £260; Club Pilot Course £260
Payment Methods:	Cash, cheque, all major credit cards
Booking Details:	Summer: 3 weeks in advance
Capacity:	6-8 hang-gliding course; 16 paragliding
Insurance:	BHPA membership (inc TPL £4 per day)
Other Notes:	Paragliding (£59 per day; £110 per weekend; SPC £250).

Company:	**Icarus School of Hang Gliding**
Address:	Hollybank, 507 Pennistone Road, Shelley, Huddersfield, HD8 8HY
Tel:	01484 841213 / 01484 604289
Price Range:	Taster £55 (+ insurance); Elementary Pilot Course £225 (+ ins); Club Pilot £50 per day (+ ins)
Payment Methods:	Cash, cheque

Booking Details:	Weather determines day; week in advance in peak periods
Capacity:	Up to 20
Insurance:	Insurance £8 per day TPL; can arrange PA if required
Facilities:	Local accommodation, café. Gift vouchers available.
Other Notes:	Open 364 days. School started in 1995; they also arrange holidays in Lanzarote (winter) and France (summer) where the speciality is long, cross-country courses and thermal flying.

Company:	**Pennine Hang Gliding Centre**
Address:	50, Dobrudden, Baildon Moor, Baildon, Shipley, BD17 5EE
Tel:	01274 531710 / 0585 482073
Price Range:	Fun taster £55; 2-day £95; 5-day EPC £200
Payment Methods:	Cash, cheque
Booking Details:	1-4 weeks
Insurance:	Must join BHPA
Facilities:	Local accommodation can be arranged. Fly on Baildon Moor, lunch in local pub or tea shop.
Other Notes:	Always check before 08.30 for flying conditions.

Company:	**Sky Systems Ltd.**
Address:	Edburton, Nr Henfield, West Sussex BN5 9LL
Tel:	01273 857700
Fax:	01273 857722
E-mail:	skyinfo@skysystems.co.uk
Price Range:	1-day taster £69; Elementary Pilots Course £290; Club Pilots Course free with purchase of equipment
Payment Methods:	Cash, cheque, all major credit and debit cards
Booking Details:	Summer up to 4 weeks; winter 2-3 days
Capacity:	20
Insurance:	BHPA membership includes TPL; can arrange PA through the BHPA
Facilities:	Local accommodation, but no on-site catering, only toilets. Corporate events organised and gift vouchers available. Paramotor display team available for promotional work.
Other Notes:	Also: paragliding, paramotoring. Open 7 days a week. Sky Systems are the biggest equipment

suppliers in the UK; they also have a repair work-shop and a mail order service, and are one of the oldest commercial organisations – they have been running for over 13 years and boast, 'We are the best, as well as the biggest'. While hang-gliding is declining in popularity, paragliding is increasing and, if what you want is the thrill of flight, it might be worth considering doing a paragliding course instead.

Company:	**Sussex Hang Gliding and Paragliding**
Address:	16 Scarborough Road, Brighton, East Sussex BN1 5NR
Tel:	01273 888443
Fax:	01273 880572
E-mail:	sussexhgpg@mistral.co.uk
Price Range:	Taster £70; Elementary Pilot's Course £285; Club Pilot's Course £285
Payment Methods:	Cash, cheque, Visa, Amex, Access, Switch
Booking Details:	Weekends 2 weeks; weekdays 3-5 days
Capacity:	12 hang-gliding (3 people per glider); 24 para-gliding
Insurance:	£15 per course for BHPA TPL; forms available in the office for instant PA
Facilities:	Lots of local B&Bs; flying shop. Vouchers available for presents. Corporate activities organised and dis-abled catered for where appropriate.
Other Notes:	Also: paragliding (£65 per taster; £230 for SPC) and paramotors. The school has been established for 20 years and teaches 300 hang-gliding students a year.

Company:	**Welsh Hang Gliding Centre**
Address:	Visitor Centre, Bryn Bach Park, Tredegar, Gwent NP2 3AY
Tel:	01873 832100
Price Range:	Taster £50; weekends £100; EPC £200 (5 days)
Payment Methods:	Cash, cheque
Booking Details:	1 week
Capacity:	8 people, 4 per instructor
Insurance:	Prices include BHPA TPL; PA can be arranged in advance
Facilities:	Local B&B. Café, changing rooms, showers and

toilets on-site. Corporate events and gift vouchers. Disabled catered for.

Other Notes: Paul Farley has been teaching for over 17 years in the beautiful valleys between the Brecon Beacons and the Black Mountains. He took over from Jerry Breen who introduced the sport to the UK.

Company: **Wiltshire Hang-Gliding and Paragliding School**
Address: The Old Barn, Rhyls Lane, Lockeridge, Nr Marlborough, Wilts SN8 4EE
Tel: 01672 861555
Price Range: Taster £55/65 (weekends); 2 days £100/120; EPC £190/220
Payment Methods: Cash, cheque
Booking Details: 1 week
Capacity: 12 hang-gliding, 12 paragliding
Insurance: Have to join BHPA: £8
Facilities: Local B&B and campsites. Disabled teaching where appropriate – please ask. Corporate events arranged and gift vouchers available.
Other Notes: In operation since 1980, equal split between the two disciplines.

Company: **Aerosports**
Address: 336 Glebe Road, Cammoney, Newtown Abbey, Co. Antrim BT36 66RL
Tel: 01232 844113
Other Notes: Part-time school. Open Fri, Sat, Sun and evenings.

Company: **Airborne Hang-Gliding and Paragliding**
Address: Hey End Farm, Luddendenfoot, Halifax, West Yorks HX2 6JN
Tel: 01422 834989
Fax: 01422 836442
Price Range: Fun day £8; 2 days £160; EPC £295; beginner CPC £495
Payment Methods: Cash, cheque, Visa, Access
Booking Details: Summer 2 weeks minimum
Capacity: 15 per course
Insurance: BHPA TPL included; arrange own PA
Facilities: Basic camping facilities; toilets and cold running

water. Local B&Bs. Paramotoring now available. Equipment sold. Discounts for groups.

Other Notes: Apr-Nov. Shop open all year. Action holidays and flight tuition arranged in Tenerife Dec-Mar. 90 per cent of tuition is in paragliding. Airborne recommend starting with paragliding and then making a 2-day conversion course when you are proficient and confident in the air. Paramotoring now available.

Company: **Cairnwell Hang Gliding Centre**
Address: Gulabin Lodge, Glenshee, By Blairgowie, Perthshire PH10 7QE
Tel/Fax: 01250 885255
Price Range: Taster day £60; 3 days £120; Elementary Pilot Course £180; 10-day course to Club Pilot £380
Payment Methods: Cash, cheque, Visa, Mastercard
Booking Details: Minimum 1 week
Capacity: 6 people per course
Insurance: BHPA, TPL included
Facilities: Bunkhouse accommodation 16-18; B&B; self-catering; gift vouchers.
Other Notes: The school is open May-Sept full-time and then the centre switches over to snow sports. Paragliding is available but it only comprises 5 per cent of flights due to the Scottish weather, which can be too wet and windy for paragliding.

Company: **Cheviot Hang Gliding School**
Address: 9 Duncan Gardens, Morpeth, Northumberland NE61 2PT
Tel: 01670 772638
Price Range: £35 per day; EPC (5 days) £175
Payment Methods: Cash, cheque
Booking Details: 3-5 days in advance
Capacity: Up to 10; 2 pilots, 2 gliders
Insurance: BHPA £3 trial flight insurance; 3 months temporary membership £28
Facilities: Café nearby, gift vouchers.
Other Notes: Will teach weekdays if group is 3+, and at weekends. Started school in 1995. Also arranges trips to Spain.

Company: **Peak District Flight Training**
Address: York House, 112 Ladderedge, Leek, Staffs ST13 7AQ
Tel: 01538 382520
Fax: 01538 382520
Price Range: 1-day taster £63; weekend £98; EPC £225. Group discounts available.
Payment Methods: Cash, cheque
Booking Details: 2-3 weeks for groups
Capacity: Up to 20, 4 people per glider
Insurance: BHPA TPL included in price; PA must be arranged personally
Facilities: Operate from half a dozen different hilltops in the area, depending on wind. Glider storage facilities. Some corporate work, though mainly sports and social clubs.
Other Notes: Open 364 days, the school has been BHPA registered since 1974 and trains between 250 and 400 people a year. Beginners can be trained in most weather conditions up to gusts of 40mph, as they are attached to a ground tether.

Company: **Peak School of Hang Gliding**
Address: The Elms Farm, Wetton, Ashbourne, Derbyshire DE6 2AF
Tel: 01335 310257
Price Range: 2-day introductory £95; 5-day EPC £219
Payment Methods: Cash, cheque
Booking Details: 2-4 weeks
Capacity: Up to 30
Insurance: Arrange own PA through BHPA
Facilities: Local B&Bs; toilets; local cafés/pubs
Other Notes: All year round, minimum age 16.

BALLOONING

I know this country did once vote for John Major, but it still requires a serious act of faith to entrust your one and only life to a bag of hot air. Particularly before breakfast. There is a moment drifting over the Bristol City goal posts when I feel in serious danger of losing the meal I haven't had.

Ballooning is supposed to be relaxing, not terrifying, and here I am suspended in a wicker picnic hamper that barely comes up to my waist, at the mercy of the fickle elements. Above my head is a giant gas bag advertising Japanese motor cars, several hundred feet below is a city that is just starting to stir. The logical side of my brain tells me I am in safe hands; the creative side decides it would rather study the mechanics of the propane burner than peek over the edge.

Fortunately my pilot, Philip Clark, is one of the best balloon pilots in the UK. He has logged thousands of hours in the air and once held the record for the longest hot air balloon flight, a very civilised trip all the way over to the champagne country of Rheims. These days, the distance records and the headlines get hogged by Richard Branson, trying to advertise some Virgin or other, but it's important to remember that Branson's balloon is sealed and full of helium gas. Philip's is open at the bottom and full of hot air.

THE WEATHER

The very first lesson takes place on the ground. It is called 'The Weather'. 'Balloonists,' explains Philip, 'believe in the weather forecast like a two-year-old believes in Santa Claus. We generally fly first thing in the morning or early evening because the conditions are calmer then.'

For days before the flight, I dutifully scour the papers, watch the news and drink in the prophecies of the weather gurus. They are remarkably consistent for only one thing – the inaccuracy of their forecasts. The sun might be shining in London, but there are thunderstorms in Bristol. A balloon pilot would rather make a forced landing in the middle of the Silverstone track during the British Grand Prix than fly into a storm. Thunderstorms kill balloonists.

Before releasing a small balloon to show how and where the wind is blowing, Philip produces maps. The largest shows all the air lanes and forbidden zones like the army artillery ranges on Salisbury Plain. It is possible to fly through controlled air space, but that takes months of bureaucratic wrangling. His local map is covered with orange blobs which indicate bird sanctuaries or land where farmers have expressed vociferous distaste for balloon landings. Ultimately, while we can choose how long we stay up (which is dependent on the amount of propane we burn), where we end up is dependent on the elements. We go where the wind blows. It is out of our hands.

It is just after 6.30am on a beautiful August morning when we arrive at the launching site in Ashton Court. The Bristol University Balloon Club is already there but their pilot is very worried about forecasted thermals. Philip reckons it is too early to worry about these sudden updrafts that can cause unplanned ascents or descents. (It's funny how thermals, which glider, hang-glider and microlight pilots deliberately search out, are hated by balloonists.) They will come later in the day when the sun has heated up the ground.

THE STUFF OF LEGEND

It is ironic how a discarded 18th-century technology has turned into a 20th-century sport. In 1783, Jacques-Etienne and Joseph-Michel Montgolfier, wealthy paper makers in Annonay, France, sent up a balloon filled with hot air; and the French physicist, chemist and aeronaut, Jacques Alexandre César Charles, released one filled with hydrogen, which made a successful 2-hour flight, covering 43km (27 miles). Later that year, the French physicist Jean François

Pilâtre de Rozier made the first actual balloon ascent by humans near Paris, first in a captive, and later in a free, balloon. Two years later, the French aeronaut Jean Pierre Blanchard, accompanied by John Jeffries, an American, made the first balloon crossing of the English Channel.

In the 19th century, ballooning was the only form of manned flight and the stuff of legend. In 1836, The Great Balloon of Nassau sailed 800km (500 miles) from London to Weilburg, Germany, in 18 hours. During the Franco-Prussian War of 1870, balloons were used for military observation by the armies of both nations, and the French minister Léon Gambetta made a dramatic escape from the besieged city of Paris by balloon. In 1914, the balloon Berliner travelled some 3,052km (about 1,897 miles) from Bitterfeld, Germany, to Perm in Russia. Armies in World War I made extensive use of balloons, especially for military observation, but after that fixed-wing aircraft proved quicker and more commercially practicable than balloons or their cousin the airship.

———— HOT AIR IS FREE ————

Until recently, most sport ballooning in Europe used hydrogen-filled balloons. But the price of hydrogen – it costs £700 to fill a balloon – and the somewhat irrational fears that still linger from the Hindenburg disaster have seen a return to the original hot air technology – with a few modifications. The Montgolfier balloon was made of paper and fuelled by burning straw; modern ones are made of nylon and fired by propane gas burners.

Although hot air is free, ballooning is not cheap. To run a gas bag for an hour costs about £100, with private tuition at £200 per hour. If you want to buy your own balloon, it will cost £10,000 plus, but then one also needs a trailer to transport it. Propane gas to fuel the heaters is relatively cheap at £15 a tankful, though a flight can use up to three cylinders. It is commercial sponsorship that puts the hot air in balloons. Philip's main sponsors were Mitsubishi motors, who also provided him with a van specially customised for their balloon. Learning to fly a hot air balloon is more difficult – but certainly more rewarding – than becoming a politician. To get a balloon pilot's CAA licence requires a minimum of 12 hours' tuition in the air, two solo flights under examination, plus written exams on meteorology, navigation, air law and aerostatics.

Until nice Mr Honda invented an efficient hot air fan, getting the empty balloon envelope inflated was almost the most difficult and labour-intensive task. Dozens of helpers were required to flap the empty carcass up and down until they had trapped enough air inside for the propane heaters to inflate it fully. The twin heaters mounted on the top of the basket resemble *Star Wars* laser guns and let forth a roar that might terrify a lion. Hot air ballooning is not that quiet a pastime.

With the envelope fully inflated, it is time to cast off. We scramble into the basket – well all right, I scramble and Philip hops in with the ease of years of practice. Suddenly we're up, up and away and the first three minutes are definitely scary. It takes a while to adjust to the knowledge that I have no control over where I am going, how fast or far I might travel. A mere 100ft in the air, people, animals, even expressions, are familiar but they are secure on terra firma and I am up here in an alien environment disobeying the laws of nature. But the higher we fly, the less the rest of the human race starts to matter. Eventually, at about 1,000ft, they become just another part of the moving carpet below, a carpet alive with termites, something to watch and enjoy.

Balloon enthusiasts are right. There is something incredibly tranquil about being up there. You are not alone because there are others sharing the same basket space with you, so together you are divorced from the rest of the world. It's not so much the silence, for that is transitory, but the stillness that relaxes. So fragile, at the mercy of the elements, yet so secure.

HAPPY LANDINGS

The hot air that gives the hot air balloon its name is created by a propane gas burner that sends powerful jets of flame into the rip-stop nylon envelope. Once the balloon is aloft, its height is maintained by opening and closing the blast valve, which controls the flow of gas to the burner. If you have sampled other methods of flying and are used to instant response technology, piloting a balloon can be unnerving. As the air cools inside the envelope, it starts to sink. I give three 5-second bursts on the burner. Nothing happens, the descent continues. I am convinced we are going to land in a primary school canteen but then we start to rise effortlessly, clearing the trees by yards. The secret lies in looking and thinking ahead.

Soon we are 15 miles out of Bristol, drifting towards Bath. It seems far too early to be thinking of landing, the open countryside unfolding below is far more relaxing to view than the urban sprawl. The sewage works – well the grass around the works – looks to be a potential landing site until Philip spots the telegraph poles and electricity cables. The only wires a balloonist likes are those connecting the basket to the balloon. Running into land-based wires can puncture the envelope or cut the basket free, with potentially fatal consequences.

Crossing the brow of a hill changes both our direction and our rate of ascent. Sheep graze contentedly below. So does a family of rabbits until the sun is blotted out by a giant shadow and the roar of the burner sends them scurrying back to their holes. Dragons obviously still exist in bunny legend.

Landing a balloon requires a flat space clear of trees, posts or other potential entanglements, for the wind and the forward momentum of the craft can drag the basket for yards. This is the point at which Philip cheerfully announces that the very basket in which we stand once succeeded in demolishing a dry-stone wall and that too much of a thump has been known to break legs. The main danger in ballooning is landing.

Naturally enough we land softly, bent legs absorbing any shock. My attempts to bail out of the basket are halted firmly, for the balloon freed of my weight would have taken off again, sending Philip up into the blue yonder and leaving me sitting in a cowpat. Having secured his passenger, he pulls the vents and the air gushes out. The envelope collapses and lies there on the ground, gasping occasionally like a beached whale, waiting to be bundled up like so much dirty washing and put in the back of the support van which had been trailing us since take off.

Gravity has re-exerted its hold. I don't feel happy to be back on solid ground. And I am absolutely starving.

WHO TO CONTACT

British Balloon and Airship Club (BBAC)
Wellington House
Lower Icknield Way
Longwick
Nr Princes Risborough
Bucks HP27 9RZ

BBAC Information Line: 01604 870025

▶ **The BBAC is a volunteer-based organisation, founded in 1965, which exists to promote lighter-than-air flying – hot air ballooning, gas ballooning and airship flying. Call them for a free copy of the *Balloon Directory*, an annual directory of all lighter-than-air services compiled by the BBAC. If you are looking for your nearest reputable pleasure flight operator, training school or manufacturer you need look no further.**

▶ **The BBAC will also give you access to the BBAC Pilot Achievement Scheme and the Crew Training Programme.**

▶ **The Civil Aviation Authority (CAA) rigidly enforces standards for all manner of flying machines. Before stepping into a balloon, check that the operators have a CAA Air Operator's Certificate which means the company has fulfilled the service and safety standards which allow them to carry fee-paying passengers. If they don't have one, stay on the ground!**

WHERE TO GO

Company:	**Virgin Balloon Flights Limited**
Address:	Head Office, 54 Linhope Street, London, NW1 6HL
Tel:	0171 706 1021
Fax:	0171 224 8353
Price Range:	Pleasure flights from £135 (valid for 12 months);

City Skyline flight £185). Tuition by arrangement.
Payment Methods: Cash, cheque, all major credit cards
Booking Details: High season at least 3 weeks in advance.
Capacity: 12 balloons (up to around 144 passengers). Can hire more for special occasions.
Insurance: Inclusive
Facilities: Details of local accommodation on request. Refreshments available include champagne, vodka, tea and coffee etc. Virgin sweatshirts, T-shirts, mugs, badges etc available. Disabled trips can be arranged. Corporate events organised, including multi-activity.
Other Notes: The largest passenger-carrying balloon company in the UK. 200 launch sites throughout the UK, including London. Also flies from sites around the world including Belgium, France, Oman, Egypt, Amsterdam, Holland and Prague. Virgin Active do multi-activity breaks (prices £65-£375).

Company: **Heaven's Above**
Address: 6 Marsh End, Howden, Goole, Yorkshire DN14 7DF
Tel: 01430 431 297
Fax: 01430 432 221
Facilities: Different launch sites throughout Yorkshire. Individual facilities vary.
Price Range: Pleasure flights £115 per person. Flying instruction – call for details.
Payment Methods: Cash, cheque, Access, Amex, Diners, Mastercard, Switch, Visa.
Booking Details: At least 2 weeks in advance
Capacity: 2 balloons at 11 people each
Insurance: Inclusive
Other Notes: Civil Aviation Authority Certificated Air Operator. British Balloon and Airship Club Member.

Company: **Aerosaurus and Exeter Balloons**
Address: National Booking Office, Southbrook House, Whimple, Exeter, Devon, EX5 2PG
Tel: 01752 690 993
Fax: 01752 822 297
Price Range: Pleasure flights from £115 per person. Flight training – call for details

Payment Methods:	Cash, cheque, Access, Delta, Switch, Visa, Master-card
Booking Details:	A few days in advance
Capacity:	5 balloons+
Insurance:	Inclusive
Facilities:	Ballooning holidays; corporate hospitality; advertising.
Other Notes:	Civil Aviation Authority Certificated Air Operator. British Balloon and Airship Club Member.

Company:	**Anglia Balloons**
Address:	Peacock Lodge, Marlingford, Norwich, Norfolk, NR9 5HU
Tel:	01603 880 819
Fax:	01603 488 862
Price Range:	Pleasure flights from £95 per person. Flying instruction prices – call for details.
Payment Methods:	Cheque only
Booking Details:	Standby only
Capacity:	2 balloons
Insurance:	Not included
Facilities:	Flights are bought on a voucher system. Once you have your voucher the company will contact you to say a flight time is available.
Other Notes:	Civil Aviation Authority Certificated Air Operator. British Balloon and Airship Club Member.

Company:	**Ascent Balloon Company**
Address:	25, Carlingcott, Bath, BA2 8AN
Tel/Fax:	01761 432 327 / (mobile) 0836 651 460
Price Range:	Pleasure flights from £110 per person; flying instruction £65 (ground school) / £130 (air) per hour
Payment Methods:	Cash, cheque, Access, Visa, Mastercard
Booking Details:	Ideally, 1 month in advance
Capacity:	2 balloons
Insurance:	Inclusive
Facilities:	Trial lessons available; corporate hospitality; advertising.
Other Notes:	Civil Aviation Authority Certificated Air Operator. British Balloon and Airship Club Member. British Association of Balloon Operators.

Company:	**British School of Ballooning**
Address:	Little London, Ebernoe, Petworth, West Sussex, GU28 9LF
Tel/Fax:	01428 707 307
E-mail:	www.bsb@globnet.co.uk
Price Range:	Pleasure flights from £100 per person. Flight training from £130 per hour
Payment Methods:	Cash, cheque, Access, Switch, Visa
Booking Details:	Ideally 2 weeks in advance
Capacity:	12 balloons
Insurance:	Inclusive
Facilities:	Private launch field; souvenir shop; toilet facilities; easy parking.
Other Notes:	Civil Aviation Authority Certificated Air Operator. British Balloon and Airship Club Member.

Company:	**Broadland Balloons**
Address:	Arboretum House, Scottow Road, Lamas, Norwich, Norfolk, NR10 5JQ
Tel/Fax:	01603 279 678
Price Range:	Pleasure flights from £99 per person. Flying instruction £120 per hour
Payment Methods:	Cash, cheque, Visa, Access, Amex
Booking Details:	Ideally 2 weeks in advance
Capacity:	2 balloons
Insurance:	Inclusive
Facilities:	Corporate hospitality; advertising.
Other Notes:	Civil Aviation Authority Certificated Air Operator. British Balloon and Airship Club Member. British Association of Balloon Operators Founder Member.

Company:	**Airborne Balloon Flights and Promotions**
Address:	74 Hillside View, Peasdown St John, Bath, BA2 8ET
Tel:	01761 437 200
Fax:	01761 822 297
Price Range:	Pleasure flights £100-£135 per person. Flying instruction – call for details
Payment Methods:	Cash, cheque, Access, Visa, Mastercard
Booking Details:	A few days in advance
Capacity:	5 balloons+
Insurance:	Inclusive

Facilities: Countrywide service; corporate hospitality; advertising.

Other Notes: Civil Aviation Authority Certificated Air Operator. British Balloon and Airship Club Member. British Association of Balloon Operators.

Company: **Cloud Nine Balloon Company**
Address: Chipchase, Ebchester, Consett, Co Durham, DH8 OTB
Tel: 01207 560 304
Fax: 01207 563 060
Price Range: Pleasure flight £105 per person. Flying instruction £250 for three hours.
Payment Methods: Cash, cheque, Access, Visa, Mastercard, Delta, Switch
Booking Details: Ideally, 2 weeks in advance
Capacity: 2 balloons.
Facilities: Corporate hospitality; advertising.
Other Notes: Civil Aviation Authority Certificated Air Operator. British Balloon and Airship Club Member.

Company: **Out of This World**
Address: 26 High Street, Sevenoaks, Kent, TN13 1MK
Tel: 01732 743 322
Fax: 01732 742 009
Price Range: Pleasure flights from £120 per person. Flight instruction – call for details
Payment Methods: Cash, cheque, Access, Switch, Visa
Booking Details: Ideally, 2-3 weeks
Capacity: 2 balloons
Insurance: Inclusive
Facilities: Corporate hospitality; advertising; fly in Austria Jan-Mar.
Other Notes: Civil Aviation Authority Certificated Air Operator. British Balloon and Airship Club Member.

Company: **West Country Balloons**
Address: 96 High Street, Nailsea, Bristol, BS19 1AH
Tel/Fax: 01275 858 830
Price Range: Pleasure flights from £95 per person. Flying instruction – call for details.
Payment Methods: Cash, cheque, Visa, Mastercard, Access

Booking Details:	Standby during winter; 2 weeks in advance during summer
Capacity:	2 balloons
Insurance:	Inclusive
Facilities:	Merchandising from office and showroom.
Other Notes:	Civil Aviation Authority Certificated Air Operator.

Company:	**The Balloon Club**
Address:	Winterstoke Road, Bristol BS3 2NT
Tel:	0117 953 1100
Fax:	0117 963 9555
Price Range:	£115 per person
Payment Methods:	Cash, cheque, all credit and debit cards except Diners
Booking Details:	1-2 weeks
Capacity:	3 balloons, 12 people per balloon
Insurance:	Inclusive
Facilities:	Toilets at all launch sites; some café facilities, depending on flight times.
Other Notes:	Run by Phil Clark of Bristol Balloons, the Balloon Club offers alternative launch sites in Bristol, Wells, the Usk Valley in South Wales and Westonbirt Arboretum in the Cotswolds.

PART TWO
WATER

JET SKIING

Jet skis don't have brakes. I discovered this simple fact during my first 2 minutes on a jet ski. Travelling at about 5mph, wobbling on my knees, I found myself in a dilemma. My choices were to hit either a large green buoy, another machine going round and round in circles, or its former rider bobbing about in the water. I took my thumb off the throttle. The machine stopped dead, my head didn't, my chin banged down on the handlebars and in slow motion the whole thing tilted slowly over to port and dumped me in the lake.

Damn it, jet skiing was supposed to be one of those activities a novice can pick up relatively easily, and here I am bobbing about waiting for the ski to come back to me like some species of homing duck. At least the water's warm. And of the other seven jet ski virgins out on the lake with me, four are also taking in the fish's eye view.

Driving down the M4 from London to the Cotswold Waterpark, where Jet Ski UK have their base, I passed another small lake with jet skiers whizzing around all standing up and looking like they're having an absolute ball. And here am I, trying to haul myself back on to my Kawasaki and getting a jet of water full in the balls. That, I can assure you, is not fun.

— NOISY AND OUT OF CONTROL —

Mention the words 'jet ski' anywhere in the vicinity of longer-established watersports and the response is decidedly sniffy. Jet skiers are viewed as noisy, scruffy and out of control most of the time, like a delinquent illegitimate son who turns up one day at the family mansion, talks his way in and shows no signs of leaving again. Now he lounges around the drawing room with his feet on the coffee table, drinking all the best brandy and pinching the maid's bottom. What's most galling is that the maid seems to like it.

Jet skiing has had a bad press and not all of its wide-boy image is undeserved. It is interesting to note that its national association has adopted the more conservative-sounding name of the Personal Watercraft Federation. The machines are relatively cheap: ranging from £2-3,000 for a solo machine to £8,000 plus for two-seater models that can reach 50mph and are stable enough to tow a water-skier. They are much more accessible financially than a speedboat, can be stored easily in a garage and towed behind a car on a small trailer. View a jet ski as a motor bike for the water and you won't be far wrong – but to drive a big bike on the road you have to pass a test. Now, add into the equation advancing technology which has led to more stable, faster machines and you have a potential for trouble.

'After ten minutes on one of those,' says Andy Archer of Jet Ski UK, indicating a slick eight grand Bombardier two-seater, 'you think you know how to jet ski. But you don't. That is like sitting in a floating armchair and it's not half as much fun as a stand-up model.' The danger, he explains, comes not on training lakes but at sea when on a calm day you can cruise for miles without seeing anyone. Suddenly, along come a group of swimmers and the novice driver panics, he is naturally frightened of hitting any of them. Instead of using his speed and steering to avoid them, he reverts to land behaviour; in a car he might apply the brakes but a jet ski doesn't have any brakes. If you take your hand off the throttle, the machine stops dead. Which is where I fell in.

— STAND UP, WOBBLE, FALL IN —

Jet Ski UK has been operating on the 35-acre Lake 11 in the Cotswold Waterpark since 1986, the first jet ski hire centre of its kind in Europe. The lake is divided into two halves, a string of bright orange buoys separating the Club course from the Novice circuit. For £15, the novice hires a Kawasaki jet ski for half an hour. The price includes wetsuit (if required), helmet and a buoyancy jacket, and 10-15 minutes tuition on land. I was told very firmly on the phone that one half hour on the water could be more than enough and to arrive at least 40 minutes before my appointed session to get properly briefed. 'We can't be out there on the water with you,' says Andy Archer, 'so, if you want to get on quickly, you have to pay attention and then come back in and ask lots of questions. There are always people who think they know more than we do, but the funny thing is they never do get to stand up!'

In my case it was a hot day and during the briefing given by Simon, a tanned, blond student on his summer vacation, I did find my mind drifting away. Surely it couldn't be that difficult, I thought, as he demonstrated the controls on a jet ski mounted on a wooden plinth, starting in a lying position, pulling oneself up into a kneeling position and then the balance required to stand up. However, once in the water with the machine started, I discovered it was a lot more difficult than I thought. I lay down, grabbed the handlebars with my hands and put my right thumb on the throttle.

The first thing I found was that these machines are pretty cramped for a fully grown adult when you lie in them. It's hard at my size to put both elbows on top of the side rails and make sure that my waist is above the jet. A jet ski works by the propulsion caused by a high-speed jet of water ejected from the stern by a pump within the hull. The pump is driven by an engine identical to the one that might drive a conventional propeller, but a propeller would mash up jet skiers' extremities. Instead, the jet can pummel your privates if you don't get them out of the way.

The trick is to get up to half throttle and then pull myself up on to my knees, using my elbows to pivot my body forward without reducing speed. My first attempt to get on to my knees is reasonably successful, but then I throttle down a bit, the machine starts to bounce about and I am back in the drink. My second ends in the ignominy described earlier.

Beginners spend a lot of time falling off jet skis. Fortunately, they do have an ingenious safety feature. If your thumb is removed from the throttle, the machine stops moving away and starts to chug round in a circle; the trick is to swim on the diagonal to intersect this turning circle. Then it's back on again. If the engine has stopped, press the green key with my left thumb for 15 seconds, throttle down, lie, lever up into a kneel then get into control. After a few goes, I learnt to keep my knees and weight forward and to keep the throttle open. The next problem was balancing when I started bouncing over choppy water. As each bounce drove the air out of my body, my natural reaction was to slow down, the slower we moved the more difficult it was to control and the easier to end up back in the water.

Eventually it was time to attempt a stand. It took a couple of circuits before I found clear water and no other bodies ahead. I put my right and strongest foot forward, pushed up and placed my left foot towards the back of the craft. So far, so wobbly, now I'm coming to a corner, so what do I do? Reduce speed and fall in. This is the continuing pattern for the next 10 minutes: stand, wobble, fall in, swim about, try again. By the time my half-hour session is over, I have managed to travel all of 30 yards in a straight line without swallowing liquid.

CRACKING IT?

Back on dry land, I suddenly realised how much I ached. My right wrist felt as if I had lifted about 300 pints, I had cuts on a big toe and on my right knee, which hurt like hell. While trying not to topple over and in, forgetting – or was it disobeying? – instructions to let go of the handlebars when that happens, I had fetched my knee a hell of a crack on the side. I tried not to limp over to Simon when I asked him about how to remain standing while turning. This time I paid attention.

The answer, it appears, is to take it like you do on a road, decelerate coming up to the turn, then accelerate out of it. At the same time, move both feet to the back of the craft so the engine is still in the water; if it's out of the water you have no forward propulsion and consequent loss of power. Then, provided you have enough speed, you can either use your body weight to lean into the turn, use the handlebars to control direction or a combination of the two. The rest of the time, keep the strongest foot forward, the other back, with your weight forward and elbows bent.

After half an hour's resting of aching limbs, I went out again. It was 5pm, the last session on a summer Tuesday, and I was determined to manage a complete circuit standing up. By now, I was hauling myself up into a kneeling position with confidence if not elegance. I was hitting a good speed – 20mph seems a lot faster I can assure you – and cornering well. Standing up still proved elusive. I made it round my first corner in one of the widest, most ungainly turns possible. I was so elated that I accelerated too fast, lost control and hit the water with a whack that drove all the air out of my body. Five minutes later, I was up and round one, two, no, three corners, then I lost concentration at the sight of another jet ski and ended up bouncing into the water. Again.

That was the best I could manage in the second session. I never quite got that mixture of balance, power, leaning and speed that I needed. The only black spot was when I was bobbing about in the water and another craft came in too close to me and the wake fetched me a bang on the back of the head – a reminder of what can happen if a jet skier loses concentration with swimmers about.

All in all, I thoroughly enjoyed it, even the next day when the aches, pains, bruises and cuts made their presence felt more firmly. It was good, cheap, fun and my son wants to try it too. I've told him he is too young to be a delinquent and must wait until he's 10. This makes him very cross.

—————— WHO TO CONTACT ——————

Personal Watercraft Federation (PWF)
CSL House
184 Histon Road
Cambridge CB4 3JP

Tel: 01223 516769
Fax: 01223 315960

▶ **The PWF is dedicated to helping its members get the best from their leisure time and craft. They are young and enthusiastic, and as a result they are backed by both the jet ski trade and media.**

▶ **As the UK's only organisation for the jet ski enthusiast, the PWF provides excitement and enjoyment for its members whilst helping the sport to grow and flourish.**

▶ **The PWF strongly promotes water safety awareness amongst all its participants. They are extremely helpful and publish an excellent and comprehensive guide to jet ski launch and hire locations across the country.**

▶ **PWF membership benefits include (for first-timers only) a joining pack worth more than £175 for only £29.90. This includes a 10-launch discount voucher, free Oakley goggles, a free legal protection policy and a free 10-point service check on your machine (if you have one) at participating dealers around the country. Thoroughly recommended.**

—————— WHERE TO GO ——————

Company:	**Jet Ski UK**
Address:	Lake 11, Spine Rd, Cotswold Water Park, Cirencester, Glos GL7 6DF
Tel:	01285 861345
Fax:	01285 861828

Price Range:	£15 per half hour (wetsuit, life jacket and helmet inclusive)
Payment Methods:	Cash, cheque, credit cards
Booking Details:	4-7 days in summer
Capacity:	8 jet skis on the water at any one time
Facilities:	Can suggest local accommodation. Hot and cold snacks available; changing rooms, showers and toilets. Shop selling leisure wear, wetsuits etc. Disabled access plus limited activities. Corporate events involving jet skiing, go-karting, quad biking, barbecuing. Gift vouchers.
Other Notes:	Jet ski hire available Mar-Sept 7 days a week. Open 08.30-21.00 all week, depending on level of bookings. Also: children's and adults' quad bikes, mountain bike hire and go-karting.

Company:	**Jetspeed**
Address:	Llewellyns Quay, Port Talbot Docks, Port Talbot, West Glamorgan, SA13 1RG
Tel:	01639 887070
Price Range:	From £15 per 30 mins (includes wetsuit, buoyancy aid, helmet and tuition)
Payment Methods:	Cash, cheque, Visa, Access, Mastercard, Amex
Booking Details:	Opening times: 10.00 till dusk all year
Capacity:	7-8 hire craft on the water at any one time
Facilities:	Changing rooms; showers and toilets; gift/equipment shop; disabled facilities. Corporate events organised; gift vouchers.
Other Notes:	Water size: 70 acres, heated water (60°F in winter and 80°F in summer).

Company:	**Middlemoor**
Address:	Nr Bridgwater, Woolavington, Somerset, TA7 8DH
Tel:	01278 685578
Price Range:	£15 for 20 mins
Payment Methods:	Cash, cheque, Visa, Access
Booking Details:	Open: daylight hours all year
Facilities:	Hotel 3 miles away. Fully licensed bar and bar snacks. Changing rooms, showers and toilets. Postcards and equipment on sale. Corporate events and gift vouchers.
Other Notes:	Water size: 17 acres. Also: karting.

Company:	**Six Hills Jet Ski**
Address:	Six Hills, Nr Melton Mowbray, Leicestershire, LE14 3PR
Tel:	01664 43080
Price Range:	30 mins. from £15.50 (includes wetsuit, lifejacket, helmet and tuition)
Payment Methods:	Cash, cheque, Visa, Access, Mastercard
Booking Details:	10.00 till dusk all year
Capacity:	6 jet skis on the water at any one time
Insurance:	PA can be arranged personally
Facilities:	Camping; disabled access; changing rooms, toilets, showers; hot and cold food; club house; gear shop. Corporate entertaining, gift vouchers.
Other Notes:	Water size: 18 acres.

Company:	**Tallington Lakes**
Address:	Tallington Lakes, Barlolm Road, Tallington, Tamford, Lincs, PE9 4RJ
Tel:	01778 346573

See page 21 (windsurfing) for details

Company:	**Church Wilne Water Sports Centre**
Address:	Sawley Road, Draycott, Nottingham, DE72 2RQ
Tel:	0973 304164
Price Range:	£15-20 for 25 mins (includes wetsuits, helmets and life jackets)
Payment Methods:	Cash, cheque
Booking Details:	Open: 0900-19.00 all year
Capacity:	6 jet skis at any one time
Insurance:	TPL inclusive
Facilities:	Corporate facilities; gift vouchers; other full facilities, but toilets not yet suitable for the disabled.
Other Notes:	Water size: 20 acres

Company:	**Crazy Capers**
Address:	Loughshore Marina, Lough Road, Antrim, BT41 4DG
Tel:	0850 554497 / 01232 833681
Price Range:	Kawasaki 440 £10 for 10 mins; 650 TS £15 for 20 mins; 750 Xi £20 for 20 mins
Payment Methods:	Cash, cheque, Access, Visa
Booking Details:	Open Apr-Sept, 12.00 till dark

Facilities:	Corporate facilities; gift vouchers; local B&B; café; shower and toilet facilities both suitable for disabled; plenty of parking.
Other Notes:	Water size: 20 x 10 miles.

Company:	**Fosse Hill**
Address:	Catwick Lane, Bandesburton, East Yorkshire, Y025 ASB
Tel:	01964 542608
Price Range:	£16-20 for 25 mins on water (includes tuition, wetsuit, and buoyancy jacket)
Payment Methods:	Cash, cheque, Visa, Mastercard, Switch, Delta
Booking Details:	Open times: 10.00 till dusk, 7 days a week, all year
Capacity:	5 hire skis at any one time
Insurance:	TPL inclusive
Facilities:	Corporate fun days; gift vouchers; local accommodation; camping and caravan site; bar snacks; BBQ; shower and toilet facilities, one toilet suitable for disabled; parking; shop with wetsuits and jet skis.
Other Notes:	Water size: 15 acres.

Company:	**Princes Club**
Address:	Clockhouse Lane, Bedfont, Middlesex, TW14 8QA
Tel:	01784 256153 / 01784 255330
Fax:	01784 255568

See page 105 (water skiing) for details

POWERBOAT RACE TRAINING

This time, I'm going to get it right. No more comments about my kneeling position resembling King Charles I preparing to have his head chopped off. No more leaning out at 50mph and getting a face full of water from that berk who drives a Porsche, while fishermen snarl at me because their piscine prey has very sensibly opted to stay 20ft under rather than get chopped into fish meal by a Yamato propeller.

Floating 2ft from the jetty, lying flat on my stomach, squashed into the sides of a floating coffin made entirely of flimsy wood and painted bright red; dead man's clip inserted in its clothes peg, left hand on the throttle at half power, right hand gripping the steering wheel from underneath at about 20 past the hour (what would my driving examiner say?), I'm ready.

Pete Kirkham pulls the engine cord. Vroom, bounce, bounce, shake and rattle them bones, keep accelerating, suddenly the boat's up on a plane and roaring towards the first marker buoy. Mustn't hit that as I haven't got £90 to replace it. Start the turn about 20ft before, move your weight forward and ease off the throttle until the back starts to swing round. Now, slide back down the boat and accelerate up the straight giving it all you can so you hardly feel the bounces at 50mph. Wide sweep at the next buoy, but not too wide as you don't want to end up in the island. Get the turn just right and you won't have to adjust your line again and you can get back up to speed.

Two laps completed and it's going just dandy. My heart has left my mouth and is now located below my vocal chords. Coming for the island turn, I'm up to full throttle for the first time but I've got my racing line wrong. I don't let off the throttle enough and I turn too much, my hand loses grip on the wheel and I've hooked the back round too far. I've lost the course completely and I'm heading straight for the grumpiest fisherman on the lake, travelling at 55mph. I have a serious problem here.

I am now confronted with two of the hydroplane's serious design flaws: it can't turn right and it has no brakes. This presents me with two choices: keep going, try to force it round to the right and risk falling in, or pull the dead man's clip. I take option two and have to endure the humiliation of seeing Pat waving a red flag – ordering the other two boats back into the pits – and awaiting the arrival of the rescue boat. Any attempt to remain anonymous by keeping my helmet on are soon dashed when Loren, the club's PR person, congratulates me on being the first person ever to hook that particular boat. I'm sure she meant it as a compliment.

──── SHINY, HAPPY PEOPLE ────

Before I went on my Team Powerboat Race Training Day, I was under the impression that people who raced powerboats were a little eccentric, perhaps a couple of marker buoys short of a full course. Driving away from it, I realised how mistaken I had been. They are, of course, just shiny, happy people having fun who are also clinically insane.

The first inkling I had was during the briefing given by Pat Ainge, who organises and runs the Race Training Days. Pat looks like a benevolent schoolmistress, a kindly granny who is still young and fit enough to show the kids a good time at Alton Towers. A genteel, suburban facade hides a fiercely competitive spirit who first took up the sport some 30 years ago when her husband Merv dragged her out to an event on a local lake. It was love at first lap. Since then she's won the Bristol – the Monaco Grand Prix of powerboat racing – and held the Formula Five speed record when she took her catamaran T750 up to 79.05mph. She held that record for a decade until the engine restrictions were relaxed.

THE BLOOD SHEET

Pat starts off by getting us all to sign an insurance waiver. 'In the trade it's called the blood sheet,' she says. The non-racing wife of one of the day's participants, who is clutching a small baby, goes pale; another wife suddenly gets very interested until Pat explains that this will absolve her from any injury claims. 'It's no good coming to me with a cut finger in a week's time.' She does not attempt to hide the fact that there have been injuries and other mishaps on training days. One man broke his arm after hitting the island and didn't realise it for a week. Pat made him go straight out again but did think he seemed a bit green. Another man lost his car keys in the lake, while another had to endure the humiliation of watching his thick roll of £100 notes being individually dried in the clubhouse oven.

Safety procedures are rigorously enforced. Life jackets and full-face motorcycle crash helmets are always worn in the boats. The most important item of safety equipment is the dead man's clip: a string attached to either your left wrist or life jacket and attached to a plug or clip. This is then attached to the boat and the moment you remove it, the engine cuts out. You stay in the boat, with your helmet on – 'in case somebody hits you' – and wait to be picked up by the 'world renowned' Osprey Rescue Team who cruise around in a very nifty, wasp-yellow inflatable. We are under race rules so must pay attention to the flags. If a red flag is being waved, we must come into the pits, but never cut across the anti-clockwise course. Overtaking is done only on the outside as overtaking on the inside is potentially dangerous. Frequent transgressors can be black flagged, which results in their reverting to landlubber status for the rest of the day.

FISHING BOATS

After the lectures are completed, we are divided into three groups and shown over the boats we will be driving later. The OSY 400 hydroplanes cause the most surprise. They're so small and seem to be constructed of little more than a few sheets of four by two, with a Yamato engine bolted on the back. In Japan, they have evolved from working fishing boats into racing machines on which millions of yen are routinely gambled. The drivers turn up, their boat and engine is drawn by lot, the only piece of equipment they are allowed to own personally is the propeller. If you are the right size (under 10 stone and 6ft) they are the perfect class to start racing in. A second-hand boat can be bought for a few hundred pounds.

We are shown over a white Formula Five catamaran (Pat's old record-breaking boat) by Mike Ashton, the Formula Four European champion. This looks more like a racing machine, it has a cockpit, a steering wheel and an accelerator pedal. Powered by a 60hp/750cc Yamaha engine it can reach 60-70mph on the straights. Once the cat gets up some speed and rises out of the water, you are really moving. Cornering takes a bit of getting used to but, as Mike explains, if you get it right you don't have to slow down at all. The other cat is a smaller, green SS45 with a 45hp Evinrude engine and a top speed of 60mph. Fortunately, the wind is not too strong today. If it gets too blowy, Pat won't let the trainees drive a cat, as there is a danger that too much wind under the hulls, coupled with too much speed, can make it flip over – backwards.

The third boat is a bright red T850 monohull (ie it looks like a normal speedboat) powered by a 70hp/850cc Yamaha engine than can hit 90mph. As Pat's monohull is damaged, this one has been brought up by Nick Vaughan, who chain-smokes more than any man who makes a living racing a powerboat filled with aviation fuel should. It also operates on conventional controls. The trickiest part of driving a monohull, Nick explains between puffs, is that the hull is covered in chines and when you are really opening it up, only the last third of the boat is actually in the water.

I discovered what he meant when I first took it out. It cornered like an angel. I was soon leaning into the bends like a TT rider and burning off down the straight. For a moment, it felt like I was flying and none of the boat was actually in the water. But because of that little contact, the boat flicks across the surface, bouncing off every ripple, flying off every eddy. At high speed, it starts to rock and roll from side to side. The natural reaction is to try to turn the wheel to compensate but, at that speed and with my experience, all you're ever doing is chasing rainbows. The only solution is to throttle down, take the next corner fast and then open up again on the stretch between the islands where the water is smooth as glass. On the third straight, speeding past the pits, the boat starts to roll again. Feeling brave, I open it up further to see whether sheer speed can overawe the pitch and yaw. Wrong move. In a millisecond I am bouncing off the sides of the boat, my head whipping from side to side. Time to throttle back before I lose my lunch or my seat.

THE GREEN CAT

While I enjoyed driving the monohull, my favourite was the little green cat. She was a frisky little devil, more responsive to the touch than the bigger, white machine. I misjudged the first bend I took at speed. By turning too early, I missed the buoy by a feline whisker and took the cat up past the lone remaining fisherman so quickly that he shook a fist at me (well I assume he wasn't waving!). Between the islands at speed and into the third bend, so tight my right shoulder slammed into the cockpit wall, I put my foot down preparing to really go for the straight and was rewarded with a cough, a splutter and then nothing. I'd run out of petrol. Audible obscenities later, I was being towed in by the rescue boat, who were getting very accustomed to my face.

CAT AND MOUSE

After breaking for lunch – two helpings of Pat's lasagne – we spent the last three hours hopping on as many boats as possible. I never got the hang of the hydroplanes, I was never comfortable or felt enough in control. On my penultimate trip, I tried to go for it and ended up nearly losing it twice. I only managed to regain control by cutting the corners of the course. 'It's not for me,' I told Pete finally. 'I like the cats.'

It's 5.15pm and the last run of the day. The fishermen have all gone home in high dudgeon, but at least no one has heaved a brick at a racer. They appear immune to the information that (a) this lake is for speedboats and (b) the boats aerate the water for the fish. The water-skiers have started to assemble their kit on the bank ready to take over at 5.30pm. It's the time of day when confidence and bravado flourish amidst the trainees and Pat usually hides away in the club house so as not to see it.

I'm in the green cat and away, hitting the corners with the G force dragging me into the cockpit wall, high on the plane and gunning it. Between the islands, I glance right and see the white cat is trying to take me. I put pedal to metal (all right, fibreglass) and stare him out. He waves a left hand in acknowledgement and I take the corner tight and fast. I'm still holding him off, the adrenaline is booming, the boat is bouncing, skidding across the water. I blow the next turn and by the time I've straightened out he's past me.

He's 20 yards clear by the second turn but I'm taking a tighter line, through the islands again. He's got a bit of extra power so I have to let him take the turn first. The long straight past the pits is getting interesting as we both have the monohull in our sights. It can burn off both of us but it's being driven by a mouse. Coming into the next turn, the monohull forces the white cat out wider. I can take them both on the inside. Yeah it's not allowed but my blood's going and I can justify it on safety reasons. It's a perfect turn. I've caught up 30 yards on the white cat, but it's not enough.

I burn out on to the straight level, the red monohull sandwiched between us. We both leave it for dead but I haven't got the power to get ahead. Overtaking two boats on the inside is probably a hanging offence. I let him take the corner first and intend to get him after the islands but I never do. Coming out into the final straight, the engine coughs and dies. High on racing adrenaline and left bobbing out in the water waiting for the rescue boat. I'm out of petrol. Again.

WHO TO CONTACT

Royal Yachting Association (RYA)
RYA House
Romsey Road
Eastleigh
Hampshire SO50 9YA

Tel: 01703 627400
Fax: 01703 629924

See page 18 (windsurfing) for details

———————— WHERE TO GO ————————

There are currently eleven powerboat circuit racing clubs approved by the RYA and eleven offshore powerboat clubs. Most importantly, the RYA checks that all Racing Drivers' Licences are checked by stringent medical examinations. It organises racing third party insurance cover of £5 million per accident, as well as boat registration and measurements for racing craft. All the rules, regulations and technical stuff you can check in the *RYA Powerboat Racing Circuit Handbook*.

Other than the Team Powerboating Race Days (see Team Powerboating entry below), the only way to get training is to get straight into a race. In order to do this, it is necessary to contact your local club direct and try to arrange the loan of a boat. The hire cost is up to the owner who normally imposes a 'you bend it, you mend it' rule. Further costs are £20 for a special day licence and an entry fee – usually £15.

Company:	**Essex Hydroplane Racing Club**
Address:	8 Firbanks, Whitstable, Kent, CT5 3EH

Company:	**London Motor Boat Racing Club Ltd.**
Address:	48 Holsom Close, Stockwood, Bristol
Other Notes:	Write for details.

Company:	**Lancashire Powerboat Racing Club Ltd.**
Address:	2 Hazelhurst Grove, Ashton in Makerfield, Wigan, WN4 8RH
Other Notes:	Write for details to Mr W Owen.

Company:	**Lowestoft and Oulton Broad Motor Boat Racing Club**

Address:	Wood Ford Villa, Honnington Road, Weston Longville, Norwich, NR9 5JU
Tel:	01603 881112
Facilities:	Private club. Canteen; changing, shower and toilet facilities in clubhouse. Small souvenir shop.

Company:	**Midland Powerboat Racing Club**
Address:	Kingsbury Water Park, Bodymoor Heath, Kingsbury, Warwickshire
Tel:	01283 812707 (Race Secretary)
Facilities:	See Team Powerboat entry

Company:	**Stewartby Watersports Club**
Address:	51 Mount Pleasant Road, Clapham, Bedford, MK41 6BU
Tel:	01234 268162
Other Notes:	It's a members' club. Also: water-skiing, sailing and angling.

Company:	**Team Powerboating**
Address:	The Old Stables, 7 Shropshire Brook Road, Armitage, Staffordshire, WS15 4UZ
Tel:	01543 492344 / 0850 421851
Fax:	01543 492344
Price Range:	Individual £141 (inc VAT); corporate days £2,680-6,750 (depending on guests)
Payment Methods:	Cash, cheque
Booking Details:	As far in advance as possible, days are limited. Non-returnable £41 deposit required.
Capacity:	Individual race days up to 15; corporate 12-40
Insurance:	TPL included; you must arrange your own PA
Facilities:	Local B&B and reasonably priced hotels. On-site catering (vegetarian meals available); toilets and showers. Corporate events and team-building organised; gift vouchers.
Other Notes:	Pat Ainge runs the only RYA approved powerboat race-training school in the UK and she only does 7 individual days! Groups can book their own days, minimum 12 people. The season runs between Mar and end Sept, so book early.

Company:	**Windermere Motor Boat Racing Club**
Address:	Bramble Hill, Ghyll Head, Windermere, Cumbria, LA23 3LJ
Tel:	01539 442722

Company:	**Chasewater Sports Centre**
Address:	9 Lilac Lane, Great Wyrsley, Walsall, WS6 6HQ
Tel:	01922 415719
Facilities:	Changing rooms, showers, toilets and catering facilities. Disabled access.
Other Notes:	Also: water-skiing, 2 ski jumps and slalom course.

DIVING

The tropical sun was burning on my back. The boat was anchored within sight of St Vincent's towering cliffs. Down in 80ft of crystal clear Caribbean waters, I could still see the outline of the wreck, still remember the family of lobsters waving their antennae, furious at this invasion of their privacy. This Scuba diving lark was proving to be fun – until I recalled being shown an 8ft nurse shark a couple of days earlier and consuming half a tank of air in 5 minutes. 'Of course, the best place to learn to dive safely is in England,' said Bill Tewes, the grizzled Texan who runs Dive St Vincent. 'The conditions you have in British coastal waters can be so difficult that after that you can cope with anything. I'm real happy to dive with someone who trained there.'

IN MUDDY WATERS

Which in part, I suppose, explained how I came to be holding hands with four other divers while swimming slowly around another wreck. It was October and the Devon seas are always chilly. This ship had sunk just off Plymouth two years ago. After a while, stirred-up mud reduced visibility to 3ft. I couldn't see it was a wreck, couldn't see anything other than the vague outline of my buddy's blue wetsuit. It was rather fun in a masochistic way, my breathing was relaxed and air consumption low. Bring on the sharks.

Fort Bovisand is an old Victorian Naval fort on Plymouth Sound that was converted into a residential diving school in 1970. Universally accepted as the premier diving school in Europe, they train commercial divers – the chaps who operate down 450ft of North Sea blackness – while servicemen from the armed forces have their own instructors. They also train civilians who want to have a look at life under the ocean wave. At a time when commercial diving is in a slump, the leisure end of the industry is booming. In the ten years since my first dive, the whole industry has changed radically, and the cost of both training and equipment has dropped to meet increased demand. When I first trained as a BSAC (British Sub Aqua Club) Sports Diver, the residential course at Bovisand did not leave much change from £500; today it is £150. Today, the majority of courses are PADI (Professional Association of Diving Instructors). In 1996, they qualified 800 PADI divers by July. PADI is a professional qualification which enables the unemployed to learn to dive for free.

In the summer, Bovisand hold regular Try Dives in the local swimming pool for free. There are literally dozens of other scuba schools that will take you for cheap – even free – introductory dives in swimming pools and inland lakes. Not everyone in Britain lives by the sea and it is possible to find evening/weekend classes for the basic qualification in most major cities. Familiarisation with the equipment takes place in swimming pools. There is nothing wrong with this except that the pool is a safe, controlled environment. It does not have tides, currents, mud, weeds or fish. The sea does. Which is why a qualified BSAC Sports Diver or PADI Open Water Diver has to make ten 'open water' dives before he or she is qualified.

MUTANT FROGS

The primary disadvantage with training in Britain is not really the weather. It is the gear. In the warm waters of the West Indies, I have dived without even a shortie wetsuit, wearing only a T-shirt and minimal weights. Standing on the harbour wall at Bovisand, waiting to jump 20ft into the sea, I felt like the bastard creation of a pack mule and a rubber fetishist's dream. A two-piece rubber wetsuit with hood and shoes (nowadays all training is done wearing a drysuit which takes even more getting used to but ends up much warmer!), 24 pounds of lead strapped round my waist, an inflatable life jacket round my neck (usually referred to as a BCV – Buoyancy Control Vest), a cylinder full of compressed air on my back, flippers – sorry fins, a diver never ever calls them flippers – on my feet, mask covering my eyes and nose, and a demand valve in my mouth.

From outside, it was not a human being who stood there but some hideously deformed mutant frog.

Dougie, my course instructor, was a former Military Police sergeant. Sometimes he forgot his charges were doing this for fun. We were not allowed to wear gloves – as 'gloves are for poofs'. He took great pleasure in ordering his ungainly herd of novices to leap off the harbour wall into the water. They, too, were a mixed bunch, from Steve, a local who works as a second mate on supertankers, to Stella, a divorced mother in her forties who was fulfilling a lifelong ambition. Although the majority of divers tend to be men, that is due to choice not discrimination. Another instructor, Andy Barber, explained later that women come to terms with their basic fear easily where the macho men try to bluff it out. In the water all are equal – and women use less air.

We all jump, teeth clamped hard on the DV (demand valve), hand cupped over mouthpiece and mask, holding them in place, falling 20ft into the chill, green, murky water. Under the water, it is all so different. As we descend, pressure increases to hurt the ears; I grasp my nose between finger and thumb and blow out every few feet. The pain ceases. (Experienced divers learn to 'equalise the pressure' just by swallowing.) Thirty feet below the surface all that weight vanishes, slow leg kicks propel me in a leisurely manner across the sea bed. If the weights are too heavy, I just inject a little extra air into the BCV and float up like a feather. It may be October and drizzling with rain on the surface, but in the sea it only starts to feel cold after half an hour. We are all playing in a near-weightless environment where up, down and the constraints of gravity are almost meaningless concepts. The only sound is my own breathing.

It is possible to become transfixed by this quiet solitude. That could be dangerous and is just one reason why only fools dive alone. Throughout the dive, you constantly check for the presence of your 'buddy'. He puts thumb and forefinger together to form an O. In divers' sign language that means he is OK. A thumbs-up means he wishes to return to the surface; a flat hand chopping at the throat means he has run out of air. If he gives me that signal, we will ascend slowly to the surface, passing my demand valve back and forth, sharing the air in my tank.

ALIEN ENVIRONMENT

Most of dive training is spent learning safety procedures, learning how to cope if something goes wrong. Sometimes it does go wrong, for a handful of sports divers die in British waters every year. Generally, it is because they panicked or forgot their training. Right now, I know the dangers of nitrogen narcosis (if you descend too quickly the nitrogen in the blood affects your brain, making you feel a bit drunk; divers suffering from the narks have been known to offer passing fish a hit of their oxygen), of the bends, gas poisoning, air embolisms, and burst lungs. I know how to prevent them happening and I know some basic decompression tables. I know not to ascend to the surface faster than 15m a minute (if I go up too fast the nitrogen will cause the bends, bubbles in the bloodstream which will cause incredible pain and possibly death), but, if I ever do run out of air 30m down and my buddy won't or can't help, it will be the longest 2 minutes of my life. Diving is potentially dangerous, because it is about human beings entering an alien environment, where the only way they can survive is by relying on man-made machines. The aqualung allows you to breathe under water, but to stay alive you must rely on your buddy and your basic intelligence. I cannot stress too much how dangerous it can be to dive alone.

Learning that discipline can be difficult; learning to inhale and exhale through the mouth can be difficult. But the reward is entry into a beautiful, tranquil, silent world – a place whose natural inhabitants consider you just to be a rather strange, ungainly fish with a bifurcated tail, that blows a lot of bubbles. Diving in the sea is a wonderful, relaxing pastime. Everybody should be encouraged to try because it will teach you a great deal about how much we need to protect our planet if our children are to enjoy the same pleasures we do.

And there is so much to see down there. Within a short boat ride from Bovisand lies a sunken U-boat and the massive wreckage of a torpedoed liberty ship. Off St Vincent lie coral reefs where the shoals of fish swim so thickly you cannot see the surface. Off the coast of Pemba in the Indian Ocean, turtles frolic, the scorpion fish puff out their deadly quills and, if you are really lucky, you might even see the mating dance of the black marlins.

Off the coast of the Yucatan, one can sometimes dive in the middle of the annual shark migration. Now that must be a sight to see. One day.

WHO TO CONTACT

British Sub Aqua Club (BSAC)
Telfords Quay
Ellesmere Port
South Wirral
Cheshire L65 4FY

Tel: 0151 357 1951
Fax: 0151 357 1250

▶ **The BSAC is considered the sport's governing body in the UK and a dive club, with its own training programme for divers and instructors. BSAC has a very wide range of primary courses and specialisations.**

The main BSAC courses (Novice/Novice II; Sport; Dive Leader; Advanced Diver) are very comprehensive. These lead to a well-qualified diver with many skills, including recovery and navigation, taught as an integral part of the syllabus – essential in the more unforgiving British waters. The qualifications are designed to create self-sufficient divers, capable of planning and executing their own dives, plus reacting appropriately in an emergency. All courses have a high theory content which is introduced at quite an early stage.

The BSAC books are first-rate manuals and make for both an excellent read and a source of background information. On the courses these manuals are used in conjunction with student workbooks.

PADI International Ltd
Unit 6, Unicorn Park
Whitby Road
Bristol BS4 4EX

Tel: 0117 971 1717
Fax: 0117 972 1821

▶ **PADI (Professional Association of Diving Instructors) is the leading world-wide professional training organisation. It's fully international with schools in 175 countries and courses in sixteen languages.**

PADI estimates that 55 per cent of all divers are trained by PADI instructors. A considerable portion have only the basic elementary qualification (Open Water) and have to dive with more experienced divers. However, PADI has a full range of more advanced courses and specialisations that produce fully self-sufficient divers, capable of organising their own expeditions and supervising others.

PADI, unlike BSAC or SAA (see below), doesn't teach advanced rescue skills during the elementary courses but has a specific rescue module. This Rescue Diver course is spread over two weekends and is very comprehensive in both theory and practice.

Remember, no matter how good the course's design, it's only as good as the tutor, so if your initial route isn't working and you're still keen to dive, don't be afraid to change tack. Better to change allegiance than never to dive.

The Sub-Aqua Association (SAA)
Northern House
43-45 Pembroke Place
Liverpool
Merseyside L3 5PH

Tel/Fax: 0151 707 0111

▶ **The Sub-Aqua Association was founded in 1976 after independent diving clubs in Great Britain felt the need for a strong voice in the country's diving affairs.**

Subsequently, a training programme and guidelines

were drawn up and the Sub-Aqua Association was born to promote the UK independent club diving system.

The SAA training programme ensures that the novice moves through the grades of competence in an enjoyable and progressive way, each new level of training building on what has previously been learnt.

Disabled trainees and divers are welcomed at the SAA, provided their medical practitioners are happy, and age is immaterial, as long as the required fitness test and medical are passed.

Magazines

Scuba World is very bright and friendly with an excellent Web site. It is the official SAA magazine.

The Diver is the official BSAC magazine with a monthly circulation of over 50,000. It is more traditional and weighty.
Both contain lots of ads for dive courses.

——————— WHERE TO GO ———————

Company:	**Dive In Ltd**
Address:	Eastrea Road, Whittlesey, Peterborough, PE7 2AR
Tel:	01733 351 288
Fax:	01733 351299)
Price Range:	Discover Scuba (lecture, video, dive) £15; PADI Open Water £99 (NVQ price normally £325)
Payment Methods:	Cash, cheque, all major credit and debit cards (except Diners)
Booking Details:	Read the manual first, then book – 1 week approx
Capacity:	16 instructors available; classes up to 24 with ratio 1:6 (1:4 in winter)
Insurance:	PADI Insurance available £10 per course, can advise on broker
Facilities:	Dive shop, B&B and caravans on-site; restaurant and bar; changing room, showers and toilets. Wheelchair ramp available. Corporate team-building events organised (4x4 and clay pigeon shooting). Gift vouchers available.
Other Notes:	PADI 5★ IDC school trained approx 2,000 stu-

dents in 1996. Training in wet and dry suits all year round; course generally take place over 3 weekends. The lake has been 'seeded with wrecks', including a coach, an aeroplane and assorted cars. There are also Dive In Centres at:

28a, Ampthill Road, Bedford MK 42 9HG (Dive Shop training course in pool), open water dives at Gildenburgh, Tel: 01234 273058

Dosthill Church Road, Dosthill, Nr Tamworth B77 1LL (training at on-site lake, dive shop) Tel: 01827 281304.

Chief Instructor, Rod Collings, insists that the training is sufficient for qualified divers to cope with British coastal water conditions. The funded courses at £99 are an undoubted bargain.

Company:	**Maenporth Scuba School Ltd**
Address:	Aqua House, 23 Tregoniggie Estate, Falmouth, Cornwall, TR11 4SN
Tel:	01326 378878
Fax:	01326 378 776
Price Range:	Try dive (pool) £10; Sea Dive Experience £40; PADI Open Water (5 days) £197 (£150 with NVQ); BSAC Novice Diver £179; Sports Diver (7 days) £263 (£200 NVQ). Custom courses by arrangement.
Payment Methods:	Cash, cheque, Visa, Access
Booking Details:	Confirm individually as demand varies
Capacity:	1:4 in water, 1:20 in classroom
Insurance:	Students are covered during training
Facilities:	All types of accommodation available locally. Catering facilities at Maenporth beach. M and F changing rooms, showers and toilets. Caters for disabled divers/students.
Other Notes:	3 miles from MSS is their sister company: The Falmouth Underwater Centre, Maenporth Beach, Maenporth, Falmouth TR11 5HN (Tel/Fax: 01326 250852), which is a BSAC Premier School and runs the diving boat operation. Together, they certify 800 PADI and 200 BSAC divers per year, making them one of the biggest dive operations in the UK. Open 7 days a week, all year round, with winter training done in dry suits. Most training is in the sea though, in rough weather, they have access to a quarry.

Company:	**Scuba For All**
Tel:	0345 125 800
Web page:	http://www.scuba-for-all.com
Price Range:	PADI Open Water £125
Other Notes:	Scuba For All is a programme initially developed by the Diving Initiative in Birmingham and now operated by some 30 colleges and participating dive centres in the UK. Prices are consistent and most offer free Try Scuba sessions in a pool. Call them to discover your local club, they will send information within seven days about your nearest centre.

Company:	**Scuba Training Ltd**
Address:	204 Fulham Palace Road, London, W6 9PA
Tel/Fax:	0171 381 5000
Price Range:	Try dive from £20; PADI Open Water £175/99 (NVQ); BSAC Novice £260
Payment Methods:	Cash, cheque, Visa, Access, Diners
Booking Details:	Week in advance
Capacity:	Instructor ratio 1:4
Facilities:	Accommodation available locally. Changing facilities and toilets available at some pools and dive sites. Corporate events organised. Dive trips arranged. Courses up to and including instructor levels.
Other Notes:	Open water dives down in Peterborough or South Coast.

Company:	**Stoney Cove**
Address:	Stoney Stanton, Sapcote Rd, Nr Leicester, LE9 4DW
Tel:	01455 272768
Fax:	01455 274646
Price Range:	Discover scuba in pool free! Discover scuba in quarry £55; PADI Open Water £199 standard (£125-99 for funded programmes / tax relief) – 6 sessions. Full PADI programme up to IDC (Instructor Development Course); with NVQ £599.
Payment Methods:	Cash, cheque, all credit and debit cards
Booking Details:	2 weeks
Capacity:	8 students per instructor, maximum 16 per class
Insurance:	Have to sign various releases and medical waivers
Facilities:	Dive shop; changing facilities; toilets, showers;

restaurant, café, bar. Corporate entertaining; groups; gift vouchers available. Career development centre.

Other Notes: PADI 5★ centre; quarry is seeded with coaches and 'wrecks' to add variety to diving. Also at Rocky Cove, 78, Oldbury Rd., Blackheath, Warley, West Midlands B65 0JS (Tel/Fax: 0121 559 0701). Same prices training in pool and then at Stoney Cove for open water dives.

Company: **The Diving Initiative**
Address: The Lakeside Centre, Lifford Lane, Kings Norton, Birmingham, West Midlands, B30 3NT
Tel: 0121 459 4549
Fax: 0121 459 4546
Price Range: Discover Scuba pool dive free! PADI Open Water £125; PADI Advanced Open Water £199
Payment Methods: Cash, cheque, Visa, Access
Booking Details: 2 weeks
Capacity: Instructor ratio 1:4
Facilities: Dive shop, equipment hire, indoor heated pool. Café, hot and cold snacks. Corporate entertaining by arrangement; gift vouchers.
Other Notes: The Diving Initiative have initiated Scuba For All (see page 78) which runs at 30 centres across the UK. They have a large, sophisticated centre and do their open water dives at Stoney Cove.

Company: **West Wales Diving School**
Address: Sessions Hall, Mathry, Pembrokeshire Wales, SA62 5HB
Tel: 01348 831526
Price Range: Try Dive price on application; BSAC Novice £200 (3 days)/Sports £250 (4 days); PADI Open Water (5 days) £99, with NVQ funding. Advanced open water (2 days) £125.
Payment Methods: Cash, cheque
Booking Details: Bookings taken any time
Capacity: 4-6 per class
Insurance: Arrange own
Facilities: Dive shop; on-site pool; showers, changing rooms in pool. Café, pubs nearby. Gift vouchers.
Other Notes: Initial training done in pool then, on third day, visits

to St. Brides Cove, 'a 6m deep sheltered cove'. Open all year, turning over 150-200 certifications a year.

Company:	**Aquanaut Training School**
Address:	23, Wilmer Crescent, Kingston, Surrey, KT2 5LU
Tel:	0181 549 0852 / 0378 298012
Fax:	0181 549 0852
Price Range:	PADI Open Water (6-8 sessions) £258 (UK completion for open water dives); £158 (open water dives completed overseas).
Payment Methods:	Cash, cheque
Booking Details:	2-3 weeks
Capacity:	3 pupils maximum, unless family of 4 wishes to learn together.
Facilities:	Corporate entertaining and gift vouchers; club house with catering facilities and shower/toilet block by lakeside.
Other Notes:	Ross Prideaux comes highly recommended by a very experienced diver friend. He is more expensive than some because, 'I will not touch the NVQ, which I feel is turning out too many inexperienced divers, not used to difficult conditions. I got out of the rat-race to do what I do and discovered I had a vocation.' Open water dives are done either in a Thames Valley reservoir or on the south coast in Weymouth. Also arranges annual club tours to Red Sea or Caribbean.

Company:	**Puffin Dive Centre**
Address:	Port Gallanach, Oban, Argyll, PA34 4QM
Tel:	01631 566088
Fax:	01631 564142
Price Range:	Try a Dive (90 mins) £30; PADI Open Water £399; Dry Suit Conversion Course £100
Payment Methods:	Cash, cheque, all major credit and debit cards
Booking Details:	1-2 days
Capacity:	6-8 per course
Insurance:	Arrange own PA
Facilities:	Largest centre in Scotland, only yards from water's edge, with on-site accommodation (18 beds), showers etc. Slipway and moorings available. Many other local attractions in Oban for non-divers!

Other Notes: Puffin is owned and run by Mike Morgan and his daughter Nicola; it is a PADI 5★ IDC Centre. All training is done in dry suits and the sea so Puffin's divers are trained to cope with currents, tides, wind and the cold. Mike does not hold with the National Vocational Qualification (NVQ) so, unlike many centres, his prices are not subsidised. He still certifies 3-500 divers a year. The conditions for diving are spectacular all year round with visibility constant at 10m. The temperature range is 4-14° degrees but the area is full of wrecks, including a vertical one that starts at 6m under and drops to 54m. Also: dive charter boats and dive shop.

Company:	**Robin Hood Water Sports**
Address:	152 Leeds Road, Heckmondwike, West Yorkshire, WF16 9BJ
Tel:	01924 444888 / 01924 443843
Fax:	01924 474529
Price Range:	Blow a Bubble – 20 mins in pool with instructor £15, deductible from course fee. BSAC Novice/ Sports Course £125/175; PADI Open Water £150 (inc drysuit course)
Payment Methods:	Cash, cheque, all major credit and debit cards
Booking Details:	4 weeks in advance for monthly courses
Capacity:	4-8 per course
Facilities:	3m-deep, dual-depth swimming pool; lecture rooms and diving in local reservoir. Also: tuition and equipment for windsurfing and snow-boarding. On-site shop. Vending-machine refreshments only. Local accommodation by arrangement.
Other Notes:	Will arrange special courses if you provide minimum 2 people. Diving courses are currently aided by the Government. Equipment provided, though you must bring own masks, snorkel and fins. BSAC is 2 evenings per week for 4 weeks; PADI, 2 evenings for 3 weeks and weekend away diving in inland quarry near Peterborough.

SURFING

The wind gusting from the north does not appear to have made much impression on the surf rolling into Newquay's town beaches. It was a beautiful, late September day, blue skies, warm sunshine and a cool breeze. Back in July, it had been a real scorcher although the surf had been flatter than a Dutch hill. I'd driven back to London in a 4-hour grump, not improved by the cheery folk on Test Match Special relating another England collapse. That had not been a good day. Lesson learnt, I'd my bags packed ready for another foray when I called my new mate Baz who runs the Surf Centre. Another millpond was forecast.

Considering that the surfers at Fistral reckon to lose no more than 14 days in five months to inclement conditions (sometime the breakers that come in from the Atlantic are so fierce that they close the beach), God was not smiling on my intentions to cut a similar dash to Keanu Reeves in *Point Break*. I may not be as good looking, but I'm certainly cheaper. This was my last chance before the school closed until May.

───── A SMIDGEN OF COOL ─────

Of all the activities I've undertaken writing this book, surfing was the one I really fancied. I can swim, and water doesn't frighten me. Most of all 'Surfing is Cool' and at my age I need to keep topping up with little smidgens of cool. I remember being in Cornwall as a kid and seeing a few hardy souls lugging giant boards around, not far removed from the monstrous tree trunks ancient Hawaiian warriors used. Back then, I used to watch them fall in a couple of times and go back to building sand castles. Now I wish I was young enough to drive a VW van and hang around beaches all summer, impressing girls with my own personalised brand of 'Sex Wax'.

The image of surfing is brilliant, tropical beaches, blond hunks surfing impossible 40ft rollers. Yet in itself it is a completely pointless exercise. What is the achievement in paddling out to sea on a piece of plastic, then turning round and coming back in again, but a lot faster?

The answer is it's great fun and very exciting – what more do you want? If you wish to understand anything about the psyche of surfing read Andy Martin's wonderful *Walking On Water*. I did. Now I'm approaching Fistral Beach, walking through the weird hybrid of a seaside resort that Newquay has become.

—— WAVES I HAVE KNOWN ——

In the past 10 years, surfing has become incredibly popular in the UK. There are now 50,000 surfers (90 per cent of whom are aged between 15 and 30) and it is increasing at a rate of 10 per cent a year. Newquay is the mecca of British surfing; it is now both a traditional British seaside resort – B&Bs, buckets and spades, chips and clotted cream with everything – and a trendy hangout for the young complete with surf shops, ethnic jewellery stores, body-piercing parlours and posters advertising rave clubs. In the evening, as elderly retired folk stroll on the beach contemplating the ocean, behind a rock a group of long-hairs will be sharing a joint.

The first sight I had of Fistral Beach was extremely encouraging. The tide was high but retreating and, best of all, there were lots of people with surfboards...and they were in the sea. Despite all its flying flags, the BSA's National Surfing Centre is not quite as grand as it sounds – it's a small wooden shack on the edge of the car park, covered with more stickers than a Formula One motor car. Inside is equally spartan – especially when one of the instructors has forgotten to turn the kettle off – with racks of wetsuits hanging like forgotten ghosts in one corner and today's surf virgins trying to cram into them in the other. Outside, racked up like toothless sharks, are more than 30 surfboards.

All surfing instructors are interchangeable beings. To qualify – aside from being able to surf – you have to have shoulder-length hair, be very tanned, incredibly enthusiastic and wear cool shades. Feeling like an impostor, I took off my cool shades and put on a surf polo neck and a wetsuit, collected my 3m board and went to sit on the sand with my class. Sitting on the sand and rapping about waves you have known is, I'm told, an important part of surfing. Never having done it, I was at something of a disadvantage.

—————— SURF'S UP, WIPE OUT ——————

The instructor for us four virgins was Sean, an Aussie whose next surf stop was to be Indonesia. He quickly ran through the parts of the board, the nose (the front), the tail (the back), the rails (the sides) and the leash (a safety tether you velcro to your back foot, which means the board is always nearby after you have fallen off and not either being urinated on by dogs halfway up the beach or emigrating to Jamaica). He explained in graphic detail the meaning of the term 'wipe out' which I still consider to be unnecessary, if prophetic. He then went through a series of safety signals, explained what the flags meant and told us very firmly we were not to go out beyond waist deep. The boards we were using were all made of polystyrene, incredibly light, very buoyant and stable. They have been around for about eight years (about the same time as the smaller boogie boards that have replaced the body surfing planks of my youth) and are a tremendous improvement. No longer does the beginner have to lug around a heavy monster that is quite capable of knocking him out. However, in a strong wind they can certainly blow you over. In the water this is expected, on the sand it's rather embarrassing.

To prevent this, Clare and I carried our boards down to the water together. Clare was a bumptious lass from Wigan who was down in Newquay on holiday and announced, 'Well I've got to try it at least once'. The other two lads had also been down all week, they had hired boards and wetsuits every day, and got precisely nowhere. 'That happens a lot,' said Sean smugly. The other class jogged past us and then entered into a stretching routine. 'It's so cold in Britain it's very important that you are warmed up and flexible when you go into the water, otherwise you can get sprains and strains. We won't do it as the object of your first lesson is to have fun and get a taste.' Having been for a quick jog along the beach before the lesson, I felt very virtuous.

The first part of our lesson was the easiest, lying flat on the board and catching the wave that way. It was important to get flat properly, feet together, toes pointing down at the end of the tail, hands underneath shoulders grasping the rails. If you put extra weight on either rail, the board would go in that direction. Get your weight too far down the board and you push the nose underwater and, yes, wipe out. Well, I didn't. Half-remembered physical memories of body surfing as a kid came back and I was soon whizzing to shore, switching direction with alacrity. The only difficulty I had was tripping over my leash when wading back out to sea. At this stage, I really believed that I would just get up on my board and surf like a master. Such illusions have happened before and will happen again. I never learn. I find that rather endearing.

—— NATURAL OR GOOFY? ——

Sean demonstrated how to stand on the board on dry land. Paddling, he explained, was the key. You have to get into position, lie down and start paddling before the wave comes, looking over your shoulder all the time to check it's still there (while waves don't go off to the pub, they can suddenly peter out). When you feel the water lift the tail of the board, you have to paddle furiously – but not dig too deep as that will turn the board horizontal to the wave and dump you in the drink again. Then, with speed up, it's hands on to the rail beneath the shoulders, count one thousand, two thousand and in one fluid movement, rising from the toes and shoulders, hit your feet, front foot at 45° to the central line, back foot at 90°.

We all practised; three of us ended up with left foot forward and one with right foot forward. This meant we were 'natural footers' and Matt was a 'goofy footer'. (I assume that in these politically correct days being a 'left footer' is just not on.) The back foot is the one you attach the tether to.

Back in the water, it all seemed rather difficult. I kept choosing the wrong wave. One that was not yet a whitecap proceeded actually to break over my head – that hurt. Third time in, I got it right and even made it to my feet for about 3 seconds. Dave, who was teaching the more advanced class, told me to point my left hand forward, to bend my knees and try to get more balance. I thought I was doing what he suggested but it just got worse and worse, and my wipe outs more and more inventive. My problem, Sean explained, was that I was bringing my left hand across my body before I tried to stand, which meant I was already out of balance before getting to my feet.

He denied it vociferously, but I'm sure Sean was having a good laugh at our expense. He called us all in and then showed us an easier way of getting up, this time on to the knees, with hands still gripping the rails and from there up to standing. It worked in practice but I found my knee too tall to go under my shoulder, even with my hands going up on to their fingers. Back in the surf, I tried kneeling a couple of times and got nowhere, except even wetter than before. Sod this, I decided, it's back to the full leap for me.

——————— I CAN SURF! ———————

For the next 40 minutes I was catching waves. Sometimes I got it right. Once I stood up and steered vaguely straight for all of 15m past a bedraggled Clare, who gave me a thumbs-up so I waved back and fell in. I got knocked over by several waves when I had forgotten Sean's instructions always to turn the board to shore with my back to the waves. OK, so he was right but somebody has to try it. I was also exhausted. My arms and shoulders were getting tired from all the paddling, my back ached from all that arching, my foot was bleeding where it had been cut by a rock. But when he summoned us in, did I go gladly? Hell, no. I was going to catch one good wave to remember. I tried and I was just getting up when some prat on a boogie board crashed into me.

Despite all those aches, I cajoled Sean into letting me stay out a while longer – like another 40 minutes. In that time, I caught three good waves, missed countless others, learnt different ways to fall off a surf board – and I got one great run. I can remember it exactly: I saw the whitecaps coming a way back and got on to the board and stable in plenty of time, I started paddling frantically, the tail lifted, I paddled furiously, one thousand, two thousand, hands back on the rails and up. I'm standing, I'm surfing. I'm going too slowly, put weight forward, speed up. Yes, it works, keep it straight, time to get off. Brilliant. I can surf.

And I'm going to do it again. I might even be hooked. Yep, surfing is cool. I'm just not going to call everyone 'Dude'. Unless I can show them my 'Sex Wax'.

WHO TO CONTACT

British Surfing Association (BSA)
Champions Yard
Penzance
Cornwall TR18 2TA

Tel: 01736 60250
Fax: 01736 331077

▶ **The BSA was formed in 1966. Many members thought it was essential to counter what was perceived as a threat from the Surf Life Saving Association to ban surfing at many popular beaches. Although surfing is most popular with the young and does have a rebellious image, the BSA constitution has been in line with other sports' governing bodies since 1969.**

▶ **The BSA is a member of the Central Council for Physical Recreation and the International Surfing Association, and is affiliated to the National Sports Council.**
It has a National Coaching Accreditation scheme to provide and co-ordinate training courses. There are currently three levels of coaching awards right from beginners to international coaching.

▶ **If you are taking up surfing seriously, it is worth joining the BSA, if just for their liability insurance. If you are involved in an accident while surfing, you are covered for claims of up to £2 million for injuries to third parties and the cost of their equipment. Replacing gear can be expensive!**

▶ The BSA has been running an Approved Surfing Schools scheme since 1990 to help the public obtain greater value for money and greater safety while learning to surf. The BSA carries out two unannounced spot checks a year and if any of the eight safety regulations has been ignored the school is removed from the list immediately.

▶ The eight regulations are:
Approved schools must be covered by public liability insurance for claims by third parties for injury or damage arising out of the operators giving surfing lessons.
Soft-skinned boards must be available for all novices.
Surfing instructors must be at least BSA level 1 accredited coaches.
No more than 10 pupils are to be coached in the water by one qualified instructor (this may be reduced to an 8:1 ratio in 1997).
All surfboards must have ankle straps.
Each instructor will have a life saving aid at hand while pupils are in the water.
A first aid kit must be available on the beach.
The names of all accredited instructors will be sent to the BSA prior to the start of the season.

▶ If the school does not have BSA Approval, go somewhere that does. Call the BSA up for a list, they are extremely friendly and helpful. Surfers love to encourage new blood.

——— WHERE TO GO ———

Company:	**Atlantic Waves**
Address:	Unit 2a, D'Amport Farm, Les Gaillettes, Jersey, Channel Islands
Tel:	01534 865492; (mobile) 0979 718150
Fax:	01534 865492
Price Range:	Taster £5 for 90 minutes; £25 per day from 09.00-17.00; £50 for weekend; £120 for 5-day course
Payment Methods:	Cash, cheque
Booking Details:	Mid-July to first week Sept. All bookings must be

Capacity:	done by 1 May; weekend courses book by end June Total capacity 40, 16 course students per day maximum; 2-4 instructors in water, plus surf lifeguard doing equipment hire.
Facilities:	Café, snacks, changing facilities, free parking available on St Ouens beach. Atlantic Waves operates out of a mobile trailer. Surfboard factory.
Other Notes:	Good beginners' waves, with other places for advanced. Every instructor is a fully qualified surf lifeguard and BSA instructor. Season 1 Apr-1 Oct. Surfboard factory so equipment turns round on three-monthly basis. Jersey has clean beach policy, St Ouens is cleanest in Europe, 5 miles long, all yellow sand. Some of best waves in UK, better (they claim) than Fistral.

Company:	**Cayton Bay Surf School and Shop**
Address:	Killerby Cliff, Cayton Bay, Scarborough, N. Yorks, YO11 3NR
Tel:	01723 585585
Fax:	01723 585899
Price Range:	£18 per 3-hour session, equipment included
Payment Methods:	Cash, cheque, Visa, Mastercard
Booking Details:	Pre-payment up to 2 days in advance
Capacity:	8 pupils per session
Facilities:	Accommodation at 'The Barn' at Ongodby, 1½ miles away; also in Scarborough and Filey. Light snacks at the Surf Shop. Changing rooms with showers and toilets. Discuss disabled access. Cayton Bay Surf Challenge held in the autumn.
Other Notes:	Cayton Bay is the only BSA-approved surf school on the east coast of the UK. It was started in 1996 by David Hindley and his family, although surf competitions have been run there since 1989. David is a meteorologist who studied the wave conditions on the North Sea and has published them in a small pamphlet available from the shop. According to his statistics, they have surfable waves 76 per cent of the time and he runs a wave report and forecast updated daily on 0891 715644. Cayton Bay itself is a long crescent which attracts the best waves in the North Sea, giving them surfing when other places don't have it. Surfing is available all year round, due to high-quality wetsuits. On Christmas

Day 1995 David's son went surfing in a snow-storm – 'He came out after 45 minutes and he was very warm.'

Company: **Sennen Surfing Centre**
Address: 4 Trevilley Farm Cottages, Sennen, Penzance, Cornwall, TR19 7AU
Tel: 01736 8771458
Fax: 01736 65091
Price Range: £18 per person; £25 per day; 2-day course £30; 3-day £45; 5-day £75
Payment Methods: Cash, cheque
Booking Details: 2-4 weeks in advance in peak season, single lessons available on the beach
Capacity: 16 in the water with 2 instructors
Facilities: Back-packers' lodge, camping and caravaning, local B&Bs and hotels. Self-catering and café/restaurant facilities. Portacabin changing rooms and toilets; gift/equipment shops in Penzance. Disabled access. Beach volleyball court and fixtures.
Other Notes: Main season: 09.00-18.00, 7 days a week from Whitsun Bank Holiday until middle of Sept. Oct-Dec and Mar-May they operate 'Winter Weekends Surfaris' which are very popular with college surf clubs.

Company: **Wight Water Adventure Sports**
Address: 19 Orchardleigh, Shanklin, Isle of Wight, PO37 7N
Tel: 01983 866269
See page 23 (windsurfing) for details

Company: **British Surf Association National Surfing Centre**
Address: Fistral Beach, Newquay
Tel: 01637 850737 / BSA 01736 60250
Fax: BSA 01736 331077
Price Range: Beginner's lesson £18; 2 lessons £30; 5-session course £70. Equipment provided. One-on-one tuition £20 per lesson.
Payment Methods: Cash, cheque
Booking Details: Book at least a week in advance during summer
Capacity: 32; 1 instructor per 8 students

Facilities:	Café, changing rooms, toilets on Fistral Beach. Lifeguard in summer.
Other Notes:	Season: 7 days a week, early May to early Oct. Always call 24 hours in advance to check weather conditions.

Company:	**Harlyn Bay Surf School**
Address:	Newbrook-Homer Park Road, Trevone, Padstow, Cornwall, PL28 8QU
Tel:	01841 533076 / 01841 521 395
Fax:	01841 533 454
Price Range:	Half-day £20; 5-day course £110; full-day Surf Safari £30
Payment Methods:	Cash and cheques
Booking Details:	Book early, 2-4 weeks
Capacity:	1 instructor to 8 surfers
Facilities:	Land Rover to transport students to different beaches, depending on conditions and abilities; most beaches have refreshment, changing and toilet facilities.
Other Notes:	Season: May to Oct. The School can also arrange surfing packages with Treyarnon Bay Youth Hostel.

Company:	**Haven Sports**
Address:	Marine Road, Broad Haven, Haverford West, Pembrokeshire, SA62 3JR
Tel/Fax:	01437 781354
E-mail:	havensports@netwales.co.uk
Price Range:	£18 per 2-hour lesson; 5-day course £150.
Payment Methods:	All credit and debit cards
Booking Details:	High season minimum of 2 weeks in advance
Capacity:	1 instructor per 8 surfers; maximum 18
Facilities:	Beach has 2 cafés, a pub, changing rooms and toilets
Other Notes:	Season: Easter to early Oct. During high season the surfing and windsurfing groups will be at opposite ends of the beach. The Pembrokeshire peninsula is huge and the surfing is every bit as good as in Cornwall. Because of the peninsula there are always good waves somewhere.

Company:	**Outdoor Adventure**
Address:	Atlantic Court, Widemouth Bay, Nr Bude, Cornwall, EX39 1NG
Tel:	01288 361312
Fax:	01288 361 153
Price Range:	Weekend £127; day £30; half-day £16
Payment Methods:	Visa, Access
Booking Details:	Gets fully booked July and August, so book 1-2 months in advance
Capacity:	20
Facilities:	Accommodation for up to 27, bar, entertainment.
Other Notes:	Season: end Mar-end Oct, 09.30-17.00.

Company:	**St George's House Christian Outdoor Centre**
Address:	Georgetown, Braunton, N. Devon, EX33 1JN
Tel:	01271 890755
Fax:	01271 890060
Price Range:	£150 per week; £30 per day
Payment Methods:	Cash, cheque
Booking Details:	5 months in advance
Capacity:	46
Facilities:	Residential multi-activity centre
Other Notes:	Licensed centre for canoeing, climbing, abseiling, mountain biking and water-skiing.

Company:	**Surf South West**
Address:	Rivington, Higher Park Road, Braunton, N. Devon
Tel:	01271 815888
Price Range:	£15 per 2-hour session inc equipment; weekend course £45 with 3 lessons; week course £144
Payment Methods:	Cash, cheque, Mastercard, Visa, Delta
Booking Details:	Book 3-4 weeks in advance during summer
Capacity:	16-20 people
Facilities:	Croyde Bay has toilets, cafés, a bar and changing facilities.
Other Notes:	Season: Apr to end Oct. Lessons start 10.30 and 13.30.

Company:	**TJ's School of Surfing**
Address:	1a The Meadow, St. Ives, Cornwall
Tel:	01736 797 348
Price Range:	£15 per 2-hour lesson

Payment Methods: Cash, cheque
Booking Details: 2 days in advance
Capacity: 12 people with 2 instructors
Facilities: Porthmeon Beach has car parking, lifeguard, toilets, cafés
Other Notes: Season: Easter to Sept; weekends only from Oct (phone for details).

Company: **Twr-y-Felin Outdoor Centre**
Address: 1, High St, St David's, Dyfed, SA62 6SA
Tel: 01437 720391
Fax: 01437 721838
Price Range: Half-day £20; full day £30; weekend with full board £140
Payment Methods: Cash, cheque, all credit cards
Booking Details: One week in advance
Capacity: 15 surfers
Facilities: Grade 2 hotel taking up to 30 guests; bar; kitchen; outdoor shop.
Other Notes: The centre is open all year, but surfing is only available 3-4 days a week in winter. Surfing takes place on Whitesands Beach. The centre is also renowned for kayaking and coasteering.

WATER-SKIING

Trapped between the M3 motorway and the back of Thorpe Park, Thorpe Waterski is a deceptive place to find. But on a warm summer day it is a delight. Arriving at 10am – 20 minutes late which is neither polite nor advisable during high season – the first thing I see is skiers being towed around a lake by trolley-bus wires. It looks strange when you're expecting a speedboat, but cable skiing is a valid and cheap alternative to water-skiing.

——————— FROM BAR TO ROPE ———————

'As it is your first time, I would suggest going out on the boat with a bar and seeing how you get on,' says Paul Seaton, the owner and three times European Champion. 'That is one-on-one teaching and it will give you confidence that you can get up on skis. Then we'll try the rope and see how you get on. I'd say 90 per cent of our first timers get up in the first two sets. Being overweight and unfit may slow down progress. Being timid won't help either.'

I was supposed to be kitted up and standing on the jetty 15 minutes before my start time. Instead, I am faffing around trying to squeeze my stomach (memo to self: lose more weight) into a tight rubber suit and then having to beg a complete stranger to zip me up. This means that I do not have time to go through some rudimentary warm ups and stretches on my legs, arms, shoulders and upper back. I may not know it yet but I am going to regret that.

My instructor Laura Beglan may look fetching in cut-off jeans but she is very matter of fact. Each set on the water lasts only 15 minutes and she intends me to make the most of it. I look at the skis which seem awfully bulky and uncomfortable as I am used to skiing over snow. I cram my feet into some battered rubber and Laura clips me in and, while she attaches a 2m-long metal pole to the left side of the boat, I roll on to my right side and slip into the water. She tells me to place my hands 50cm apart, the right inside the cable and the left at the end of the pole, then to lean back into a fetal position with the ski tips 50cm out of the water. My knees are tight into my chest, my arms straight and my eyes looking straight up, pleading to the sky.

Laura starts the boat and as if by magic I start to rise out of the water remembering to keep going up in 15cm stages. My right foot feels pretty wobbly but I'm up and skipping over the water, with Laura shouting at me to keep my arms straight and to keep rising. Now this is pretty easy. I continue in this belief even though my arms are beginning to complain. Laura shouts words of encouragement and after three tows on the bar, as I lie floating on my back watching the traffic thunder past towards London, I learn that it is time to go on the rope. Nervously, I place the rope between my skis and resume the crouch with my arms outstretched either side of my knees.

—— THE BIG SPLASH SCENARIO ——

Confession time: I did have a go at water-skiing once – about 20 years ago on the Med when I was allowed three goes behind a speedboat. I actually managed to be towed for about 20m, unfortunately it was face first, underwater, with the skis somewhere else entirely. Like back on the beach. It wasn't much fun.

The boat accelerates up towards 18mph. Yes, I'm up first time, hooray, whoops; my legs wobble, so I sit back, bounce on the water, wobble, sit back a bit more, water spraying up into my face, bounce, wobble, swallow half the lake, sink. 'Leaning back comes later on,' says Laura helpfully, as I cough out several minnows. Second time up, I lean forward too much to compensate, the right ski tip goes underwater and my face follows it. Third time lucky, I get up, travel 20m before my confidence goes and I return to the sit back, wobble, bounce, big splash scenario.

This is beginning to piss me off. I get in the fetal position again, arms out straight and I hold the position. Yes, I'm up and we're rolling, I keep going up and suddenly I'm a fully erect Homo

Water Skier. We get to the end of the lake and somehow – I still have no idea how – I stay up doing a turn and we're heading back to the other end. My arms feel as if they have been stretched so far my knuckles will brush the ground, if I ever make it to dry land again. 'Follow the ski pylon,' shouts Laura, as we get to do another turn. But I'm going the wrong way, I'm whipping into the wake from the boat and losing speed, I lean too far forward, lose both skis and subside gracelessly into the water.

—— A CARBOHYDRATE BREAK ——

Laura picks my skis up and I roll into the boat. The first set is over. 'Take at least an hour's break,' advises Laura. ' Go to the café, get some carbohydrates and sugar into your body.' I nod as speech is beyond me. I've done 15 minutes water skiing and I am shattered. One bacon roll and high carbohydrate drink later, I feel a lot more human. Unfortunately, I still cannot grip my pen.

I'm lucky because the weather is so warm I can lounge around in shorts and a T-shirt. I don't need the thermal tracksuit in my bag, but there is one minute when the sun goes behind a cloud and a breeze sweeps up the lake when it gets chilly. If you are going water-skiing, make sure you have a set of warm clothes, maybe even take a thermos flask. If you get too cold – and you can do that very quickly in what passes for a summer in this country – it will sap the strength from your muscles and make the next set very hard work.

—— CROSSING THE WAKE ——

An hour later, I'm leaping into the skis, slipping in the water and raring to go. I get up first time and reach the other end of the lake without incident, until I decide to go in the opposite direction from the boat. 'Exactly where were you going?' inquires Laura, while I cough and splutter. Next time up and it's all wrong from the word go, so I collapse back into the water. 'Now let's try going from side to side but stay within the wake of the boat,' suggests Laura. 'To turn left, put your weight on your right ski, to turn right, put it on the left one.' Off we whizz and I make some rather tentative movements from side to side, until we come to the end of the lake and go round a corner. Once again sheer strength keeps me vertical, my arms hauling me upright, my legs refusing to split.

'Now let's try crossing the wake,' says Laura, after I have finally sunk. 'Look straight out at the side of the lake you're aiming for. Don't look down. Don't bend your arms.' First crossing of the wake, I look down. Guess what? Splash. Next go, I cross the wake, bend my arms and splash right down on my backside. Ouch. Next time up, I go right with no problem, coming back, I cross the left wake, looking fixedly at a truck on the M3, then I bend my arms. Face plant.

'Last chance,' says Laura firmly. 'We're going in. I want you to cross the wake both ways before we get there.' Time has gone so much quicker on this set, I feel like I've hardly got wet and it's already over. Huh, I'll show her. Cross left, no problem, cross right, perfect, she cuts the engine and I glide in next to the jetty, perfect timing and placing – just like the experts. The only problem is my arms don't have the energy to lift my body out of the water.

——— GAME, SET AND MATCH ———

I spend the next hour relaxing in the sun and watching the experts showing off on the slalom course on the Arena, leaning right back on a mono ski, gliding from side to side, swapping hands, hair blowing in the slipstream. It all looks so elegant. It's just not that easy. The Arena is an artificial lake with steep banks that make it a natural amphitheatre. It is one of the best competition sites for professional water-skiing anywhere in the world and has been host to the World Championships three times. Laura, who has been skiing for five years, is showing her stuff by doing jumps off a ramp. So for my third set I am left to the gentle ministrations of Chris Mayhew. Chris is on crutches with his right leg in plaster – the legacy of a water-skiing accident! 'I was going rather fast,' he admits – the top men will travel at 36mph across the water compared to my more sedate 19mph. 'I was unlucky; I broke several bones in my foot and ankle.' Beginners, he assures me, are unlikely to do something so drastic unless they leave the lake and end up trying to cross over the motorway. The majority of injuries are minor: muscle pulls and strains caused by over-exerting long-dormant muscle groups.

I get up first time no problems and get to the far end when, wham, it's face plant time again, both skis ripped off. Chris is not impressed, 'Go and pick them up then get them on.' This takes about 5 minutes as the bindings are too tight and I am so buoyant that I keep floating away from the skis, getting more and more irate in the process. Eventually I manage to get them on and Chris decides to confuse the issue by making me change my grip. One hand has to be on top of the handle, the other beneath it, knuckles facing in opposite directions – it doesn't matter which way, just the one that is most comfortable. My first attempt to get up with the new grip is an unmitigated disaster.

The next time I'm up and it feels peculiar, but I'm bouncing over the wakes without too much trouble. Chris keeps yelling at me and making various obscene gestures with his hips. The first time the sight of a man in plaster humping the air makes me giggle, so I fall in again. He tells me to bring my handle in closer to my thigh, not so far out, and use my hips to keep my body upright. It's about using the body to keep balance, and the speed and momentum to keep you going with minimum effort.

We're up and Chris gives me a fearful battering as we go round the lake twice, three times with me criss-crossing the wake, with confidence increasing simultaneously with the pain in my arms. 'I am not going to give up,' I say through gritted teeth as he does another turn; my grimace of pain is obviously interpreted as a grin of sheer delight and so we do it again. Eventually, after nearly 10 minutes of criss-crossing wakes and water, my arms simply lose all sensation and I subside. I lie on my back, arms outstretched in the water staring at a blue sky thinking, 'This is wonderful.' Then I have to try to get on to the boat again.

—— THE LEARNING CURVE ——

'Not bad,' says Chris. He is not as encouraging as Laura but then some women are used to telling a man he's great when they don't mean it. I'm thrilled to have made it up behind the boat after all these years. It was exhilarating to be up and moving over the water, if not totally relaxing. I even feel confident enough to try cable skiing next time. But not today, for my arms are shot and I know I am going to be very stiff in the morning.

The upshot of my first three sets is that, if I was to come twice a week for a month, I could get pretty good. Maybe even try and mono on one of the next two sessions. Water-skiing is a good sport for a beginner. There is a very fast learning curve, if you're fit and dedicated enough. After that it just takes more time, more practice and lots of money.

WHO TO CONTACT

British Water Ski Federation (BWSF)
390 City Road
London EC1V 2QA

Tel: 0171 833 2855
Fax: 0171 837 5879
E-mail: info@bwsf.co.uk

▶ **There are approximately 135 water-ski clubs affiliated to the BWSF, which will happily supply you with a list of them.**

▶ **The BWSF publishes a set of safety recommendations which all affiliated clubs must adhere to.**

▶ **Facilities vary – some have superb club houses and offer other watersports, while others just provide a water-skiing area for private boat owners to launch in. Some, like Alwen Water Ski Club (see page 104), are literally miles from anywhere. If you wish to take lessons, check the club has a qualified instructor and that they have equipment for you to borrow or hire.**

▶ **As a member of the BWSF, you receive the *British Waterskier* magazine five times a year, personal accident cover while skiing and a range of other benefits.**

WHERE TO GO

Company:	**(North) British Disabled Waterski Association – Whitworth Water Ski Centre**
Address:	Tong Lane, Whitworth, Rochdale, OL12 8BE
Tel:	01706 852534
Price Range:	Call for details
Payment Methods:	Cash, cheque
Booking Details:	Disabled asap – bookings taken 6 months to a year in advance
Capacity:	Full-size, championship lake
Facilities:	Accommodation available locally; catering on courses; full changing, shower, toilet facilities; parking for approx. 40. Fully adapted for disabled access. Corporate events organised.
Other Notes:	Purpose-built to cater for all disabilities. Able-bodied and disabled memberships. Venue for the European Disabled Championships, 1996.

Company:	**(South) British Disabled Water Ski Association**
Address:	The Tony Edge National Centre, Heron Lake, Hythe End, Wraysbury, Middx, TW19 6HN
Tel:	01784 483664
Fax:	01784 482747
Price Range:	£5-11 per 10 mins. Groups £36 per boat per hour.
Booking Details:	Beginners/novices 2 weeks ahead in spring, summer
Capacity:	5-6 per hour
Facilities:	Accommodation available locally; catering on courses; full changing, shower, toilet facilities; parking for approx. 40. Fully adapted for disabled access. Corporate events organised.
Other Notes:	Mid-Apr-Oct: Mon-Fri. (except Tues), noon-dusk; weekends 09.00-dusk. 1 Nov-mid-Apr: Sat, Sun, 09.00-dusk. The BDWSA will arrange courses for special needs groups, the physically and visually impaired and people with learning difficulties.

Company:	**Cirencester Water Ski Club**
Address:	Lake 37, Cotswold Water Park, Gloucestershire, GL7 5TL
Tel:	01285 861776

Price Range:	£8 per ski – 15 mins (tuition included)
Payment Methods:	Cash, cheque
Booking Details:	Ring in advance, 2-3 days at least.
Capacity:	Water size ½ mile
Facilities:	Caravan accommodation for club members. Temporary members during the week may use catering/changing facilities of clubhouse.
Other Notes:	This is a club. Temporary weekday membership only.

Company:	**Heany Water Ski School**
Address:	6 Hawkhope Hill, Falstone, Hexham, Northumberland, NE48 1BZ
Tel:	01434 240072
Price Range:	Wakeboarding: £10 full instruction lesson. Water-skiing: £10 per instruction lesson.
Payment Methods:	Cash, cheque
Booking Details:	2 days in advance
Capacity:	Lake: 7 x 3 miles – the biggest man-made reservoir in Europe
Other Notes:	The school is run by Nick Heany – National Water Ski Champion, 1995 – and his brother Julz, and is closed during the winter months. The boys retired from professional water-skiing in March 1996 to take up wakeboarding – a cross between snowboarding and surfing. They are now amongst the top five wakeboarders in Europe. Although the school still teaches water-skiing, Nick says, 'Once people see wakeboarding, the thought of water-skiing goes straight out the window and they want to wakeboard instead.'

Company:	**Liquid Leisure**
Address:	Handley Barnes, Little Hyde Lane, Ingatestone, Essex, CM4 0E8
Tel:	01277 352245 (office)/01277 821554 (home)
Price Range:	£18 per lesson (15-20 mins)
Payment Methods:	Cash, cheque
Booking Details:	Pre-booking essential
Capacity:	50-100 per day
Facilities:	Local hotels. Catering by arrangement; changing rooms and toilets; gift shop; corporate events and gift vouchers available.

Other Notes: Open 7 days a week Mar-Oct. Also: club membership, wakeboarding and jet ski launching facilities.

Company: **Royal Docks Water Ski Club**
Address: Gate 16, King George V Dock, Woolwich Manor Way, London, E16 2PA
Tel: 0181 858 0442
Price Range: Lesson £20; 4 lessons £55
Payment Methods: Cash, cheque
Booking Details: 48 hours
Capacity: 2 boats
Facilities: Light refreshments; bar; showers and toilets; equipment on sale. Corporate events organised (outside caterers). Gift vouchers.
Other Notes: Only club in central London for past 11 years, next to London City airport. Membership £160 per annum.

Company: **Scottish National Water Ski Centre**
Address: Town Loch, Townhill, Dunfermline, KY12 0HT
Tel: 01383 620123
Price Range: Non-members £12 per day; £10 children/students/OAPs. Membership and group discount details available on request.

Company: **Stoke on Trent Water Ski Club**
Address: Trentham Gardens, Trentham, Stoke-on-Trent, Staffordshire
Tel: 0831 472077
Fax: 01782 633907
Price Range: 30 min ski £7 (equipment and tuition provided); day tickets £7.50
Payment Methods: Cash, cheque
Booking Details: 2 weeks in advance, minimum
Capacity: 2 boats towing skiers at any one time; 10 boats on the lake maximum
Insurance: Extra cover made available for corporate events
Facilities: Accommodation available locally: club house; changing rooms; showers; toilets. Hot and cold snacks. Parking at water side; disabled access. Corporate entertaining/groups; gift vouchers.

Other Notes: Instruction in recreational, mono, tricks, jumping and barefoot skiing. Also available is Ski Boat Driver Award (SBDA), a day course for non-drivers. All equipment provided if necessary.

Company: **Tallington Lakes**
Address: Tallington Lakes, Barlolm Road, Tallington, Tamford, Lincs, PE9 4RJ
Tel: 01778 346573
See page 21 (windsurfing) for details

Company: **Thorpe Waterski**
Address: Staines Road, Chertsey, Surrey, KT16 8PN
Tel: 01932 561171
Fax: 01932 567622
Price Range: Single lesson £15 (Apr-Oct); £13 (Nov-Mar); week-end course £96/112. Cable Ski 1-hour pass £9; 2-hour pass £13; all day £26.
Payment Methods: Cash, cheque, Visa, Access
Booking Details: Boat lessons 7-10 days depending on season
Insurance: Insurance available through British Water Ski Association; there are signs up saying you water-ski at own risk
Facilities: On-site café, changing rooms, showers and toilets. Accommodation available locally. Corporate activities organised.
Other Notes: Thorpe Waterski has hosted the World Championships and thus has superb facilities – it says it's the best in Europe. The cable ski is closed Dec-Mar. The lakes are open all year round except Mon, Tues and Fri in the winter season.

Company: **Yorkshire Water Ski Club**
Address: Welton Waters, Common Lane, Welton
Tel: 01482 666133 / 01482 631627 (secretary)
Price Range: Non-members £10 (10-15 mins) includes tuition. Reductions for members, children and families.
Payment Methods: Cash, cheque
Booking Details: Closed between 1 Nov and 28 Feb. Ideally 2-3 weeks in advance.
Capacity: Water size: 80 acres. Only one boat at a time.
Facilities: Clubhouse with changing rooms, showers and toi-

lets (disabled access). Corporate events organised and gift vouchers can be arranged.

Other Notes: Club run solely by members. Tournament-oriented. Also: windsurfing by arrangement.

Company: **Alwen Water Ski Club**
Address: Tyn yr Erw, St George Road, Abergele, Clwyd, LL22 9AR
Tel: 01745 824898 (h)
Price Range: Tailor-made lessons – call for details
Payment Methods: Cash, cheque only
Booking Details: Essential to call in advance
Capacity: One boat only
Facilities: Corporate entertaining; use of kettle; shower and toilet block suitable for disabled as well.
Other Notes: This is a remote club on a reservoir surrounded by dense forest in the heart of North Wales. It is vital to call before you arrive to ensure that the club is manned, and to get directions to find it. There is only one boat, which runs on propane gas so it doesn't pollute the drinking water of the reservoir. On a good day, in the words of the secretary, Eddie Booth, the skiing is 'beautiful.' On a bad day it is 'like the Arctic'.

Company: **National Water Sports Centre**
Address: Adbolton Lane, Holme Pierrepont, Nottingham, NG12 2LU
Tel: 0115 982 1212
Fax: 0115 945 5213
See page 116 (white water rafting) for details

Company: **Blackwater Watersports**
Address: Fox Lane, Eversley Cross, Hook, Hampshire, RG2 ONQ
Tel: 01252 871182
Price Range: £12 per tow (includes tuition), tow lasts around 10 mins
Payment Methods: Cash, cheque, Access, Visa
Booking Details: Open times: 09.00 till dusk all year
Capacity: One boat at any one time
Facilities: Gift vouchers, toilet and parking facilities.

Other Notes: Water size: 30 acres.

Company:	**Princes Club**
Address:	Clockhouse Lane, Bedfont, Middlesex, TW14 8QA
Tel:	01784 256153 / 01784 255330
Fax:	01784 255568
Price Range:	Membership prices on request. Non-members cable ski £11 – 1 hour, £13 – 2 hours £26 – all day. Beginners' course morning (3 tows) weekday £45, weekend £50, afternoon (2 tows) £35, day course (4 tows) £55, 3-day course (12 tows) £140. Also: jet ski £18 per half an hour for 550cc solo craft; £20 for 650cc. Call 01784 240625 for further details.
Payment Methods:	Cash, cheque, major credit cards (Amex and Switch cannot be taken over the phone)
Booking Details:	Beginners' course 2-3 weeks
Capacity:	4 per hour on ski boat
Facilities:	Corporate days out organised. Club includes changing rooms with showers, restaurant, bar, gym, aerobics and squash courts. Four ski lakes plus 800m cable tow.
Other Notes:	Princes is the oldest water-ski club in Britain – over 40 years old.

WHITE-WATER RAFTING

'It's not exactly *The River Wild*, is it?' announces the Semi Spy, staring at a dead flat, dead straight 2,200m stretch of water. 'How exactly do you propose we go white-water rafting on that?'

'That's where they do the Olympic Rowing trials. We're going on the canoe slalom course,' I retort somewhat sharply, tired after the 2½ hour drive from London, and wondering exactly where we are going. The River Trent, after all, is not exactly world-renowned for its rapids. 'It's down there,' I say gesturing beyond a narrow concrete bridge. As we look, a canoeist drops 10m down into the water with a loud crash and promptly turns turtle. The Famous (but resting) Actor goes pale.

Originally, I had intended to tackle white-water rapids in a canoe. Enquiries soon revealed that it would take a minimum of two to three days before any instructor would be inclined to let me loose on any liquid with froth on it. Even then it was most likely to be a pint of beer. 'Try rafting,' was the advice. 'That way you get the adrenaline rush without having to work so hard.' Unfortunately, while the UK has plenty of white-water sites for canoes, those available for large, inflatable rafts are limited. I had intended to go to Snowdonia, the River Dee or Scotland to sample the delights of a real river but deadlines and other events had conspired otherwise. So instead of navigating the gorges, gullies and wild waters of the Colorado River piloted by Meryl Streep I was at the National Water Sports Centre, near Nottingham, under the command of a raft guide called Julian, ready to tackle a man-made 700m course.

God knows what Julian Clapham made of the three

reprobates I had inveigled up from London to fill the raft with the promise of a 'Daring Day Out' – but then he has taken on eight-man rafts full of aggressive, tattooed drunks from Hull. It didn't help that we were running late as the Famous Actor and the Semi Spy had refused to change into their wetsuits until they had received an infusion of beans and chips. Then he had to fetch a larger buoyancy aid for the Semi Spy after he proved too broad across the beam for the original, much to the mirth of his companions.

—— THE GIN AND TONIC CURE ——

Julian then asked if any of us had any experience rafting. The Property Developer 'fessed up to having been on a rafting trip in Australia a few years back. The rest of us agreed that we could swim 50m but that the Semi Spy had evolved the unique ability to get seasick on a floating restaurant. Undaunted, Julian set about explaining the various techniques and safety procedures. The raft is divided into compartments, in each compartment are two paddlers who are responsible for each other's safety. You wedge your feet either into a stirrup (at the front) or under the raft divide and then sit on a yellow stripe on the side of the raft. (The stripe is made of a different material which is not so slippery.) At the top of the paddle, the thumb goes under the T, with the rest of the hand over the top; the bottom hand goes down as far as the blade.

As the river water used on the course has just flowed through Nottingham, it is not the cleanest in the land and Julian advised keeping one's mouth shut when – not if – one fell in. He also advised having a large gin and tonic after finishing – apparently the quinine in the tonic zaps the nasty bacteria. On falling in, one should never let go of the paddle, and then try to grab the handles or rope that run around the raft. You fish your buddy out by hauling in on the shoulder straps – not the helmet or arm. If for some reason you find yourself underneath an upturned raft, sink down to where the current is faster and it will carry you away.

Now it was time to try the water, so we hop in and head out on to the glassy flat Trent to try out the manoeuvres. He soon has us paddling hard forward and then spinning the raft with one pair paddling back ('use the hips for more power') and the other forward. In rough water areas, where the raft is at sharp angles, water starts coming in. If it comes in your side you lean into the raft, if it isn't your side, you lean out. I note with some alarm that the Semi Spy does not seem too thrilled at the idea of leaning out. Charitably, I blame this on the size of his bottom.

It's time to go and we paddle along a nice flat stretch of water that suddenly narrows under a concrete bridge. Approaching it, we see that the water suddenly goes into a series of ridge backs. Julian steers us so we are sideways on and we are sliding over the edge. Four hearts stop. Down up, down up, whew, it's time to breathe again. Then we're heading straight for a series of metal slalom poles, suspended from overhead cables and used by canoeists. If you don't pay attention they can fetch any extremities a vicious crack; the object is to take them on the helmet or chest or, if they are coming at your face, use the paddle to ward them off.

Although the course is short, it is cunningly designed with lots of concrete pyramids and shallows to create eddies where the water runs counter-clockwise and, with a bit of nifty paddling, you can go over the same areas several times, until either exhaustion or a miscalculation lets the current drag you further down. We're going well for a first run, bouncing up and down, paddling when ordered, through the Cheese Grater and on to the Mangle (don't ask me where they get the names from) when disaster strikes.

Everything is fine, then the raft is at an angle, water is pouring into my side, I lean in, the Semi Spy leans out, or rather tries to. Next thing I know, I'm in the water, holding my paddle with one hand and the other hooked on to the rope. The Semi Spy hauls me back and announces solemnly, 'I have just saved your life.' The others cackle. So do the people on the river bank.

SPECTATOR SPORT

It may be October but there is still an audience gathered to watch what is obviously the local spectator sport – people falling off rafts. In high summer, the banks are packed with people having picnics or barbecues, some waiting for their own 2-hour slot, others just along for a laugh. It can get packed on the course, too, with up to eight rafts and dozens of canoeists battling the white water. The skill of the guides enables them to take parties of children, or those with special needs, down the course with no mishaps. As we carry the raft back up-river for 150m before getting back in the Trent for a leisurely paddle, I feel that somehow we are all going to get wet today.

For the second run, after we have negotiated the rollercoaster bumps, Julian introduces a new variation – the 'pop out'. The Famous Actor and the Property Developer, up in the front compartment, put their paddles down and sit on the nose of the raft facing us, with their hands on the rope. At a given command, we paddle furiously and they lean back, their helmets hovering over the water. If the raft has been fully inflated, the back will rise and the guide on an eight-man craft can find himself 4m above the water contemplating a belly flop. We don't manage that, though I do miss a stroke and am toppling overboard when the Semi Spy grabs me before I hit the water. 'That's twice now,' he says ominously, 'so don't mock.'

For the third run, it's our turn to be up the nose. On command we lean right out, my helmet is brushing the surface, then I can see the back lift as my head goes under. When we pop back up again, we see that the Famous Actor has disappeared. We fish him out and continue down the course. Julian does some cunning steering and, instead of me being the one sliding in, I'm leaning out. Like a giant redwood tree, the Semi Spy is toppling overboard. Instinctively I grab him. 'What did you do that for?' his close friends ask me. I'm not sure, so I just mumble something about payback.

Julian asks us if we fancy 'surfing the stopper wave' in pairs. The Famous Actor and I promptly volunteer the others and watch from the bank. Basically, Julian controls the angle of the raft with his weight and the others have to go from side to side, to commands of, 'High left,' and, 'high right,' and lean out to stop the raft from flipping. It doesn't. So, the Famous Actor and I decide to really go for it, riding the waves like bucking broncos, screaming 'yee ha' and howling with laughter. After what seems like hours, but is probably only a couple of minutes, one of us makes a mistake and the raft flips over on its back. Wet again.

A MOUTHFUL OF TRENT

By the last couple of runs we're a real crew, pulling together, working a rhythm and obeying the commands instantly. I'm up at front right with the Famous Actor, my left foot hooked under the strap, when Julian calls 'All in deck' or something like that. The raft is at a sharp angle to the water and as I slide in the little finger on my left hand smashes straight into the other side. It hurts like hell. 'I've broken it,' I whimper, and then I forget the pain as I'm upside down gulping in a mouthful of Trent. My foot is stuck and I experience a flash of panic until it comes free. I come up coughing and spluttering under the raft. Still floundering and gasping, I turn round to see Julian and the Famous Actor trying to right the raft; it slips out of their hands and comes down on my head. The impact drives me underwater, inhaling another mouthful of bacteria as I go. The current whips me away and when I resurface I am spinning round and round and heading straight for a large concrete block at high speed. I manage to bash into it feet first, but my momentum turns me round again so my shoulder and head bang into it. 'Thank God for helmets,' I think in-between coughs.

There is no chance of getting back on to the raft so I find an eddy, get my breath back and then float on down-river feet first, my paddle grasped in regulation position. Naturally enough, I miss the landing site and the Property Developer has to haul me out. Sitting on the bank, we notice Julian sprinting down the far bank to collect two paddles – one of them his – before they reach the North Sea. 'Anyone would think the paddles were more important than us,' grunts the Property Developer sardonically.

That was a suitably watery end to our 2-hour session. The spectators had been entertained with some spectacular falls and we'd had a great time. The downside was that as I had to drive back to London, I was the only one who didn't get to slurp down a brace of gin and tonics. And I had to come to terms with the fact that by this time next year the Semi Spy would be telling all and sundry how he'd saved my life from a man-eating hippopotamus while rafting down the Zambezi.

I'd also learnt a salutary lesson. Even in the most controlled conditions, with safety-conscious guides and the proper equipment, nature has the ability to make fools of us all. On a real river, the rock I banged into could have been jagged, the currents could have created an undertow and, while I was coughing out the water, I could have been swept hundreds of yards away. It didn't happen, but it reminded me that all adventure sports require one thing in common: always keeping a part of your brain alert for danger.

WHO TO CONTACT

This is still a new sport in transition with a small but growing number of practitioners, who in 1996 introduced a code of practice for river rafting. A new raft guide training structure has been developed with the close assistance of the Scottish Rafting Association. The best rides are to be had abroad but for a taster of what's in store try the following for information:

The English White-Water Rafting Committee
Mike Devlin
c/o Current Trends
Adbolton Lane
West Bridgford
Nottingham NG2 5AS

Tel: 0115 981 8844
Fax: 0115 9822033

The Scottish Rafting Association
Dave Horrocks
Ythan Centre
Station Road
Ellon AB41 9AE

Tel: 01651 851215

The Welsh Rafting Committee
Tony Howard – Tel: 01978 790485

CANOEING

If white water is your thing but you think rafts are boring, you might wish to take up canoeing or kayaking in its various guises, whether on lake, sea or rapids. In which case contact the BCU (British Canoe Union, see below) for a list of their affiliated clubs and approved centres that teach canoeing. Like most big organisations, they are not very helpful in recommending specific places – there are dozens – but persist and you, too, can get both wet and happy.

British Canoe Union
Adbolton Lane
West Bridgford
Nottingham NG2 5AS

Tel: 0115 982 1100
Fax: 0115 982 1797

If you live in Northern Ireland, Scotland or Wales contact:

The Canoe Association of Northern Ireland
c/o SCNI House of Sport
Upper Malone Road
Belfast BT9 5LA

Scottish Canoe Association
Caledonia House
South Gyle
Edinburgh EH12 9DQ

Welsh Canoe Association
Frongoch
Bala
Gwynedd
North Wales LL23 7NU

National Canoeing Venues (Sports Council)
Plas Y Brenin

Capel Curig
Betws y Coed
North Wales
Tel: 0169 04 720280

Plas Menai
Caernarfon
Gwynedd. LL5 1UE
Tel: 01248 670964

Glenmore Lodge
Aviemore, Inverness-shire
Scotland
Tel: 0479 86256

WHERE TO GO

Company:	**Canolfan Tryweryn**
Address:	Frongoch, Bala, Gwynedd, LL23 7NU
Tel:	01678 521 083
Fax:	01678 521 158
Price Range:	Raft Experience (20 minutes) £10 adult, £7 junior; Raft Extravaganza (2 hours) £141 weekdays, £188 weekends (per raft). Wetsuit hire £4, wetsuit boots £2
Payment Methods:	Cheque – £20 deposit, balance 15 days in advance
Booking Details:	Experience: bookings can be made only 2 days in advance; Extravaganza: check with centre for days when water is being released – this is sometimes confirmed only a few days beforehand.
Capacity:	4-7 per raft
Insurance:	Participants advised to arrange their own PA
Facilities:	Local accommodation; changing facilities, showers, toilets, cafés, restaurants and pubs close by. Corporate entertaining; groups; gift vouchers.
Other Notes:	Closed for maintenance 18 Oct-30 Nov. Water releases are never 100 per cent guaranteed.

Company:	**Pioneer Activities**
Address:	Waensawr, Pentrecelyn, Ruthin, Denbighshire, LL15 2HW

Tel/Fax:	01978 790485
Price Range:	£21 per person for 2-hour session that includes all equipment
Payment Methods:	Cash, cheque
Booking Details:	One week minimum
Capacity:	6 per raft, 3 rafts plus '2 man ducky'; 20 max
Insurance:	Arrange own PA
Facilities:	Changing, shower, toilet facilities available at launch sites.
Other Notes:	Also: kayaking, climbing, abseiling, archery, Canadian canoe expeditions. Multi-activity weekends inc 2 nights' accommodation and food at £100 per person (max 10).

Company:	**Clywid Outdoors**
Address:	The Centre, 65 Harwoods Lane, Rossett, Wrexham, WI12 0EU
Tel:	01244 570 157
Fax:	01244 571 244
Price Range:	Bala – 8-man raft £142; Llangollen – 6-man raft £90. Wetsuit hire £4.
Payment Methods:	Cheque, cash
Booking Details:	1 week for Llangollen; 1 month for Bala
Capacity:	18 (3 rafts) in Llangollen; 24 (3 rafts) in Bala
Facilities:	Dragon boat racing and white-water rafting corporate days; gift vouchers; Christmas and birthday parties; local accommodation. Catering and toilet facilities at 2 sites.
Other Notes:	Also: mountain biking, Canadian canoeing, kayaking, dragon boat racing. White-water rafting takes place either at Bala, or on the Dee at Llangollen; canoeing at Llangollen and dragon boat racing in Chester.

Company:	**Croft-Na-Caber**
Address:	Croft-Na-Caber, Kenmore, Loch Tay, Perthshire, PH15 2HW
Tel:	01887 830 588
Fax:	01887 830 649 (hotel)
Price Range:	Chinese run £18 per person (big groups only); Grandtully/Stanley trip £24
Payment Methods:	Cash, cheque, Access, Visa
Booking Details:	2 weeks

Capacity:	8 per raft, max 8 rafts
Insurance:	Company liability; arrange own PA
Facilities:	Corporate entertaining and gift vouchers; self-catering chalets and small hotel; restaurant lounge and coffee shop. Separate changing facilities; parking; craft and gift shop. Some chalets and hotel suitable for disabled.
Other Notes:	Open all year. Best in autumn and spring when the river is running: Also: canoeing, kayaking, sailing, windsurfing, mountain biking, jet bikes, river sledging, clay shooting, archery, quad bikes, canyoning.

Company:	**Current Trends**
Address:	Adbolton Lane, West Bridgford, Nottingham, NG2 5AS
Tel:	0115 9818844
Fax:	0115 9822033
Price Range:	Weekdays £75 + VAT (per raft), higher rate evenings and weekends
Payment Methods:	Cash, cheque, Visa, Access
Booking Details:	As much as possible, 8 weeks plus for weekends
Capacity:	8 per raft, up to 3 rafts
Facilities:	Corporate entertaining, gift vouchers; local B&B; on-site changing, shower, toilet facilities (not suitable for disabled); on-site catering with ramp access; parking; canoe retail shop.
Other Notes:	Also: kayaking, canoeing, windsurfing, sailing, climbing, caving. Mostly groups of 6-8 oriented.

Company:	**Four Seasons**
Address:	Tees White Water Course, Tees Barrage, Stockton, TS18 2QW
Tel:	01642 678000
Fax:	01642 677334
Price Range:	Summer £60 for 2 hours (includes helmet, buoyancy aid, paddle and guide). Winter £60 for 1 hour, includes wetsuit.
Payment Methods:	Cash, cheque, Visa, Access
Booking Details:	Summer 2-3 months in advance
Capacity:	4 6-man rafts
Facilities:	Corporate facilities, gift vouchers; caravan and camping site; full catering facilities and shower/

toilet facilities – everything suitable for disabled; retail shop.

Other Notes: TWWC is a 350m artificial course in a U-shape – so you don't have to carry the raft far. Also: canoeing, kayaking, bell boating.

Company: **National Water Sports Centre**
Address: Adbolton Lane, Holme Pierrepont, Nottingham, NG12 2LU
Tel: 0115 982 1212
Fax: 0115 945 5213
Price Range: 8-man raft £77.50 (inc guide, buoyancy aid, helmet, paddle); 4-man raft £55. Wetsuit hire £4 + £25 deposit.
Waterskiing £10 per 10 min lesson
Payment Methods: Cash, cheque, Visa, Access
Booking Details: Summer, weekends 4-6 weeks in advance
Capacity: Five 2-hour sessions a day, 7 days a week
Facilities: Corporate entertaining. Gift vouchers for certain activities such as white-water rafting and waterskiing. On-site 70 bed hotel (1, 2, 3 and 4 bunks/room). Disabled facilities.
Other Notes: Windsurfing: 2-hour taster sessions available Mon-Thur 18.00-20.00 Apr-Oct. Call for junior details. Water-skiing cableway open May-Sept. Also: canoeing, sailing, rowing, powerboat handling courses.

PART THREE
EARTH

CAVING AND
POTHOLING

Barbara is extremely dubious about descending into Giant's Hole. This decision is not based on the tyranny of fashion, though wearing a sludge-green plastic oversuit, plum-coloured wellington boots and a white helmet with attached torch does not generally contribute to a person's self esteem. As we are all dressed in similar eye-catching and sweat-enhancing ensembles – ranging from banana yellow to jaffa orange – that cannot be the problem. No, Barbara suffers from claustrophobia and she is concerned that if she goes into the cave she will freak out.

I'd always thought of caving as a peculiar sort of sport. I've been into a fair few tourist caves. Places with concrete walkways, electric lighting and guides to point out the most interesting stalagmite and stalactite formations which, while they have dramatic names like The Devil's Handmaidens, The Drowning

Eagle or Father Christmas' Beard, usually look like interesting shapes of slimy rock. In tourist caves, guides always like to play the 'let's get really dark' game which involves turning off all the available lights so we can see how incredibly dark it can be in a place where there is no available light, no reflections, no luminous anythings. It's very scary to realise how much we depend on our vision. When there are only five of you standing in Base Camp Chamber and each one turns their helmet light off in turn, it seems a whole lot darker and much more scary.

———— DUBIOUS PLEASURES ————

Giant's Hole is to be found on Peakshill Farm, a few miles west of Castleton in the Peak District. For the faint-hearted, there are plenty of 'show caves' to visit, including one that can only be reached by boat, but Giant's is a good place to sample the delights of caving. There is a 4 to 5 hour trip or, on an afternoon visit like mine, you can sample some of the dubious pleasures of the sport in 2 hours. We are all reassured to learn that our lights are powered by Oldham's lead acid cells which will give us 14 hours of illumination.

Giant's Hole is technically known as a solution cave, formed when seeping rainwater, surface and underground streams wear away the rock over the course of hundreds and thousands of years to create underground labyrinths. As it flows, water absorbs carbon dioxide from the soil; water and carbon dioxide react chemically to form carbonic acid. Although a very weak acid, carbonic acid will dissolve limestone. The drip, drip of the water is perpetually re-depositing dissolved limestone carbonate, which over the years will form into wonderful and grotesque shapes – stalactites or stalagmites. The best-known structures are the stalactites, which hang like icicles from the roofs of caves, and the stalagmites, which extend upward from the cavern floors. Sometimes two growths meet and join into a pillar form, helping to support the roof. Less well-known forms of carbonate deposition include flowstone and dripstone. These rock formations can vary in colour from ghostly alabaster white to dusky red and muddy brown, the result of mineral deposits brought by the water.

Over the years, a stream may work down several levels in a cave, leaving dry chambers behind as its path is redirected. If after several unusually wet years the water table starts rising, old cave chambers become flooded and new ones begin forming at higher levels. During a long drought, chambers will begin forming at lower levels, closer to the declining water table. Over thousands of years, climatic fluctuations produce multi-level cave systems which brave souls like to explore.

—— BASE CAMP CHAMBER ——

The entrance is easy enough – a slow gradual descent into the bowels of the earth, walking upright for 90 per cent of the time, following the path the water has gouged in the limestone over thousands of years. John Thomas, our guide from Rock Lea, leads us into what appears to be a dead end. 'That used to be the way down,' he says, pointing at what seems to be little more than a crack in the wall. Peering down, all I can see are piles of small rocks and stones and a puddle of water. Once upon a time this was the only route to Base Camp Chamber, slipping crawling and sliding through water and mud. It would take between 3 and 5 hours to travel a few hundred yards. Now a different route has been blasted through that only takes 10 minutes and the old passage is clogged up by rocks.

The value of the helmet is soon apparent as I bang my head every few yards. Some of this clumsiness is because, while my body is intrinsically aware of how tall I am, it has yet to come to terms with the extra couple of inches the helmet has conferred upon me. A seasoned caver and guide like John hardly ever bonks his bonce.

Base Camp Chamber (so-christened because in the old days, before the new passage, cavers would camp there overnight before heading on for further explorations) is a vaulting place reaching 40ft into the ceiling. The walls are decorated by flowstone that has twisted itself into grotesque and varied shapes, in colours that range from murky brown to a spectral white. Everywhere I can hear the drip, drip, drip of water gouging away another micron of limestone or adding it to another natural sculpture. Deep cuts and troughs in the rock show where the water level reached in different eras.

We head on to Garland's Pot, where the water has created a natural circular well. It is a pothole but only 20ft deep. Going down into it is a wire ladder, attached to a bolt permanently fixed into the rock, with a blue safety rope running parallel. John explains there is a group down there on the 5-hour excursion. We, however, are going back to Base Camp Chamber in search of alternative excitement.

PANIC ATTACK

I'm rather disappointed for a few minutes; then we hop up on to a platform and John gestures at a gap in the wall. The prosaically named 'Water Inlets' are between 12 and 15ft high but no more than a couple of feet wide. The inlets have created a spiral passage carved from the limestone that winds its way up to the roof of Base Camp Chamber. Katie, being the smallest, goes first; I being the widest have to bring up the rear. John warns it may well prove too narrow for me at the top. In fact, it nearly proves too narrow at the bottom.

I have to wait a few minutes for the other four to slip-slide their way through the gap, minutes in which I feel strange palpitations in my chest. I don't feel comfortable. Then it's my turn; I slide in and get stuck; I breathe in and get stuck a bit more. I don't like this at all, my breathing gets fast and shallow, I'm having a minor panic attack. Barbara asks if I'm alright. Not really, no. I pull myself back out and learn its easier to go back down than uphill. I know I can escape. Now I know I'll be OK, I can control my breathing, nice and slow, deep breaths and go up again. I'm not comfortable at all but I go on up, ducking under some outcrops, hitching myself up on to a ledge to slide past another on my bum. I catch up with the others as Katie has announced that the next entrance is a little tight for her. We're crammed together like sardines in a limestone coffin. I'm not going through that. No way.

I have to lead the way down. I think rats may go down drainpipes faster, but not much. The sooner I can get out of this, the happier I shall be. This isn't adrenaline coursing through my body, it's a touch of panic which is much more frightening. After we come back into Base Camp Chamber, John decides to tell us all about the route from Giant's into Oxbow Cavern, which involves an extremely narrow tunnel 100 yards long. That's fine except the tunnel is also flooded and the only way to traverse it is to crawl along on your back so your face is out of the water. Finally, there is a sharp S-bend which sometimes proves too narrow for larger members of the party (why is he looking at me?) and, if someone gets stuck, the only way out is travelling back up the tunnel feet first. People do this for fun?

TO FIT A 42IN CHEST

Ten minutes later, John shows us a little tunnel off the main passage. It's quite safe, he assures us, as it comes out about 15 yards further down. I go to look at the exit, which looks uncomfortably tight. My chest starts to constrict again. Peter has already dived down it. He does fine until his battery pack gets stuck. 'Don't break it,' I suggest helpfully, ' you don't want to get sulphuric acid everywhere.' He wriggles round the bend and gets stuck, helmet wedged one way, body the other. For a moment, he panics, then he takes the helmet off. With one wriggle, his shoulders are through the gap – and wherever they go the rest of him can follow.

'It's pretty narrow,' says John looking at me. 'About a 42in chest. What size are you?' '44 plus,' I gasp, adding at least an inch for safety, 'I don't think I fancy that.' Neither do the ladies, so we head back up with me half cursing my lack of courage, half praising a wise decision. Close to the entrance, John hops up into the roof and rigs up a rope for us to climb up. I think he's being overcautious until I try to get a grip and nearly fall flat on my muddy green arse. We're now up in the Upper West Passage which, despite its name, could never pass for a Yuppy hangout in Manhattan. I'm in the lead and I have something to prove to myself. After about 100 yards, I come to a fork in the passage – 'Go right,' shouts John. It starts to get narrower and the roof comes down. But it's wide enough and not pressing on my body, so I'm feeling alright. Until we have to start crawling and my breath comes in shorter, sharper bursts. I bang my left knee, right below the patella on the tendon that's been giving me gyp all summer. A sharp dose of pain focuses the mind perfectly and suddenly the fog of incipient panic lifts. A brace of wriggles, another crack on the knee, and I'm back where we started.

Ten minutes later, we're back in the fresh air, a little soggy and with hands stained brown (except for Katie who has been wearing a pair of bright yellow washing-up gloves throughout). I am both relieved and disappointed. Been there. Done that. Don't want to do it again.

Two weeks later, I find myself dreaming about caves, cursing my frailty, wondering whether this was a primordial fear I cannot conquer. There is only one way to find out, so perhaps one day soon I'll pull on the overalls and the helmet and try again. But don't hold your breath.

WHO TO CONTACT

National Caving Association

Mailing address only:
Monomark House
27 Old Gloucester St
London WC1

E-mail: nca@ukonline.co. uk

Secretary:
Fran Baguley
White Lion House
Ynys Uchaf
Ystradgynlais
Swansea, SA9 1RW

Tel: 01639 849519

Training Officer:
Alan Butcher
Priddy Green House

Priddy
Wells, BA5 3BE

Tel: 01749 870157
Fax: 01749 870857

▶ On first investigations, the NCA appears to be a top secret organisation which, although it has no listed telephone number, does have an E-mail address. According to their Hon Secretary, a Mr Fran Baguley, there are no commercial centres that offer caving training but there are some 400 caving clubs spread around the country.

▶ There are only nine areas in the United Kingdom and Ireland where geology allows caving actually to take place (Yorkshire Dales, Peak District, South Wales, Mendip Hills, South Devon, Sutherland and Appin in Scotland and, in Eire, County Fermanagh and County Clare) so local clubs often have to travel many miles.

▶ Aside from the five places we have discovered which do offer caving trips, joining a club is the only way to go caving safely. It provides an opportunity to meet other people with the same interests. Clubs often have a hostel in a caving area, with reciprocal arrangements with club huts in other regions. They arrange 'meets' or caving trips as well as evenings in their local home towns and they may also have a library.

▶ For a beginner, the best clubs to join are those that have a training programme involving surface practice, rather than just expecting people to join in with the normal trips. Some clubs have a minimum age for joining, 16 or 18, so it is best to check!

▶ If you have access to the Internet, Andrew Brooks' caving Web site is well worth a visit on:
http://www.sat.dundee.ac.uk/~arb/speleo.html

Magazine

If you want to see some great pictures of caves and underground features to whet your appetite, try *Underground Photographer* magazine – a specialist publication for photographers who take pictures of caves and caving.

WHERE TO GO

Company: **Mendip Outdoor Pursuits**
Address: Laurel Farmhouse, Summer Lane, Banwell, Weston-Super-Mare, BS24 6LP
Tel: 01934 820518 / 01934 823666
Fax: 01934 820518
Price Range: Half-day caving from £8 per person; 5-activity weekend £90
Payment Methods: Cash, cheque
Booking Details: 2 weeks in winter; summer – as much as possible
Capacity: Caving: 3 groups of 8; other activities vary; max for weekend is 200 people
Insurance: Can arrange PA on request
Facilities: Local accommodation and catering available by arrangement. Changing rooms, showers and toilets; equipment and outdoor clothing shop; disabled access; corporate events; specialise in tailor-made packages.
Other Notes: Multi-activity 'Underground and Overground' packages include climbing, abseiling, windsurfing, canoeing, archery, assault course, dinghy sailing, raft building, orienteering and initiative exercises.

Company: **Mere Mountains**
Address: 10, Keldwyth Park, Windermere, Cumbria, LA23 1HG
Tel: 015394 88002
Fax: 015394 88288
Price Range: Try Rock Climbing Weekends £90-120 (exc accommodation); other courses on request
Caving, climbing, white-water canoeing from £60 per day for 2 persons (discounts for groups of 4+)
Payment Methods: Cash, cheque, Visa, Access, Amex (+3 per cent charge)
Booking Details: Weekends 6-8 weeks ahead in summer

Capacity:	4 full-time instructors; groups no larger than 8 with 2 instructors
Insurance:	PA cover available at £6 for 4 days
Facilities:	Local accommodation and catering by arrangement. Changing rooms and showers for canoeing only. Disabled access if pre-booked. Corporate events; team challenges; tailor-made activity days/weekends/weeks.
Other Notes:	Chief Instructors John and Elspeth Mason have 30 years of experience between them. Also: Multi-pitch rock climbing, scrambling, winter weekends, private guiding and tuition – prices on request. Activity weekends including: kayaking, open canoes, abseiling, gorge scrambling and windsurfing.

Company:	**Edale YHA Activity Centre**
Address:	Rowland Cote, Nether Booth, Edale, Derbyshire, S30 2ZH
Tel:	01433 670302
Fax:	01433 670243
Price Range:	£84 beginners' caving weekend (accommodation and meals included). Same prices for camping/activity weekends.
Payment Methods:	Cash, cheque, Visa, Access, Switch, Delta
Booking Details:	2-3 months in advance
Capacity:	12 per course
Insurance:	PA available at £6 per day
Facilities:	Corporate entertaining, gift vouchers; dormitory accommodation; on-site catering and shower/toilet facilities; parking and gift shop.
Other Notes:	Beginners' courses include 2 contrasting trips, plus evening lectures. More intensive courses available to improve skills. Also: climbing courses, canoeing, archery.

Company:	**Freetime Activities**
Address:	Sun Lea, Joss Lane, Sedbergh, Cumbria, LA10 5AS
Tel:	015396 20828
Price Range:	Half-day (2-3 hours underground) from £13; weekend courses £50-60 per person. Group discounts available.

Payment Methods: Cash, cheque
Booking Details: Summer, as much advance warning as possible; rest of year, call to check availability
Capacity: Minimum size 4; maximum 6 per instructor. Total 24.
Insurance: Can advise on PA
Facilities: Local accommodation available.
Other Notes: Paul Ramsden is a nationally-qualified caving instructor who has run Freetime since 1988. Specialist equipment is provided, but cavers need their own warm and old clothes, waterproofs and either boots or wellington boots. Also: abseiling, specialist training courses.

Company: **Rock Lea Activity Centre**
Address: Station Road, Hathersage, Peak National Park, S30 1DD
Tel: 01433 650345
Fax: 01433 650342
Price Range: Climbing weekends £99-149 (inc B&B); improvers' climbing weekends £149; personal instructor for exclusive tuition £140 per day. Caving weekends £129-149. Multi-sports weekends £99-149.
Payment Methods: Cash, cheque
Booking Details: 2-3 months in advance
Capacity: Depends on activities
Facilities: Accommodation (shared rooms); hot showers; toilets; TV lounge; cooked breakfast and sandwich lunch included in price. Many pubs, restaurants; outward bound shop in Hathersage.
Other Notes: Rock Lea specialise in activity holidays, climbing and caving weekends, mountain biking or multi-activity weekends.

CLIMBING AND ABSEILING

'Is that all?' It slips out before I can stop myself but, let's face it, on first impression the Overhanging Buttress at North Burbage hardly lives up to its name. I am expecting to be confronted with towering rocks 100ft high and all I can see are some gritstone slabs dotted along a hill which a child could scramble up. Half an hour later, I would like to eat that first impression, but I am much too busy trying to find some crack in the rock face wide enough for my fingers, while praying that 20ft below Kate on the belaying rope is paying attention. Rock climbing is not as easy as it looks. And this rock is only classified as 'diff' (short for difficult) which – perversely enough – is about as easy as the sport gets.

Rock climbing is the first item on the agenda for my Rock Lea Multisport Weekend up in the Peak District. We are only 5 miles from Sheffield and 25 from Manchester, but at 9.30 in the morning the population seems to consist mostly of very persistent midges whose bites continue to itch for days. John Thomas is our instructor once again (see Caving and Potholing). He dumps his bag at the base of the rocks and hands us a bag containing climbing harnesses and hard helmets, and leaves us to sort them out while he sets some ropes 30ft above our heads. There are four of us (two female and two male) and, while the law of averages decrees that one person should manage to get the harness on correctly, this law obviously does not apply in North Derbyshire. The thigh buckles, John explains patiently, should not be on the inside of the leg as we would not want to risk cutting our femoral arteries.

CLIMB WHEN READY

For safety, we are top roping. John has secured the rope at the top of the rock face using various 'nuts' (originally climbers used motorbike nuts threaded into rope to wedge into cracks in the rock face. Nowadays, a climber carries hexagonal metal clips and expandable wedges in various sizes) and safety devices. One end of the rope is tied in a figure-of-eight knot and attached to the carabiner in the waist harness, the other end is threaded through a metal clip and attached to the 'belayer'. The belayer's job is to keep the rope tight when you are climbing, pay it out when you are descending, and to act as a brake and stop you hitting the ground if you fall.

John then makes us go through the standard call and response language used by climber and belayer. It seems a bit silly when we are standing 2ft apart, but he points out that this will not always be the case. 'Take in,' I say and Katie, a secretary from Jersey, pulls in the slack. When the rope is taut I say, 'That's me'. She replies, 'Climb when ready'. I come back with the incisive 'Climbing' but do not actually start until I hear her call, 'OK'. What we are doing is free climbing, which means that the rope is used solely as a safety device. We climb up and down the rock face by sticking our hands and feet in cracks in the rock.

As a kid, I was always scrambling up cliffs and trees and so the first climb starts easily enough. To catcalls of, 'What are you, some kind of goat?' I make the first part easily enough. Then the cracks get narrower and I start to worry whether my lightweight walking boots are as suitable as trainers when it comes to climbing. A quick stretch and I've reached the top, oblivious to the rope. Descending is trickier as it involves looking down.

The second face is a craggy chimney that looks easy enough. But to get to it, I do a push up – like on the edge of a swimming pool – and use my knee for extra leverage. This, John explains, is a total no-no. He demonstrates that if you can reach a ledge with your knee, you can do so with a foot, but that if you end up with both knees on a ledge you could actually be in trouble. Both Pete, a London electrician, and I find that our longer reach makes climbing easier for us than for the girls and, initially, we feel more comfortable about leaning out to get a better grip.

It still requires a serious act of faith to entrust your one and only life to a bag of hot air.

I always said I would never do anything this stupid.

**Above: The Zip Wire, a lad on the edge.
Left: 'This is how you do it,' said Dave, showing off all the way across.**

My eyes are open wide, probably because I want to see my last moments on this planet.

Motocross: you can't just sit down and let the bike do all the work, the body is constantly shifting, up and down, left and right.

Do try to remember when cycling was a relaxing pastime, not an exercise in urban survival.

**White water rafting
at Canolfan Tryweryn, Gwynedd.**

What a 4 x 4 driver loves most is a great big wallow in mud, mud and more, glorious mud.

Crammed tightly into the Swift cockpit, I am not exactly in the right frame of mind to go out and race.

Trial flights are generally towed up by a light aircraft to around 2,500 feet. 'You have control,' says Phil. This is tricky and we start flying out to one side like a water-skier on a slalom course. 'No I haven't,' I retort.

The natural
inhabitants
underwater
consider all
divers to be
rather
strange,
ungainly fish
who blow a
lot of
bubbles...

Although my climbing exploits amount to little more than a taster....it was hard work and great exercise, culminating in a sense of achievement far higher than the height of the climb.

I don't think I fancy that cave.

Even in the largest caverns there is no available light, no reflections, no luminous anythings.

Main picture: Even with two instructors attached, most first-time jumpers forget to pull the ripcord.
Inserts: Tandem jump. The student is attached to the instructor.

Flying over
Tintagel. Even
Merlin couldn't
do this.

BLADE 582

MAINAIR SPORTS

This cockiness is soon blunted when a solo 'free' climber comes along (solo climbers don't use ropes or any safety devices) and pulls himself up around a difficult overhang without even bothering to do up his shoe laces. When he takes his shirt off as well, we feel suitably useless, though the ladies seem rather impressed.

STICKIES

Sporadic showers of rain make the rock slippery just as we progress on to a couple of 'severe' climbs. One requires hooking the right hand into a crack, balancing the left foot in a tiny hole and then moving the right foot up to a ledge at thigh height. As there is nowhere for the left hand to grip, it can only be used for balance. Fortunately, this all takes place 3ft above the ground. I try it three times but my boots slip straight off the slippery surface. Both the women slip off too and Barbara, who has a bad back, refuses to go on.

Because it is wet, John lets us put on 'stickies', special climbing boots with thick, sticky rubber soles. New they cost about £60 and are always bought a size small so you can feel the rock properly. They are extremely tight and I feel as if I am in ballet shoes, forced on point. I am first up on the next climb and, once again, the first 10ft are the most difficult. The big cracks are tantalisingly out of reach; it seems to take ages to get up there. I slip off twice and each time I have to rub off the grit that sticks to the rubber soles. If I don't, its like I've put ball bearings on my feet.

My left hand finds a crack, my right foot a tiny ledge, my left foot is in a pocket, all of which I would never have noticed unless my face was inches from them. I've already broken two nails on my right hand scrabbling for grip. It feels like I've been stuck kissing this rock for hours (though it's probably only 3 minutes) and unless I do something soon, I'm going to be stuck forever 4ft from the ground with a million midges snacking on my hands and face. I push off on my left leg, the climbing boots grip superbly, my fluttering fingers grab a hold and I'm off. Now I've got a rhythm and I'm up and away. By the time I reach the top, I am sweating profusely and shattered, taking in great breaths of air like a drowning man.

That third climb is the most difficult for all of us – and would not have been possible without the climbing boots. Katie, being the smallest, has the most difficulty with the first bit but refuses to quit until she's made it. I'm belaying, so I give her as much help as I can; every time she moves, I haul in the slack so she can't slip down. Barbara gets tired arms and stuck. She eventually escapes from that position by getting angry, scaling the rock while abusing it with some choice language. We all know how she feels and so she, too, gets a huge round of applause when she reaches the top.

John is determined that we should all manage to complete four climbs successfully, so it's back to the one that we all slipped off first time around. The trick is not to hug the rock as if you were making love to it (the women are frequently asked what gritstone has that we chaps don't) but to lean out making the best use of our legs. That's all very well, but when you are trying to stick your right knee past your right ear while hoping that your fingers don't fly out of a crack smaller than a 10p piece, and balancing your left foot on the head of a pin, it's not the most natural thing to do. Eventually, my right foot finds some hold – bless those stickies – and I heave up, my left hand grabs a crack and I've made it.

ABSEILING

After four hours, we're all starving hungry and very relieved that the faces were not 100ft high. Having learnt a little bit about how to get up, the next thing to learn is how to get down quickly. Which is why the following afternoon we're back in harness and helmet, learning to abseil off the edge of an old railway bridge 100ft above the River Wye, while Rock Lea director Iain Jennings cracks jokes and threatens to dunk Peter in the water for treading on his rope. 'To a climber, that's the equivalent of spitting in his beer,' he glowers.

Abseiling (or rappelling) is the quickest way to get down rock faces, but we are using a bridge because you get a longer descent. The hardest part is actually getting through the bridge railings and making those first tentative steps off the edge. I have two carabiners on the harness now, one attached to a safety rope, the other to a metal thingummy that acts as a friction brake. My left hand grips the rope above the device while the right goes below and controls the speed and rate of descent. To brake, I pull the rope behind my bottom; to release it, I push it forward. Then you either step or bunny hop down the side of the bridge.

That first step off is tough, accepting that you are in control and won't plummet. We all do one nervous abseil where faces and knuckles are white and then everyone is raring to go. I'm so keen on my third abseil that I very nearly go over without having clipped the friction device on to my carabiner – thank heaven for safety ropes.

While we are all getting cocky, Iain rigs a second abseil rope. This time there is only brick to walk on for 10ft, then you have to drop into space and slide down the rope with feet dangling. Once again, the hardest part of that is the first time, when Iain secures the waist harness so tight you can hardly breath. Reaching the lip of the bricks, you lower your bum until it is way below your feet and your weight is all resting on the harness. 'I bet you're glad I tightened that harness now,' shouts Iain sarcastically. If I'd had any breath left, I'd have sworn at him. Abseiling down the rope alone is surprisingly easy and then I am pulled in by Barbara to avoid getting my feet wet in the stream.

For the second water descent, I practise abseiling over an overhang. Obviously what you don't want to do is to crack your head when abseiling. Being unconscious makes braking tricky. The idea is to walk down to a couple of inches above the overhang (or the end of the bricks), ask for some slack on the safety rope and then bunny hop out as far as possible. I give an almighty push with my legs, push my right hand forward and drop 10ft. I felt very pleased with myself. Even more so when Iain chose not to dunk me in the river.

Although my climbing exploits amount to little more than a taster, it was enough. Abseiling was exhilarating and fun, while actually scaling the rock faces was hard work and great exercise, culminating in a sense of achievement far higher than the height of the climb. Less than a month after my weekend in the Peak District I was back in harness. On a climbing wall in South London. It's great fun on a wall, but I miss the exhilarating views on offer in the Peak District.

Now I hear there are some great solo climbing spots off

Portland Bill in Dorset. If you fall, the sea acts as a safety net. I wonder if there are midges there?

——————— WHO TO CONTACT ———————

British Mountaineering Council (BMC)
177-179 Burton Road
Manchester M20 2BB

Tel : 0161 44 4747
Fax: 0161 445 4500
E-mail: bmc – hq@cix.compulink.co.uk.

▶ **According to a recent survey, there are currently 150,000 rock climbers in Britain. It is also one of the fastest-growing popular sports, particularly among children fascinated with the TV show *Gladiators,* which regularly includes a race up an artificial wall.**

▶ **There has been a massive increase in the number of indoor climbing walls in the country, allowing city-dwellers to practise the sport inside. However, climbing indoors is no substitute for the real thing and, in my case, after a day's climbing and abseiling in the Peak District it took a while – and the onset of winter – before I decided to venture indoors. I'm glad I did. The options for a 'wannabe' climber are vast and so the recommendations made here only skim the rock face of what is available.**

▶ **If you want to start climbing, the first thing to do is call the BMC, who will send you a starter pack. Your choice then is either to join a climbing club – as of 9 October 1996 there were 219 clubs affiliated to the BMC – visit a local climbing wall for an introductory course, or take your courage in your hands and go on a course run by a BMC approved guide. I enjoyed two half days at Rocklea as part of a multi-activity weekend, which is a good way of doing it if you're not convinced you'll like it.**

▶ The BMC has 50 years of experience and over 35,000 members. The 1997 membership fee is £14, which includes insurance cover of £50,000 personal accident and up to £2 million personal liability.

▶ There is also a BMC information service and an increasingly useful Internet site that can be reached on www.thebmc.co.uk.

WHERE TO GO

National Climbing Centres

There are three National Climbing Centres, funded by the Sports Council, that provide introductory rock climbing courses.

Company:	**Glenmore Lodge**
Address:	The National Mountain Centre, Aviemore, Inverness-shire
Tel:	01479 861276
Fax:	01479 861212
Price Range:	5-day beginner course £355 inc accommodation, food and equipment
Payment Methods:	Cash, cheque, Visa, Access
Booking Details:	6 weeks
Capacity:	4 to a course, instructor ratio 1:2
Insurance:	Advised to arrange own PA through BMC
Facilities:	80 beds on-site with catering facilities; changing rooms, showers, toilets; small shop with essential items; parking. Disabled access. Corporate events organised.
Other Notes:	The Centre has been open 50 years and is open all year round. Also: canoeing, Canadian canoeing, kayaking, mountaineering, skiing, indoor climbing wall and gym.

Company:	**Northern Ireland Mountain Centre**
Address:	Tollymore, Bryanford, Co. Down
Tel:	013967 22158
Fax:	013967 26155
Price Range:	Intro weekend £90; Go Climbing weekend £100;

Learn to Lead weekend £100. Hire of professional instructor £85 per day. Summer nights rock climbing: 3 nights £15.

Payment Methods: Cash, cheque
Booking Details: Booked and paid for 2 weeks in advance
Capacity: 12
Insurance: Participants encouraged to get own PA
Facilities: Corporate groups catered for. Dormitory-style accommodation up to 30. Disabled facilities.
Other Notes: Direct access to the Crags of the Mournes. In operation for 25 years, funded by the Sports Council for Northern Ireland.

Company: **Plas y Brenin**
Address: The National Mountain Centre, Freepost CS77A, Capel Curig, Gwynedd, LL24 0BR
Tel: 01690 720280 / 01690 720363
Fax: 01690 720394
Price Range: Rock climbing £165 for 2 days; £365 for 5 days
Payment Methods: Cash, cheque, Visa, Access
Booking Details: As far in advance as possible
Capacity: Instructor student ratio 1:4 (first day), then 1:2 for 2 day course
Insurance: Policy with Harrison Beaumont Insurance included as part of course fee covers up to £5,000 PA and £1 million liability
Facilities: Corporate days out and management training courses available. Accommodation: 66 beds – mainly twin; bar.
Other Notes: Courses run from end Mar-end Oct. Also: canoeing and kayaking. Plas y Brenin is The National Mountain Centre owned by the Sports Council Trust and operated as a centre of excellence.

BMC Approved Courses

This is a selection of BMC approved courses, generally conducted over a weekend and often tailor-made for individuals or small groups. If you wish to find others closer or more convenient geographically call the BMC.

Company: **Mere Mountains**
Address: 10, Keldwyth Park, Windermere, Cumbria, LA23 1HG

Tel: 015394 88002
Fax: 015394 88288
See page 124 (caving) for details

Company: **Snowgoose Activities**
Address: The Old Smiddy, Station Road, Corpach, Fort William, Scotland, PH33 7LS
Tel/Fax: 01397 772467
Price Range: Rock climbing: 1 day £45 (min 4 people); weekend £90; 3 days £135; 5 days £225. Prices do not include accommodation.
Payment Methods: Cash, cheque, Access, Visa
Booking Details: At least 7 days
Capacity: Ratio: 1 instructor to 4 climbers
Insurance: PA insurance available on request or direct through BMC
Facilities: Self catering/bunkhouse accommodation. Lecture rooms; drying and laundry rooms; equipment store; showers, toilets. Corporate/company days; gift vouchers.
Other Notes: Snowgoose has been operating for six years and also offers courses in hill walking, winter skills, mountaineering, kayaking.

Company: **Ardclinis Activity Centre**
Address: High Street, Cushendell, Co Antrim, Northern Ireland, BT44 0NB
Tel: 012667 71340
E-mail: ardclinis@aol.com
See page 23 (windsurfing) for details

Company: **C-N-DO Scotland**
Address: 77-78 Stirling Enterprise Park, Stirling, FK7 7RP
Tel/Fax: 01786 445073
Price Range: Day £40; weekend £75 (ratio 1:5); 5 days £270 (ratio 1:4, first 2 days, afterwards 1:2)
Payment Methods: Cheque in advance, Visa
Booking Details: Day course 2 days in advance; weekend courses (or longer) 1 week in advance
Capacity: 1:5 beginners, larger groups by arrangement
Insurance: PL; PA arranged on request
Facilities: Corporate/PR/sponsored events. Accommodation

and catering by arrangement. Some disabled activities by consultation.

Other Notes: Also: walking holidays, snow and ice climbing, cross-country skiing.

Company: **Calshot Activities Centre**
Address: Calshot Spit, Fawley, Southampton, SO45 1BR
Tel: 01703 892077
Fax: 01703 233063
See page 24 (windsurfing) for details

Company: **Edale YHA Activity Centre**
Address: Rowland Cote, Nether Booth, Edale, Derbyshire, S30 2ZH
Tel: 01433 670302
Fax: 01433 670243
See page 125 (caving) for details

Company: **Mountain Ventures**
Address: 120, Allerton Road, Liverpool, L18 2DG
Tel: 0151 734 2477
Fax: 0151 734 2997
Price Range: Intro rock climbing weekend/activity weekend £100 (inc accommodation, food and equipment). Prices quoted are for groups of 4+. Individual prices on application.
Payment Methods: Cash, cheque
Booking Details: Summer weekends 2 weeks; winter 1-2 days
Capacity: Instructor/student ratio 1:4 or 5
Insurance: PA available £10 for 3 days
Facilities: Corporate events and school groups
Other Notes: Mountain Ventures has been in operation for 14 years. The climbing centre is at Llanberis, Snowdonia. Also: canoeing, orienteering, hill walking.

Company: **Open Door Outdoor Activities Centre**
Address: Penmaendovey Country Club, Pennal, Nr. Aberdovey, Powys, Mid Wales, SY20 9LD
Tel/Fax: 01654 791326
Price Range: Rock climbing: single day on application; weekend £130 (inc food and accommodation); 5-day mid-

week £300; 7-day £400

Payment Methods: Cash, cheque
Booking Details: Groups 2-4 weeks, individuals on application
Capacity: Up to 30
Facilities: Corporate entertainment as well as residential corporate team-building, management training etc. with Castle Management up to NVQ level 5. Accommodation in 5-acre country club. Also organises courses at other locations.
Other Notes: Also: canoeing, mountain biking, quad bikes, clay pigeon shooting.

Company: **Outer Limits**
Address: Pwll-y-Garth, Penmachno, Gwynedd. N. Wales, LL25 0HJ
Tel/Fax: 01690 760248
Price Range: Climbing: 1-day £75 (1:1); £40 per person (larger groups); weekends £150/£80. Longer course prices on application.
Payment Methods: Cash, cheque
Booking Details: Groups 6 weeks; individuals 3-5 days
Capacity: 1-12 (2 instructors)
Insurance: PL; arrange own PA
Facilities: Corporate groups, local accommodation.
Other Notes: Chris Butler is a former Royal Marines Physical Training Instructor who started Outer Limits in 1996 and specialises in small groups and individuals. Also: mountain walking, kayaking, mountain biking, gorge walking, horse riding and trekking available through Ty Coch Farm Riding and Trekking Centre.

Company: **Peak Odysseys**
Address: 11 Garden Cottages, Walton Hall, Eccleshall, Staffs, ST21 6JR
Tel: 01785 850314
Price Range: Single day 1:1 £90; groups up to 4 £50 per person per day; prices for weekend/week course on application
Payment Methods: Cash, cheque
Booking Details: 4 weeks in summer
Capacity: 1-8 (above 5, second instructor)
Insurance: From 1997 PA will be included in price

Facilities:	Training done on location, using local cafés and pubs for instruction.
Other Notes:	Mike Reynolds has 20 years' experience in outdoor education and specialises in individuals and smaller groups. He instructs all year round and will give instruction in winter mountaineering, navigation training and scrambling. Also: canoeing.

Company:	**Rock Lea Activity Centre**
Address:	Station Road, Hathersage, Peak National Park, S30 1DD
Tel:	01433 650345
Fax:	01433 650342

See page 126 (caving) for details

Climbing Walls

There are literally dozens of climbing walls around the country. This is a small selection of walls which offer instruction by Single Pitch Supervisor Award qualified staff, in accordance with BMC guidelines.

Company:	**The Castle Climbing Centre**
Address:	Green Lanes, Stoke Newington, London, N4 2HA
Tel:	0181 211 7000
Fax:	0181 211 7720
Price Range:	Beginners' courses £20 for 2 hours. Subsequent visits £4.50. Kit hire: boots £1.50, harness £1.50, belay device 50p.
Payment Methods:	Cash, cheque, Visa, Access
Booking Details:	1 week in advance
Capacity:	1 instructor to 6 students
Insurance:	PA through BMC
Facilities:	Changing rooms; showers and toilets; climbing shop; hot and cold snacks. Corporate entertaining; gift vouchers.
Other Notes:	The Castle is probably the state-of-the-art climbing wall in Britain. Courses run Mon-Fri. at 19.00, and in the afternoons at weekends.

Company:	**The Cragg**
Address:	Mid Suffolk Leisure Centre, Gainsborough Road, Stowmarket, Suffolk, IP14 1LH

Tel:	01449 674980
Fax:	01449 770763
Price Range:	3 week (3 x 2½ hours) introductory course £18.50 inc equipment; improvers' course £18.50; subsequent entries £2.75 (must provide own equipment)
Payment Methods:	Cheque in advance, cash, Visa, Access, Switch on day
Booking Details:	4 weeks
Capacity:	1:6 ratio
Facilities:	Changing rooms, showers, toilets; climbing shop; hot and cold snacks. Corporate entertaining; gift vouchers.
Other Notes:	Courses run 06.45-08.15 and 08.15-09.45. Cragg is open 10.00-22.00.

Company:	**The Edge Climbing Arena**
Address:	Queen Elizabeth Leisure Centre, Blandford Rd, Wimbourne Dorset, BH21 4DT
Tel:	01202 888208
Fax:	01202 848242
Price Range:	1 day taster for children (POA); 4 week courses on Wed evenings (90 mins) £19; personal instruction £20 per hour
Payment Methods:	Cash, cheque, Visa, Access
Booking Details:	4-6 weeks for beginner courses
Capacity:	10 per course (1 instructor + 1 assistant)
Facilities:	Locally available accommodation; changing and toilet facilities; snacks from vending machines. Disabled catered for and corporate events organised. Also: pool, weights, bar, squash, tennis etc.
Other Notes:	The wall was opened in 1995. It is open weekdays 17.30-23.00; Sat-Sun 09.00-19.00. Registration to use climbing wall only available Mon-Fri (no equipment hire available).

Company:	**The Rock Face**
Address:	The Birmingham Climbing Centre, AB Row, Birmingham, West Midlands, B4 7RB
Tel:	0121 359 6419
Price Range:	£20 per hour per lesson (3 people max); shoes hire £2
Payment Methods:	Cash, cheque, Access, Visa
Booking Details:	Week in advance – avoid Wed during college terms

Facilities: Café, changing rooms, showers and toilets. Specialist outdoor shop – largest in country. Disabled catered for. Corporate events and gift vouchers.

Other Notes: Europe's largest climbing wall with international competition facilities. Lessons can be arranged any time. The centre is open 10.00-22.00, 7 days a week. It gets very full on Tues, Wed, Thurs evenings and less so on weekend nights.

Company: **The Rope Race Climbing Centre**
Address: The Engine Room, Upper Hibbert Lane, Marple, Stockport, Cheshire, SK6 7HX
Tel: 0161 426 0226
Fax: 0161 427 7300
Price Range: Introductory sessions 2 hours £8 inc all tuition and equipment. Membership £4, £4.50 admission; hire charges £2 each for boots and harness.
Payment Methods: Cash, cheque
Booking Details: 5-6 days
Capacity: 3-12 on intro nights; wall takes 150
Facilities: Catering facilities, changing rooms and toilets on site; gift shop. Corporate events organised as well as junior climbing sessions and parties.
Other Notes: Open Mon-Fri 10.00-22.00; Sat-Sun 10.00-19.00.

Company: **The Tower**
Address: Leicester Leys Leisure Centre, Beaumont Way, Beaumont Leys, Leicester, LE4 1DS
Tel: 0116 233 3074
Price Range: Try it – 90 mins £5.60 (inc all equipment); 8 week course (weekly session) £39; weekend course (compressed 8 weeks) £39
Payment Methods: Cash, cheque
Booking Details: Call for details of different courses
Capacity: Min 4, max 8
Facilities: Part of leisure centre providing all usual catering and changing facilities. Disabled catered for. Corporate events and gift vouchers available.
Other Notes: The Tower is a custom-built wall opened in 1995. It is open Mon and Fri 12.00-22.30; Tues, Wed, Thurs 11.00-22.30; Sat 10.00-17.30; Sun 10.00-20.30.

Company:	**Glasgow Climbing Centre**
Address:	Ibrox Church, 534, Paisley Road West, Glasgow, G51 1RL
Tel:	0141 427 9550
Fax:	0141 427 9551
Price Range:	£18 per initial 2-hour session (inc equipment hire and registration). Kit hire: boots £2, harnesses £1.50.
Payment Methods:	Cash, cheque, Visa, Access at a push
Booking Details:	At least a week for private lessons (min 4 people)
Capacity:	The wall takes 200; 1 instructor to 4 people
Facilities:	Changing rooms, showers, toilets; restaurant; equipment shop; parking nearby. Group bookings (have included police and educational).
Other Notes:	Novice lessons are 18.30-20.30 Mon-Fri; 17.30-19.30 Sun. Lessons for min 4 people can be arranged at other times. The wall has been open for 2 years and is inside an old Victorian Church.

Company:	**The Edge**
Address:	John Street, Sheffield, S2 4QU
Tel:	0114 275 8899
Price Range:	Taster £12 1 hour; climbing intro (2 x 2 hours) £40; Edge Experience (2-hour session for groups) £8-15 per person. Rental: boots £2.50, harness £1.50, belay £1.
Payment Methods:	Cash, cheque, Visa, Access, Switch, Delta
Booking Details:	1 week in advance
Capacity:	1:6 ratio, no more than 12 in class
Facilities:	Café, changing rooms, showers, toilets; climbing shop nearby.
Other Notes:	Custom-built wall, open 3 years, also runs courses for children from 7 years old.

Climbing clubs

The fourth alternative is to join a climbing club – there are over 200 BMC affiliated clubs in the UK. Call the BMC for a list, or access their Web site on www.thebmc.co.uk.

MOTOCROSS

I'm late arriving at Wild Tracks. By the time I actually make it over to the Kennett Track, 'Curly Chief Mechanic' (as he is always referred to) has already walked half-way round the course. From a distance he appears to be addressing a group of jockeys, some of whom are very small but all are clad in outfits of bright pink, electric blue and yellow that would not be out of place at a race meeting at nearby Newmarket. Being tardy I'm still in shorts and T-shirt and, although it is over 80°, the track has been watered down, so I find myself squelching through muddy puddles to catch up with Curly.

'Do your braking before you make the turn here,' he says, looking straight at a 10-year-old boy, who nods wisely while simultaneously flexing his right brake hand. 'If you are going too fast, just keep on going and turn at the bottom there.' *There* is a large muddy puddle surrounded by enough soft sand to recreate Hadrian's Wall. The other class members, comprising another small boy, a larger 13-year-old, a teenage brother and sister, a young man and an older bloke in his mid-40s, all nod their agreement.

Curly and Daniel Parker are the instructors in charge of the Geoff Mayes Motocross Try-Out Day that operates on most Tuesdays and Sundays at Wild Tracks in Suffolk. Each session lasts 2 hours 45 minutes and guarantees at least 2 hours on a bike. Geoff, a former British Motocross Champion, who wears a perpetual smile under his beard, is teaching another group over on the main track but promises we can join him if we get good enough.

—— BUTCH BOOTS AND ARMOUR ——

First, I have to get dressed. This involves putting on more protective gear than most knights of old. Knee and shin guards, a combined breast and back plate with reinforced pads that flap over the shoulders, and a belt-cum-back-protector. Then I pull on my 'jeans', which are unlikely to feature in any Levis ads seeing as they are garishly coloured and laden with logos, followed by a similar turtleneck shirt that nearly strangles me and a pair of rather butch boots with metal rimming on the front of the sole. This eye-catching ensemble is then topped off with gloves, a white crash helmet with a peak and mouth guard and a pair of goggles. All I need now is my own lean, mean, green racing machine.

Geoff uses new Kawasaki KX 60, 80, 100, and 125 motocrossers. The 60s are weeny little machines, ideal for kids, but because I was late I am offered the choice of an 80cc or a 200cc Enduro bike, which seems much too big to start with. I settle on the 80cc. I have driven small bikes in my time – nothing bigger than a 250cc road machine – so at least the controls are familiar. The recommended riding and driving style is not. For a start, you never seem to use first gear: you start in second and change up and down without using the clutch. When cornering, you need to sit far forward, right on the petrol tank, allowing the front wheel enough traction. If cornering right, you have to put your weight on your left foot and extend the right leg forward, to help with balance and control. When accelerating on a straight, or going over a bump, you stand up with your weight slightly forward.

— TERRORISING THE SPECTATORS —

We start off going around a small, flat circuit to get the feel of the bikes. I soon learn that at my height it's difficult to sit right forward, that the size of my boots and that of the back brake are not compatible, and that it's difficult to go round a corner, stand up, sit down, change down and go round another corner in less than 25m. The bike also has a tendency to stall if I take it above third gear. Perhaps I'll do better on the real track.

I suppose it would be possible to tackle the track more slowly than I did the first time, but I doubt it. If I'd been going any slower around a couple of the corners, sliding through the soft sand, I'd have been eating it. Having completed that successfully, confidence soars and I start to open up the throttle. After my first bump and getting airborne, I learn why it is important to stand up, the impact of bike seat on posterior is sudden and sharp enough to make me yell. A spectator laughs but their humour turns rapidly to terror when my attempt to skid through a muddy puddle does not quite work. Instead of swinging through the curve, I head straight for the edge of the track and the watching pedestrians. Who's laughing now?

It is exhausting work, you can't just sit down and let the bike do all the work, the body is constantly shifting, up and down, left and right. As with anything new, you are not relaxed but tense so movements tend to be jerky or extreme. The fingers on my left hand are constantly twitching, wanting to work the clutch (a common problem with those who drive road bikes). I have decided against trying to use the back foot brake and am having problems remembering to apply the front brake, using only the first two fingers of my right hand. However, after half a dozen circuits, I have settled into a routine, trying to pick the same line and to maintain a constant speed, to brake or change down before the corner, get the weight right by sitting forward and extending the foot into the turn. A few times it works and then, buoyed by enthusiasm, I over-gun it next time round and end up pivoting on my leg to complete the turn. After half an hour, I am drenched in sweat and aching all over so I come off to guzzle a litre of water.

– CONFIDENCE AND AGGRESSION –

Curly proffers some advice and then a bigger machine. The Kawasaki 200cc Enduro is a full-sized bike, altogether more what I am used to. For a start, I can operate the back brake and the extra power is enough to get me out of most corners. A quick test circuit and then I'm back on the Kennett Track, really catching some air on the bumps, using the extra weight and power to pull out of the corners. Twice in quick succession I nearly come to grief. The first is by applying the front brake too hard. The bike stops sharply and my momentum almost carries me over the handlebars into the blackberry bushes. The second time, I don't apply enough brake or change down in time and I have to go straight on instead of taking a sharp left: no problem, I just have to power out of a muddy puddle and grab some more air.

After another 20 minutes Curly calls me in as he needs the bike to escort one of the youngsters round the track. He's having confidence problems – primarily due to being overweight and not being able to restart his bike easily – but after a couple of circuits escorted by Curly he, too, is happy, even daring to open up on the straights. By the end of a session, Mayes reckons on having everybody travelling around the Kennett Track – though smaller children may have to have an instructor on the back. Further progression depends on a combination of confidence and aggression.

SERIOUS FUN

We have about 45 minutes of our session left – and I've run out of drinking water – when Curly calls me over. With two other riders, he leads us over to the 'Big Track' – an altogether different proposition. It's a sand-based track that can be used in all weather conditions for national and championship race meetings (one of the problems with motocross is that it appears to be run by a bewildering variety of committees and governing bodies, like heavyweight boxing without the multi-million pound purses) and from the moment we followed Curly over the first bump I realised this was going to be serious fun.

The course seemed to go on forever, twisting and turning back on itself with wide sweeping bends and hillocks so steep that if you didn't get airborne at the top you didn't have enough speed to get up there in the first place. On one long straight, I really opened up and spent the whole time standing up as I hit six bumps in succession, gaining more height with each one, hitting the ground with a thump and opening the throttle in time for the next one. At the last bump, the pros twist in mid-air so they are already halfway through the turn before they've even landed. I am more circumspect, changing down and sweeping the turn wide before opening up to take another bump with an oomph that caught me by surprise.

For the first circuit we followed Curly – though not exactly, as he has a habit of taking some corners wide on the gravel where the sand has been packed down by two years of pounding. On one corner he went into it too fast, his back wheel slid into deep sand and, try as he might to accelerate out of the hole, there was to be no recourse. He was still moaning about the hole in his black Levis (no protective gear for this pro today) in mid-afternoon. The three of us nearly came to grief laughing.

After that comic interlude, we were on our own learning the track, getting the turns, trying to plot a course as close as possible to the most direct route. On race days and when the course is wetter, the best line rapidly becomes very rutted and in some ways easier to follow – provided you have enough speed. Not enough and you soon find the back wheel slipping away. After a few laps, it becomes routine, you pick out the same landmarks to aim for, open up the throttle at the same place a little bit more each time, trying to conquer your natural inclination to slow right down for corners. Too slow and it's all such an effort using your body to pull the bike round; too much speed and you are using your body to pick the bike out of the sand. I worked on the theory that if I felt safe going round the bend, I was driving too slowly. If I could remain mildly terrified at all times, this was a good sign. The downside of this was that with each lap I had to go a little faster to maintain the correct terror quotient.

The other problem I never managed to correct was getting the right line going through a tight bend with loads of sand in the way. Every time I saw the sand I thought, 'Oh hell I'm going to get stuck now,' and slowed some more. It was also very hard remembering to keep my bum right forward, as with every turn it naturally gravitated towards the bike's rear which made the turn more difficult.

I was just thinking to myself, 'One more lap and I'm done' when Curly called me in. Time was up and so were my arms – once I stopped driving they felt sore and bruised and were very stiff the next day. Getting out of my kit was most unpleasant as my T-shirt was soaked through – I wonder how many calories you use up on motocross – and I had a thirst on me caused by inhaling tons of sand and dust that didn't leave me for days. I have a desire to go back and do it again, but this time it will have to be faster and dirtier.

——— WHO TO CONTACT ———

Motocross governing bodies

If you have any queries about clubs in your area, or want to know more about any off-road motorcycle sport, the main organising bodies for the various genres are as follows:

Auto Cycle Union (ACU)
The ACU deal with motocross, enduro, trails, grass track or youth.

Address: Wood Street, Rugby, Warks. CV21 2YX
Tel: 01788 540519
Fax: 01788 573585

Amateur Motor Cycle Association (AMCA)
The AMCA deal with amateur motocross, enduro or trials.

Address: 28 Mill Park, Hawks Green Lane, Cannock, Staffs WS11 2XT
Tel: 01543 466282
Fax: 01543 466283

British Schoolboy Motorcycle Association (BSMA)
The BSMA deal with youth motocross.

Address: Lil Hill, 20 Glen Park Crescent, Kingscourt, Stroud, Glos GL5 SDT
Tel: 01453 766516
Fax: 01453 764877

Motor Cycle Union of Ireland (MCUI)
The MCUI deal with Irish motocross, enduro, trials, grass track and youth.

Address: 24 Sallyminstragh Road, Killinchy, County Down BT23 6RE

Scottish Auto Cycle Union (SACU)
The SACU deal with Scottish motocross, emduro, trials, grass track and youth.

Address: Block 2, Unit 6 Whiteside, Bathgate, Edinburgh, EH48 2RX
Tel: 01506 630262
Fax: 01606 634972

Youth Motorcycle Sporting Association (YMSA Ltd)
The YMSA Ltd deals with youth motocross, trial and youth.

Address: PO Box 931, Sheffield, S31 BUX
Tel: 01909 770558

Trial Riders Fellowship (TRF)
The TRF deal with trial riding only.

Address: 6 Tennyson Place, Checkheaton, Bradford, West Yorkshire, BD19 3DJ
Tel: 01274 870162

—————— WHERE TO GO ——————

Company:	**Geoff Mayes Motocross School**
Address:	Team Green Starter School, 17 Broad Street, Harleston, Norfolk IP20 9AZ
Tel:	01379 854291/(mobile) 0585 731713
Price Range:	Half-day £52 per adult; children over 7 from £42; full day £90 adults; children from £70
Payment Methods:	Cash, cheque, major credit cards
Booking Details:	3-4 weeks
Capacity:	6-14 depending on bike availability and group sharing.
Facilities:	Local B&B and Travelodge. Catering facilities available on certain days, depending on track. Changing facilities, showers and toilets. Disabled access – ring to check beforehand. Corporate events organised at Wild Tracks. Gift vouchers available at Christmas.
Other Notes:	Regular sessions at Wild Tracks (see Off-Road

section) Tues and Thurs between Mar and Oct and other locations include Mildenhall, Suffolk; Doncaster, Reading and Oxford. Sessions 10.00-13.00; 13.30-16.30 – call for details. Operates Mar-end Dec most weekends and sometimes twice in midweek. Sponsored by Kawasaki.

Company:	**Dave Watson MX School**
Address:	Yauncos Cottage, Tillers Green, Dymock, Glos GL18 2AD
Tel:	01531 890496
Price Range:	£70 2 days; £70 bike hire
Payment Methods:	Cheque
Booking Details:	2 months
Capacity:	Maximum 20 riders
Facilities:	Track facilities vary, most have toilets and some have café/snack outlets.
Other Notes:	Have to be able to ride a motorbike; sponsored by Honda. Primarily 2-day schools, midweek in school holidays, 10-15 times a year either in Cambridgeshire or around Shropshire/Gloucestershire area.

Company:	**Moto Action**
Address:	The Winchester Project, 21 Winchester Road, London NW3
Tel:	0171 586 8731 / 0860 876171
Fax:	0171 911 0412
Price Range:	Intro 3 hour session £65 inc bike and equipment; children 10-15 £55
Payment Methods:	Cheque, cash
Booking Details:	Summer – individuals 4 weeks in advance, groups 4-6 weeks
Capacity:	Groups of 1-6
Facilities:	Training tracks at Dartford or Mildenhall, Suffolk and Washbrook Farm, near Cambridge, or near Bournemouth, depending on weather. Facilities vary. Mobile unit has changing facilities and tea, coffee. Being re-done, hopefully to cater for disabled. Ring to check. Gift vouchers. Corporate activities including filming for advertising and record companies.
Other Notes:	Courses from complete beginner to semi-advanced. Season all year round, 2-3 times a week;

have been running courses from 1982 using Suzuki bikes.

Company:	**Team Green Training School**
Address:	Kawasaki Motors UK Ltd, 1 Dukes Meadow, Millboard Road, Bourne End, Bucks SL8 5XF
Tel:	01628 851000
Fax:	01628 850886
Price Range:	£50 own bike; Kawasaki owners get special rates from £20
Payment Methods:	Cheque, major credit cards, cash on day
Booking Details:	Book as early as possible
Capacity:	Maximum 3 instructors at 10 riders per instructor – seldom more than 20 on a course
Facilities:	Vary according to track, generally toilets and some catering.
Other Notes:	Bike owners only. Course for novice motocrossers from semi- to fully advanced run approximately 20 times per year from Mar to end Sept.

Company:	**Barry Johnson MX School**
Address:	10 Harebell Close, Heath Hayes, Cannock, Staffs WS12 5XA
Tel/Fax:	01543 271675
Price Range:	Yamaha off-road bike experience – 1 day inc bike, clothing, refreshments from £99; also 4-day courses (prices on application)
Payment Methods:	Cash, cheque
Booking Details:	Minimum 2 months to ensure specific dates
Capacity:	10 per course
Facilities:	Coffee and light lunch provided; on-site toilets; car parking. Corporate off-road experience events organised.
Other Notes:	Barry, who has been racing bikes of all kinds for years, uses three tracks – near Bolton, the West Midlands and near Brighton. He runs courses nearly every weekend throughout the year. Yamaha owners get 10 per cent discount.

Company:	**Geraint Jones Enduro School**
Address:	Glynhafren, Old Hall, Llanidloes, Powys SY18 6PS
Tel/Fax:	01686 413324

Price Range: Yamaha Off Road Experience £99 (bikes, equipment included); 2-day Enduro Schools £130 + £10 equipment, £50 (bring own bike)
Payment Methods: Cash, cheque
Booking Details: Essential as much advance warning as possible
Capacity: Maximum 10 with 2/3 instructors
Insurance: PA through Bowrings Motorsport Insurance Company. Tel: 0181 300 4000
Facilities: Local B&B/hotels. Lunch provided. Toilets and changing facilities. Corporate events organised.
Other Notes: Off Road Experience runs May-Oct approx 30 times; 2-day courses winters by application only.

Company: **Motozone**
Address: Bulls Head House, Nantwich Road, Audley, Stoke-on-Trent, ST7 8DH
Tel: 01782 721922
Fax: 01782 723910
Price Range: £25 for 2 hours inc bike and all equipment; £99 full day
Payment Methods: Cash, cheques
Booking Details: 2-3 days
Capacity: Max 22 on track
Facilities: Mobile café at weekends and Portaloo, but hoping to upgrade
Other Notes: Track: Redhall Lane, Halmer End, Audley, Stoke-on-Trent, open 7 days a week 10.00-18.00.

Company: **Reading Trial Park**
Address: Island Road, Smallmead, Reading, RG2 0RP
Tel: 01734 314976
Fax: 01734 314976
Price Range: £50 per 2 hours inc bike and equipment
Payment Methods: Cash, cheque, Visa, Access
Booking Details: One month
Capacity: Up to 20 in a group
Insurance: Offers PA cover
Facilities: Corporate events (karting relay races or heats). Café and toilets on-site.
Other Notes: Tuition from ACU National Coach, Andy Nicholls. 4-wheel driving, karting, kart hires, quad bikes, skid pan. Deal with Yamaha to do 2-3 courses per week starting in 1997.

Company:	**Mervyn Anstie Quad Squad**
Address:	32a Andover Road, Ludgershall, Nr Andover, Hants SP11 9LZ
Tel:	01264 791056 / 0973 909592
Fax:	01264 791056
Price Range:	Quad bikes £25; quads/pilots £35; full day £46
Payment Methods:	Cash, cheques
Booking Details:	Minimum one month
Capacity:	1-100
Facilities:	Locally available accommodation; on-site barbecue to full silver service catering; changing rooms, showers and toilets. Suitable for some disabled. Full and half-day corporate events; junior quad squad 6-15 years; children's birthday parties (from age 6).
Other Notes:	Not really motocross or off-road driving or go-karting, but a day out driving with a difference! The Quad Squad offer quad bike racing, Honda pilot rallying and mini bikes for raw beginners to experts, and children 6-15. They operate out of circuits near Andover and Walton-on-Thames approx 4 times a week. Specialising mainly in groups, there are individual open weekends twice a month.

MOTOR RACING

They have all been here before me: Hill, Brundle, Herbert, Senna. World champions, great drivers, shooting stars, ghosts of the past and hopes for the future. And now I know why they are all so small. It's the only way to fit in the damn car.

Jim Murray from the Silverstone Driving Centre is kindly letting me go first because I'm, as he delicately phrases it, 'the biggest'. Indeed, at first sight, the only thing that the racing crimson Formula Ford Swift SC96F-Z has that is bigger than me is its spare tyres. The steering wheel is smaller than the one I gave my son to play with when he was 18 months old – and the mechanics have to take that out before I can get in. Standing on the seat I then have to slide both feet simultaneously into this cavernous hole. Now I am sitting on a piece of moulded plastic which is so tight it is digging into my hips. It hurts. I'm not wearing the best shoes – the soles are too wide and I'm in danger of applying the brake and accelerating simultaneously. And now they are strapping me in.

I am trussed like a Christmas turkey with straps over my thighs, around my waist and over my shoulders. I know there is a quick release buckle but, if anything happens, I'm wedged in so tight the rescue squad will have to bring a crowbar. Not that there is much chance of that, as I'm much too scared to take the car up into fourth gear – if I can find it.

─── DANGEROUS DRIVING ───

At Silverstone, all the race training is done on the Stowe track, which though not as dramatic as the full track is quite scary enough. Its advantages are that if you lose control there isn't much to hit beyond a few tyre walls. Before being let loose, all the group members were shown round the track in a saloon car and given a couple of laps to get used to the idea. Rob, my instructor, asked whether I had done anything like this before and then demonstrated the most basic techniques – most of which would get you arrested for dangerous driving on the roads.

To help the novice, there are coloured cones on each corner. 'When you come to the red, start braking gently,' said Rob. 'Change down into third gear if you are coming off the straight. Keep applying the brake gently until you reach the first yellow cone, where you start to make your turn, the second yellow cone is the apex of the turn. Get as close to it as possible and accelerate out when you feel comfortable. Use the whole width of the road at all times. If you are keeping your racing line that makes it very difficult for anyone to overtake you. Keep both hands on the wheel – unless you are changing gears. The other thing to remember is that you are used to a front wheel drive car and the Swift is back wheel drive so that might take a bit of getting used to.'

Formula Fords are now raced in some 20 countries. Since 1967, when it began as a low-cost alternative to Formula Three, it has provided the first start on the racing grid for six Formula One World Champions. Formula Fords are the strongest, most technologically advanced entry-level racing cars on the market today – however, if you decide to take it up and if you have the talent (which is the big 'if') a budding driver needs to find £75-100,000 worth of sponsorship for his first year on the circuit. There is a choice of three chassis made by Swift, Mygale and Van Diemen, while the engines are standard 130ps, 1.8 litre Zetec Ford engines, the same model that powers the Fiesta, Escort and Mondeo. The Escort that cut you up at the weekend could never reach 120mph, but nor would the engine need to be rebuilt every couple of races.

MISSING THE GEARS

Crammed into the Swift cockpit, concerned that my Timberlands are too big for the pedals, I am not exactly in the right frame of mind to go out and race. I spot the gear lever which is a small chrome thing on the right side of the wheel. 'Is it standard shift change?' I enquire. The answer that comes back is contradictory –

yes and no. I start off believing that first and second and third and fourth are back to front from my Cavalier. This is not only wrong but is to prove rather embarrassing. 'Remember don't go up above 4,000 revs,' shouts Jim. The rev counter is concealed directly behind the steering wheel and, as I can't see the dial anyway, I decide that if I ever can see the needle I'm in trouble.

My start is most inelegant. Confused by the gears, I start in third and stall. Second time, I limp out on to the track. The first lap I'd have done quicker on my mountain bike, I brake before the red cones and come round the steepest hairpin in warp factor tortoise. Looking in my mirror I notice the other driver on the circuit is already behind me and, as he's not allowed to overtake on these training laps, I decide I'd better speed up. After another nine laps I'm starting to get the hang of it, hitting fourth gear and 60mph on the two straights, then holding in third while I negotiate the turns. The car handles easily though I can feel every bump in the road, particularly if I let one of the wheels drift over the verge. After nine laps they wave the black and white flag to tell me to come into the pits, I see it and celebrate by changing down into second gear. Completely confused, I limp around the circuit again.

In the pits, they tell me, 'You are having problems changing gear'. It is made clear to me that it is a standard gear shift – and that I must be some sort of idiot for thinking otherwise. This time I can take it up to 4,500 revs and, for nine laps, I try and fail to do so. By now, the turns are smoother, I am accelerating out of the bends faster, desperately trying to hold my neck steady. On one hairpin, I lose the back slightly and my helmet cracks into the side of the cock-pit. Now I understand why Grand Prix racing drivers have to be fit.

My turn is over all too soon but now I have the pleasure of watching the others. A couple of them even have their own racing overalls and special shoes – tight racing boots with incredibly thin soles so they can feel everything. One manages a 360° spin coming out of the hairpin, which makes us slow-coaches feel better.

SKIDDING

Before lunch, we are all taken off to the skid car, a left-hand drive automatic Jaguar which is placed on a chassis that changes the weight of the car and makes it skid. Rob takes us on a couple of circuits of the course, weaving in and out of the cones with a dexterity that leaves me, sitting in the back, feeling very nauseous. It is blowing strong gusts across Silverstone and the grey clouds are threatening the rain Michael Fish has promised. While waiting my turn, I watch some of the lads playing with a Caterham 7, doing turns and skids that are illegal in most countries. In the Jag most of my colleagues manage at least one complete spin or a series of cone annihilations.

Alan Ring, the Irish Formula Ford 1,600 champion, has come along for the day (he is the only one allowed to overtake on the laps) and he takes the cones aggressively, moving the Jag around as I bounce about in the back. He manages 1:06.8 seconds on his first lap, the fastest by a full 2 seconds.

On the second, he's going for it so fast that he completely loses it and the car does a complete rotation. The next driver makes even more of a hash and then it's my turn. I think I'm going to be dreadful so I take it slowly, clipping one plastic bollard because I haven't worked out the width, but soon I find that I can steer into the skid, brake slightly before turning and hold control. My first lap is 1:08, plus a 2 second penalty. Second time, I've got confidence and have taken the pro's advice of using only one hand on the steering wheel. I'm going a bit faster but holding it steady, dabbing the brakes, making small adjustments. I lose the back end slightly and then pull it out and go through the final zigzag without a mistake. My time is 1:06.6, the fastest by the huge margin of 2/100ths of a second. A serious result.

———— HITTING 5,500 REVS ————

After lunch, it's back to the Swifts, allowed up to 5,000 revs. I'm first out, once again, and now the conditions have changed. I'm on slicks (dry weather tyres) and the weather has moved from drizzle to light showers. This makes driving much more interesting, the racing line is now essential: if I oversteer or accelerate too fast I'll lose the back. A couple of occasions out of the hairpin, I put my foot down early and the back slides out. The skid control car laps come into physical memory and I steer through the skid and speed up to the next red cone. The rain is coming down harder now but I only notice it because my helmet visor is fogging up, otherwise my concentration is absolute. In these conditions, there is no margin for error.

After five laps, we are called into the pits and drive to the workshop to have 'wets' fitted. Back in the pits, 15 minutes later, we are told very firmly, 'If you lose it, spin, or come off the track we will bring you in, the conditions are too bad to run any risks'. First lap on the wets, I'm driving very gingerly but they just stick to the surface. It's incredible, like wearing rock climbing boots. They grip the surface like super-glue. Within a couple of laps, I'm taking the corners as fast as I was in the morning session, oblivious to the tumbling rain.

The routine is now second nature. Give it as much welly as I dare down the straight, brake at the red cone, change down, brake, turn, accelerate out, up a gear if it's the second straight, hold the line, make the turn, accelerate, check the mirror, open it up again. This time on the main straight, I don't let my foot off the accelerator until after the red cone, coward, make sure it's better next time. Another pit stop and I can take it up to 5,500 revs – that doesn't seem so impossible now. Out of the pits, back into the routine. The rhythm is the thing, once settled into that, the speed inches up, I have faith in the car and I've learnt some faith in myself too, so it's down to what I do now that determines the outcome. I can even see a little white arrow flickering about one o'clock above the steering wheel, I think it reads 5,700 revs but I'm not going to confirm this because my eyes need to be on the road.

The rain is now heavy and constant, my overalls are soaked through, and I don't notice a thing. My concentration is total: through the spray, through the corner, change up, brake, change down, foot off brake into the turn, accelerate out of it, and so on. Physical discomfort is irrelevant, a dull ache somewhere at the back of my mind that might relate to my hips. It's all eyes, hands and feet. Nothing else matters. Damn, there's the black and white flag. Perhaps I could pretend not to see it? If I had the choice I'd still be out there now. Instead I have to sit on the M25 and dream of better days.

WHO TO CONTACT

The RAC Motor Sports Association Ltd (RACMSA)
Motor Sports House
Riverside Park
Colnbrook
Slough
Berkshire

Tel: 01753 681736
Fax: 01753 682938
E-mail:100350.347@compuserve.com

▶ **The RACMSA is recognised as the governing body of motor sport in Great Britain by the world governing body, the Federation Internationale de l'Automobile (FIA) in Paris. It governs most forms of four-wheeled motor sport in the UK.**

▶ **To race you must first be over 17 with a valid RTA driving licence (or be 16 with at least one year's experience in karting). Before you apply for a race licence you must purchase a 'Go Racing' starter pack from the RACMSA, obtain a medical certificate and complete a one-day RACMSA course for novice drivers (cost £135) run only by members of the Association of Racing Driver Schools (ARDS).**

WHERE TO GO

Company:	**Ian Taylor Motor Racing School**
Address:	Thruxton Circuit, Andover, Hants SP11 8PW
Tel:	01264 773511
Fax:	01264 773441
Price Range:	Standard course £99; Super course £145; 5 additional laps on day £55
Payment Methods:	Cash, cheque, Visa, Access
Booking Details:	6 weeks in advance
Capacity:	21 per session, 6 sessions per day

Facilities: Accommodation and on-site catering, changing rooms, showers and toilets. Disabled access by arrangement. Corporate events; gift vouchers.

Other Notes: Each course lasts approximately 3½ hours and all racing takes place on the 2.4 mile track, universally regarded as the fastest in Britain. The Super course enables participants to drive a Formula Renault or Sports 2000 racing car, much faster vehicles which get closer to the real thrill of Formula 1.

Company: **Jim Russell Racing Drivers School UK**
Address: Donington Park, Castle Donington, Derby, DE74 2RP
Tel: 01332 811430
Fax: 01332 811422
Price Range: Introductory race (2 hours) £9; half-day super trial £195; full day £235; week course £2,250
Payment Methods: Cash, cheque, Visa, Access, Amex
Booking Details: 2 months in advance
Capacity: 100 people per day
Insurance: PA available on day
Facilities: Local accommodation, restaurants, cafés, bar, changing facilities and toilets. Corporate days and gift vouchers.
Other Notes: Founded in 1957 at Snetterton in Norfolk, it was the first racing school in the world and moved to Donington in 1988. Graduates include double Formula One World Champion Emerson Fittipaldi. The week-long race drivers' courses end with a race and hopefully a National B Licence.

Company: **Knockhill Racing Drivers School**
Address: Dunfermline, Fife, Scotland, KY12 9TF
Tel: 01383 723337
Fax: 01383 620167
Price Range: Half-day racing course £79 weekdays, £89 week-ends single seater; £99/109 Rally; £169 Master Drivers Super Trial
Payment Methods: Cash, cheque, major credit cards (exc Amex)
Booking Details: 4-6 weeks in advance
Capacity: Race Training: 30 per session; Rally: 18
Facilities: Two restaurants, club house, licensed bar, toilets, parking. Corporate entertaining, gift vouchers.

Other Notes: Knockhill is the only full-time circuit-racing and rally driving course in Scotland. Driving Formula First single seaters and Ford Fiesta XR2is.

Company: **Nigel Mansell Racing School**
Address: Brands Hatch, Fawkham, Nr Longfield, Kent DA3 8NG
Tel: 0990 125 250 (central office)
Price Range: Brands Hatch and Oulton Park Initial Trial Bronze, £85 weekdays, £105 Sat; Super Trial Bronze £155/179; Off-Road Initial Bronze £75; Super Bronze £115
Payment Methods: Cash, cheque, Visa, Access
Booking Details: As much as possible for weekends
Insurance: Bronze prices include vehicle insurance, Silver and Gold vehicle and personal
Facilities: Corporate entertaining and gift vouchers for a day's racing. Food on-site and hotels nearby. Showers etc for drivers. Disabled spectator facilities.
Other Notes: There are now 4 circuits under the Nigel Mansell banner: Brands Hatch; Oulton Park; Snetterton and Cadwell Park (for motor cycle race training). Courses are 5 laps in a BMW 318i with an instructor and then laps in a Formula First. Also: rally car driving and off-road courses at Brands; multi-activity days; karting.

Company: **Tom Brown Racing Drivers' School**
Address: 40 Clydeford Road, Cambuslang, Glasgow, G72 7JF
Tel/Fax: 0141 641 2553
Price Range: Introductory lesson £65; racing car super trial £99.
Payment Methods: Cash, cheque
Booking Details: 4-6 weeks in advance
Capacity: 6 sessions per day
Facilities: East Fortune Airfield has full catering and toilet facilities, disabled access. Corporate entertaining, gift vouchers.
Other Notes: Tom Brown, 7 times Scottish Champion, has recently moved his operation from Ingliston racing circuit to East Fortune.

Company:	**Aintree Racing Drivers' school**
Address:	1 Fairoak Court, Whitehouse, Runcorn, Cheshire WA7 3DX
Tel:	01928 712877
Fax:	01928 790086
Price Range:	Introductory race car trial £95; super race car trial £125; advanced saloon car £95; skid car £59.
Payment Methods:	Cash, cheque, Access, Visa, Switch
Booking Details:	Book in advance for weekend sessions. 40 race meeting days a year.
Capacity:	60 people maximum at summer weekends; 50, winter weekends; 30-40 midweek. They have 10 Formula Fords, 5 saloons and 25 pro go-karts.
Facilities:	Corporate entertaining; gift vouchers; local accommodation; shower and toilets; parking; catering, small gifts. Disabled toilets and viewing platform.

Company:	**Castle Combe Racing School Ltd**
Address:	Castle Combe Circuit, Chippenham, Wilts SN14 7EY
Tel:	01249 782417
Fax:	01249 782392
Price Range:	Initial trial £92; advanced course £165
Payment Methods:	Cash, cheque, Visa, Access. Credit Card hotline 01249 782929.
Booking Details:	Minimum of 4 weeks in advance
Capacity:	25 people per session, 4 sessions per day
Insurance:	PA cover available direct from Bowring Motorsport Insurance Company on 0181 300 4000
Facilities:	Cafe, corporate facilities, gift vouchers.
Other Notes:	Off-road facilities, skid pan and motorcycle race days also available. Race training is done on Fri in spring/summer, Fri or Sat in autumn/winter.

Company:	**Everyman Motor Racing**
Address:	Mallory Park Circuit, Kirkby, Mallory, Leics LE9 7QE
Tel:	01455 841670
Fax:	01455 850433
Price Range:	Half day £105; full day £165
Payment Methods:	Cash, cheque, Access, Visa, Amex
Booking Details:	4-6 weeks in advance

Capacity:	18 people per session; full days (3 sessions per day); half days (2 sessions per day)
Insurance:	PA available
Facilities:	Corporate entertaining, gift vouchers. Local accommodation; on-site catering facilities; limited shower/toilet facilities; parking; shop.
Other Notes:	Also available: pro karts, off road, rally school, tank driving, trucks. Race days are approx every 2 weeks all year, usually on a Saturday.

Company:	**Palmer Promo Sport**
Address:	The Old Post Office, Worthing Rd, Southwater, West Sussex RH13 7DT
Tel:	01403 733999
Fax:	01403 733222
Price Range:	£325 per person in a shared event (1-11 places); £295 (12+). An exclusive event starts at £8,000 for up to 24 people. Catering is £20 per person. All prices are exclusive of VAT.
Payment Methods:	On application
Booking Details:	3-4 months in advance
Capacity:	1-100 guests
Insurance:	TPL and vehicle damage insurance (with a £350 excess) included. Additional cover plus PA can be arranged if required.
Facilities:	Corporate entertainment, toilets, catering, gift vouchers.
Other Notes:	The Motorsport Experience is geared primarily at corporate clients and is intended to pack in as many different types of fast driving as possible in one day. Other extras include trying to change the tyres on a Formula One racing car in the Pit Stop Challenge, driving a 40-ton articulated lorry, racing go-karts and a reverse steer contest in a mini that turns right when you steer left. It is an expensive day out but brilliant for entertaining corporate clients.

Company:	**Peter Gethin Driving Courses Ltd**
Address:	Goodwood Motor Circuit, Chichester, West Sussex PO18 0PH
Tel:	01243 778118
Fax:	01243 533498

Price Range:	Trial racing courses £80-99; Performance course £195-595 (inc full written report)
Payment Methods:	Cash, cheques, major credit cards exc Amex; no Switch over the phone
Booking Details:	4 weeks for weekends, 2 weeks for weekdays
Capacity:	15 people per session, 4 sessions per day
Insurance:	PA available for £10 per day
Facilities:	Corporate days out. Restaurants on site.
Other Notes:	Course run twice a month during the year, one weekend, one midweek; call for details.

Company:	**Richard Peacock's Race School, Ireland**
Address:	Mondiale, Balloo Crescent, Bangor, Co Down, Northern Ireland BT19 7WP
Tel:	01247 452322
Fax:	01247 450932
Price Range:	Half-day race training £95; Formula B £129; Formula B+ £169
Payment Methods:	Cash, cheque, Visa, Access
Booking Details:	2 weeks in advance
Capacity:	30 people
Insurance:	PA included in price
Facilities:	Corporate days out. Refreshment available.
Other Notes:	Course are run at Kirkistown Circuit, County Down or Nutts Corner Circuit, County Antrim approximately once per month.

Company:	**Silverstone Driving Centre**
Address:	Silverstone, Towcester, Northants NN12 8TN
Tel:	01327 857177
Fax:	01327 858268
Price Range:	Single Seater Racing Car Experience £99; Intensive Race Tuition Course £2,250
Payment Methods:	Cash, cheque, Switch, Visa, Access, Amex, Diners
Booking Details:	6 weeks in advance for summer weekends, 2-3 weeks for midweek
Capacity:	Check with Driving Centre, minimum 6-8
Facilities:	Café, toilets, gift shop, car parking, wheelchair access. Corporate entertaining packages.
Other Notes:	Silverstone also offers single day experiences in saloon racing cars, rally driving, 4x4s and road skills for £99. The centre is open all year round.

MOUNTAIN BIKING

I know all about riding a mountain bike. I ride one around London. Three or four days a week, I arrive at my destination contented, perhaps a little puffed, sometimes a little damp, but with rosy cheeks and so much more relaxed than those who have chosen to do battle with the Northern Line. However, one day a week – invariably a Monday – I arrive in a psychotic rage, babbling incoherently about how people are out to get me.

I am not a paranoid schizophrenic. There really are motorists out and about on the streets of London who are trying to kill me. I try to avoid confrontation by taking back streets, or cycling along the South Bank pavements but sometimes the red mist overcomes my Oakleys and I subside into cycle rage. The other Monday I was crossing Vauxhall Bridge just after 9am. I had to get into the right-hand lane, so I stuck my arm out and started to move across. Two cars ignored the signal and I scurried back into the curb. Finally, I spotted a 50 yard gap in the traffic and went for third time lucky. Even though the lights were red, a Telecom truck accelerated into the empty space for, as all motor vehicle drivers know, cyclists do not exist. He missed me by a ballerina's foot.

I lost my temper. I caught the driver up at the lights, banged on his window and cast aspersions upon his relationship with his parents. 'You don't have right of way (expletives deleted)' was the gist of his reply, emanating from behind clouds of cigarette smoke. 'I don't have to let you cross the road because I am bigger, faster, nastier and greyer than you are.' After a final reference to illegal sexual practices, he roared off, pausing only to readjust his wing mirror which had mysteriously come loose during this reasoned exchange of views.

Most drivers do not deliberately aim to mow us down, it is just that bicycles are a blind spot. Anybody who has chosen pedal power in London knows that it is potentially dangerous. I love the freedom it gives me and I see no reason why I should have to stop just because every day I am a potential target for a murderous motorist. We irritate if we cycle in the safest place – the middle of the road – but we are no slower than cars. During daylight, the speed we travel (10mph) is certainly the average for Central London. I minimise my risks by wearing a helmet and luminous strips, I am constantly aware of just how badly people drive, and am alert for trouble.

A NICE RIDE

One can take only so much. So I thought, when I was up in the Peak District staying at Rock Lea, I'd go out for a nice ride. Try to remember when cycling was a relaxing pastime not an urban survival exercise. I'd reckoned without Iain Jennings, who runs the centre. Iain is rightly concerned about the safety of the groups who stay with him and, although three of us had experience of riding regularly – Peter cycled to work in London, Barbara had a racing bike in Jersey – he felt it was necessary to go through basic bike information and safety procedures.

'You might learn something,' he said, looking straight at me for some reason. And I did. Most of the information was stuff you never get told at the high street shop where they just measure you up, give you the bike, wave goodbye and cash the cheque. The first thing I learn is that mountain bikes have smaller frames than traditional racing bikes. To check it's the right size, stand legs astride over the bar. If the bar is physically and sexually abusing your reproductive organs, the bike is too big. If you can see acres of daylight betwixt crotch and bar, it is too small. When sitting on the bike with the ball of your foot on the pedal, the leg should be slightly bent at its fullest extent. It is important to adjust the seat to get it right, otherwise it can get very uncomfortable or cause extra strains on the leg.

Most mountain bike specs talk lovingly of the twenty-one

gears you have at your disposal – seven ratchets on the rear wheel and three settings by the pedals. This, Iain, explained, is somewhat misleading as there is a great deal of crossover. What you should not do is have the pedal gearing in high and the wheel in low (or vice versa) as this stretches the chain too far and can cause it to break. Chains always break when you are half-way up a mountain path in a thunderstorm.

Similarly, use the brakes sensibly: the front one does most of the work but if you jam it on too fast, you will fly over the handlebars. There are also safety considerations involved in cycling in groups, so be careful about crossing main roads and don't be ashamed of getting off and walking across the road.

Iain's final word of advice before leaving us in the capable hands of our transplanted Cornish guide, Simon, was, 'In the Peak district, the rain washes all the gravel to the bottom of the hill. Do not ride down a hill at full speed screaming and hollering and then brake suddenly. This may involve you in a sudden impact with a lot of gravel. This in turn may necessitate a visit to the local Casualty where you will wait a long time before they remove the gravel, stone by stone. This takes ages, and it hurts.'

Suitably chastened and following a 5-minute spin around the car park to check the bikes were okay and that everything fitted – including the helmets – we took off on the main road from Hathersage towards Castleton. We'd covered 2 miles – reaching a pub certain of the party had staggered home from two nights earlier, but in rather quicker time – when Peter discovered that one of his front brake pads was rubbing on the wheel rim. Simon fixed it quickly and we headed off up the 3-mile climb towards Ladybower Reservoir.

OFF ROAD

One of the joys of mountain biking is that the machines are tough enough to go off-road and that is what you should do. In the United States, they were originally designed for intrepid Californians to cycle along mountain paths, through rocks and dust traps without getting punctures and falling off without bending the frame. The sophisticated gearing system allows you to climb steep hills like a Land Rover – the most serious mechanical problem comes when your legs pack up. One other thing I learnt is that a padded tube along the cross bar is not to prevent any major testicular injury but is for resting the frame on your shoulder when you are climbing a very steep hill!

Instead of taking us up the road, Simon led us down a little track, past a Quaker retreat and on to a path that followed the old railway line to Glossop. Disused railway lines are great for cyclists because, since trains can only follow the slightest geographical inclines on the terrain, they simply can't go up steep hills. After a couple of miles of path we came back on a narrow tarmacked lane for a wonderful speedy descent through an old-fashioned landscape of woods and streams. The only downside was that after the bridge at the bottom we came across a steep 400 yard climb.

After recovering our breath and taking off most of the excess clothes we'd all worn in the damp morning, we headed on past Ladybower Reservoir, turning left towards Derwent which meant we never did get to cross Cutthroats Bridge. Then it was off the road again on a gravel bridleway that skirted up the side of Derwent Reservoir. (Simon sternly pointed out that bikes are allowed on bridleways but not on public footpaths.) It is a great way to travel fast enough to cover ground but slowly enough to take in the beauty of the landscape. We had another technical stop when Barbara's pedal came out (moral: if you are into off-road cycling, carry a tool kit) but soon we passed the ruined walls of what was Derwent village before it was abandoned and flooded. During the Second World War, the dams were the training ground where 617 Squadron practised with Barnes Wallace's bouncing bomb before the legendary Dambusters' Raid.

The nearest our party came to bouncing was when Simon offered to show us how to come down a very steep grassy hill on a mountain bike. 'When it gets wetter, the whole path is mud,' he grinned, pointing at a strip of bare earth about 12ft wide coming straight down what appeared to be a sheer hill decorated with sheep droppings. 'I lost it once and fell over the fence.' The technique he demonstrated is very simple, if a little inelegant. Basically you sit back, right back, your bottom behind the saddle hovering above the rear wheel, then you control your rate of descent by the judicious application of the brakes. It works and actually it's pretty easy to do once you have started rolling towards the bottom. Peter loved it and spent his second and third descents trying to slide his bike into a terminal skid.

The next couple of hours were fairly uneventful. Apart from when I decided to mount the kerb. Now, pavements in Derbyshire are different from those in London. In London, any biker is used to bouncing on to pavements. As I discovered, Peak pavements are higher, wider and then they drop off a few inches before you get back to smooth tarmac. The result was damaged pride and sore bits. I can feel them wince as I write this. The ride back down through Bamford was a wonderful winding, curving descent. Cyclists can get up a fair old speed. It is not often you see a near-accident because two cyclists are overtaking a car that is driving too slowly.

I had a great day, fresh air, exercise, a little drama, enjoyed some history and some personal pain. Two days later, I was back on my bike in London with a new attitude. Live and let live, relax, smell the diesel, all that sort of stuff. It lasted a while. Unfortunately, last week I had an altercation with a van in Soho. I hope the driver has found his ignition keys by now!

If you can ride a bike, you can ride a mountain bike. And you can ride a mountain bike pretty well anywhere. If you have a bike you can organise it all yourself. If you want to try it out, there are several multi-activity sports centres that offer guided mountain bike activities. In addition, bikes can usually be hired in towns where there is a flourishing tourist industry. So, instead of listing all the places where you can hire a bike, the best bet is to buy your own.

WHO TO CONTACT

Cyclists Touring Club
Cotterell House
69 Meadrow
Godalming
Surrey GU7 3HS

Tel: 01483 417217
Fax : 01483 426994
E-mail: cycling@ctc.org.uk

OFF-ROAD DRIVING

Damn this perverse English weather. All summer I've been praying for dry, sunny days and getting enough rain to drown a rat, I need wind and I get calm, calm and I get wind. Now, when I need lots of rain and wet to make mud, all I get is dust. Off-road driving conditions are at their worst in the summer. There is nothing to get stuck in!

Like the hippopotamus, what a 4x4 driver loves most is a great big wallow in mud, mud and more glorious mud. Show a serious off-road driver a swamp and say to him 'Don't go in there under any circumstances, there is a serious danger of getting stuck,' and you might as well start warming up the tractor now. Point at a very steep slope which can only be tackled at a teetering sideways angle, suggest the car could easily topple over, and you can see the danger lights flashing red in their eyes.

For years, four-wheel drive vehicles were either ancient Land Rovers with post-war accessories owned by working farmers or Range Rovers driven by rich country folk. Things changed during the 80s when first the Japanese, then all the car manufacturers, started making serious 4x4 vehicles. Owning one became a status symbol for city-dwellers who were more likely to get stuck on the M25 in the rush hour than a muddy puddle. Alex, the appalling merchant banker who stars in a *Daily Telegraph* cartoon strip, would regularly spray his Range Rover with liquid mud to give the right impression. Despite the large increase in the number of 4x4s on the road, it is obvious that most people who drive one have no idea how to use it properly for driving on off-road circuits or 'green laning' (travelling across country) safely.

Wild Tracks, just off the A11 near Newmarket, has two off-road tracks providing different degrees of difficulty to suit both beginners – like me – and more advanced drivers. You can either take your own 4x4 vehicle or use one of the three Wild Tracks vehicles – a diesel Land Rover, a Toyota or an ageing Range Rover. Alan, my instructor for the session, suggests we take the Range Rover.

DRIVE SLOWLY

In many ways, off-road driving requires you to forget everything you do on the road. Sadly, there is no James Bond style driving at 60mph up hill and down dale. It is much more leisurely than that. The first thing I learn is that if you are driving off-road you drive slowly. From the moment I engage the four-wheel drive, I only use first and second gears, and probably never go more than 15mph even on the flattest dirt track. 'You use second gear for everything, except going down steep slopes,' insists Alan, 'then you use first gear. Try not to use the brake and use the clutch as little as possible – if at all. The moment you put your foot on the clutch, you lose control of the vehicle, for the wheels are then freewheeling and you are at the mercy of the conditions. Keep your hands relaxed on the steering wheel, but don't put your elbows on the wheel or hook your thumbs around the wheel rim.'

That is all easier said than done. I quickly learn to keep my thumbs out of the way when we hit a deep rut and the vibration goes straight through my hands. Ouch. At Wild Tracks, the easier course is the yellow one, skirting the motocross track, through the woods where an outbreak of myxomatosis has left many rabbit corpses across the track. I soon become aware of the dangers of overhanging vegetation and trees when a particularly sharp branch whips in the open window and nearly takes my ear off. By the time we have returned to the main bowl, I am getting pretty cocky.

Until, that is, we take a slope at an angle and I'm leaning over so far I feel like I'm on a racing yacht in high seas. 'Steer straight through,' commands Alan, but too late as I have pointed the front wheels slightly downhill and find the vehicle sliding out of control.

Fortunately, we are soon back on level ground. Back on the main area, we approach the two hills, steep artificial creations. Alan asks me to stop the car. 'Whenever you come to a slope or hill for the first time, stop the car, get out and walk to the top. You need to see what is at the top and what is at the other side. Look out for tree roots, potholes, anything that might cause a problem. When you get to the top, always stop before going down the other side.' In case there is a sheer drop, I suggest facetiously. 'Exactly.'

When you can't see the top, you have to fix your sights on a particular point – a fence post, a tree, an ancient cowpat – and aim for that. On the shallower slope that is easy enough, though the blue hill turns out to have a descent at a different angle. Once I've reached the top, I realise I can't actually see my angle of descent as the slope is too steep. So I get out and have another look. To go down is simple in theory but really hard in practice. Put the Range Rover in first gear, then take my feet off both clutch and brake simultaneously. I start moving, then gingerly raise my feet, which both hover uncertainly above the pedals. It works, the gearing in the engine does all the work and we go straight down the slope in full control.

We stop again and Alan gets out to demonstrate the theory, using a piece of plank. The approach angle is the angle of ascent between the ground and front bumper, the departure angle at the back will be affected if you have a tow bar or hook. The ramp break-over angle sounds rather impressive but is really just about making sure that at the top of a hill you don't go straight over a sharp summit and crunch the floor of the vehicle. The Range Rover has good ground clearance because the differential is not in the dead centre of the chassis but underneath the driver's left knee. Owners of 4x4s should also remember that they are probably driving on road tyres which could be damaged by some off-track conditions. Finally, when driving into water – 'During the winter, this whole bowl is covered in water and mud,' says Alan proudly – the wading depth of the car is the height of the bumper. However, if you start to drive through water and keep a steady pace, this creates a bow wave in front of the car – the 4x4 equivalent of the parting of the Red Sea – enabling you to drive in deeper water.

LOOK OUT FOR TANKS

Life on the hills and the bowl has now been complicated by clouds of dust set up by the two Wild Tracks Chieftain tanks and an Abbot self-propelled gun, which are hurtling about the place looking very frightening. When a 60-ton tank goes up and over one of the hills, I feel sorry for the ground. As they are being driven by a group from Nottingham, Alan advises steering well away. Range Rovers are tougher than most cars but a brush with a tank will leave only one winner. I make a mental note to come back another time to drive the military fleet – it may not have any practical benefits but it looks great fun.

BREAK EVERY RULE

Next-off, we practise a 'failed hill climb'. Alan demonstrates it first and, once again, it involves breaking all the normal driving rules. You get most of the way up the hill and discover you can't make it to the top, so you leave the car in second gear and turn off the engine. This holds the Range Rover in position. Then you look round to make sure that there are no other vehicles close behind. 'Always keep at least 50m behind the car in front,' say Alan, ' to avoid just this eventuality.' Having checked the back, you put your feet on clutch and foot brake, then turn the engine back on. Once it has caught, you change straight down into reverse, release both pedals and steer back down the hill looking behind you. It sounds easy on paper but on the ground at a 30° angle it requires another leap of faith. The first time I snatched at reverse, missed it completely, and found myself freewheeling down the hill. That was when I realised how easy it was to lose control. Second time around and everything worked perfectly.

The best fun of all is another hill descent in first gear. In winter, this is straight into a muddy puddle deep enough to drown a Mini. It gives a splash that would not be out of place at Alton Towers and covers the whole car in a brown viscous substance that would give mud a good name. Even into a tiny summer puddle, it was most satisfying.

Due to the good conditions, Alan was not able to give full

tuition on other basic driving techniques to cope with ruts, slippery slopes and especially water and wading, and how to handle getting stuck in mud. On really muddy days Alan claims he just goes and parks the tractor by the mud hole and waits for the hippos to get stuck. Some drivers who have a winch on their vehicle deliberately get stuck so they can play with their toy. They usually get pulled out by the tractor too. The really serious players push it and try to turn their vehicles over. I, however, am happy to remain upright.

Although the conditions in which I did my 4x4 training were too hospitable to get the full benefit from the instruction, I soon found that the lessons learnt have a use on the road too. A few days later, I was in the Lake District negotiating steep semi-tarmacked tracks in a Vauxhall Cavalier. By using clutch and brake much less than before, I soon found I was both more in control and more successful than I had anticipated.

Next time the weather is really bad I'm off to Wild Tracks again. Perhaps they'll let me drive a tank. That would be an excellent way of negotiating Central London during rush-hour traffic jams.

WHO TO CONTACT

The Federation of Off-Road Driving Schools (FORDS)
Martin Chester-Bristow
PO Box 9
Hoyland, Barnsley
South Yorks S74 0YY

Tel: 01226 748822
Fax: 01226 740151

▶ **FORDS is a loose association of off-road schools formed in 1995 to try and set industry standards and weed out the cowboy operators.**

▶ **There are now some sixty recognised centres in the UK and Republic of Ireland. They will happily give you details of your closest FORDS member.**

Off-Road Clubs

There are 48 Land Rover Clubs (Association of Rover Clubs, c/o Andrew Stavordale, 65 Longmead Avenue, Hazel Grove, Stockport, Cheshire SK7 5PJ (Tel: 0161 456 8224) and 65 other Off-Road clubs. Perhaps the most famous is the All Wheel Drive Club (PO Box 6, Fleet, Hants GU13 9YR).

Magazine

Off Road & 4 Wheel Drive is excellent, informative and helpful. It contains a monthly list of Off-Road clubs and centres.

—————— WHERE TO GO ——————

Company:	**Wild Tracks Offroad Activity Park**
Address:	Chippenham Road, Kennett, Newmarket, Suffolk CB8 7QJ
Tel:	01638 751 918
Fax:	01638 552173
Price Range:	Half day (3 hours) £110; full day £155 (extra people at £30 per person)
Payment Methods:	Cash, cheque
Booking Details:	3-4 weeks in advance
Capacity:	3 vehicles; 3 passengers per vehicle in 4 x 4, more in military vehicles
Facilities:	'Wild Snacks' restaurant. Shop with small selection of gifts. Toilets. Will arrange tailor-made events.

Company:	**Edge Hill Shooting Ground**
Address:	Nadbury House, Camp Lane, Warmington, Banbury, Oxfordshire OX17 1DH
Tel:	01295 678141
Fax:	01295 670100
Price Range:	Full day £140 (inc lunch and coffee); half day £60 (inc lunch); group £200 (max 6)
Payment Methods:	Cash, cheque, major credit cards
Booking Details:	2 weeks in advance to be sure
Capacity:	Clubhouse can seat 50 for lunch
Facilities:	Clubhouse, hot and cold snacks, toilets. Corporate entertaining and groups; gift vouchers.

Other Notes: CPSA affiliated. Also: clay pigeon shooting and archery. 100 acres.

Company: **Fresh Tracks**
Address: Haultwick Farm, Ware, Herts SG11 1JQ
Tel: 01920 438758
Fax: 01920 438 729
Price Range: Shared day (3 drivers in car) £99 per person; £199 exclusive use of car; £49 half-day hire of quad bikes
Payment Methods: Cash, cheque, major credit/debit cards (exc Diners)
Booking Details: Vouchers next day, otherwise 14 days
Capacity: 4 cars on-site at one time (12 people); up to 200 for corporate days
Insurance: PA available at £9 per day. Cars and PL covered. Private cars have to be insured by owner.
Facilities: Hotel on-site; changing, showers and toilets. Disabled access. Corporate events; gift vouchers.
Other Notes: 3 large sites in Bristol, between Leeds and Manchester and in Hertfordshire. Also have access to 40 other sites. Also: rally cars, Ferraris, tanks.

Company: **Ian Wright Off Road Driving School**
Address: Pickwell, Bolney, West Sussex RH17 5RE
Tel: 01444 881190 / 0850 486888
Fax: 01444 881677
Price Range: Full day 1 person £238.50; half day £176.25; 3 persons sharing £94/64.63 per person
Payment Methods: Cheque, cash, Amex
Booking Details: 2 weeks in advance
Capacity: Up to 400 on multi-activity days. Eight 4x4 vehicles.
Facilities: Camping, caravaning, local hotels, guest houses; hot and cold meals; changing rooms and toilets on-site. Showers at extra charge. Motorised activity days, 4x4 driver training, family fun days etc.
Other Notes: Ian Wright has been a competitive trials driver for 20 years and Pickwell Country Estate is set in 400 acres of parkland and wood with 15 miles of green lanes and tracks.

Company: **Leisure Pursuits**
Address: Chartin House, Hammerwood Road, Ashurstwood, East Grinstead, West Sussex

Tel: 01342 825 522
Fax: 01342 824722
Price Range: Super start (2 hours) £85 (Sun and weekdays); Challenge half-day £280 for 3 people; Off-Road Challenge day £125 per person. Individual tuition £40 (not Sat)
Payment Methods: Cash, cheque, major credit cards
Booking Details: Saturdays busy, short notice sometimes available
Capacity: Up to 50 off-roading events; up to 200 in mixed activity events
Facilities: Accommodation at inn 1 mile away. On-site catering, changing rooms, showers and toilets; disabled access; corporate events organised.
Other Notes: Also: team-building, challenge events, archery and clay pigeon shooting. Endorsed by FORDS, Member of AWDC (All Wheel Drive Club) and RAC Motor Sports Association.

Company: **Motor Safari**
Address: Chester and Welsh Borderlands, Robin's Nest, Mold Road, Caergwrle, Wrexham LL12 9HA
Tel: 01978 760679
Fax: 01978 762370
Price Range: Half day £75; full day £129. Professional courses, fun days etc prices on application.
Payment Methods: Cheque, cash, Visa, Delta, Switch
Booking Details: 14 days in advance
Capacity: 1-60, though can handle up to 1,000
Facilities: Local accommodation; varied catering; bars; toilets; showers; leisure-wear for sale. Corporate entertaining; product launch; gift vouchers.
Other Notes: Motor Safari have 50 sites across the UK. Their three main sites are near Newbury, near Birmingham and a quarry just outside Wrexham in North Wales.

Company: **Spectrum 4x4 Outdoor Pursuits**
Address: PO Box 9, Hoyland, Barnsley, S. Yorks S74 0YY
Tel: 01226 748822
Fax: 01226 740151
Price Range: Shared day from £89 per person; individual tuition 1-day £200
Payment Methods: Cash, cheque, all major credit cards

Booking Details:	4 weeks
Capacity:	9 Land Rovers
Insurance:	Participation Insurance included, PA £10 per day
Facilities:	Local hotel. Toilets. Corporate entertaining, groups and stag parties, gift vouchers.
Other Notes:	Current Land Rover and hill climb champions, have been in operation 6 years.

Company:	**Tuf Trax**
Address:	Westerings, Station Road, West Haddon, Northamptonshire NN6 7AU
Tel:	01788 510575 / 0585 587648
Price Range:	1-day course £238.50 (1-2 people sharing); £352.50 (3-4 sharing); Bedford 4x4 truck £58.75 per hour. Stalwart 6x6 amphibious 8 tonner available for £250 + VAT.
Payment Methods:	Cash, cheque
Booking Details:	2-4 weeks
Capacity:	Groups from 4 upwards
Insurance:	Optional PA
Facilities:	Local B&Bs and hotel. Small canteen. Cranfield Hall available for corporate activities. Gift vouchers.
Other Notes:	Challenging natural scenic locations near Kettering, with dramatic terrain. Also: group days, laser shooting, archery, quads, off-road karts and hovercraft.

Company:	**Yorkshire 4x4 Exploration**
Address:	The Green Dragon Inn, Exelby, Bedale, North Yorkshire DL8 2HA
Tel:	01677 427222
Fax:	01677 427222
Price Range:	From £95 to 165
Payment Methods:	Cash, cheque, major credit cards
Booking Details:	1-2 months in advance
Facilities:	Local accommodation, pub, hot and cold food, toilets. Corporate entertaining; gift vouchers.
Other Notes:	Richard Fawcett uses ex-military vehicles, ex-Camel Trophy Defenders and Discoverys.

Company:	**Nigel Mansell Racing School**

See page 160 (motor racing) for details

Company:	**N. Herefordshire Off Road Driving School**
Address:	The Vauld, Marden, Hereford, HR1 3HA
Tel:	01568 797372
Price Range:	1-day course school vehicle £85; 1:1 tuition £125
Payment Methods:	Cheques, cash
Booking Details:	2-4 weeks for weekends
Insurance:	Have to sign disclaimer
Facilities:	Super B&B next door. Food available at base. Corporate events up to 16 (8 vehicles at 2 per vehicle).
Other Notes:	Serious driving course (they train Oxfam and International Rescue drivers).

Company:	**North Yorkshire Off Road Centre**
Address:	Bayness Farm, Robin Hood's Bay, Whitby, N. Yorkshire YO22 4PJ
Tel:	01947 880371 / 0831 694294
Fax:	01947 880371
Price Range:	Discovery 1-day £176 per person, £29.50 per hour: Land Rover 1-day £141. Own vehicle £82.50.
Payment Methods:	Cash, cheque, major credit cards
Booking Details:	6-8 weeks for weekends; a few days for weekdays
Facilities:	Corporate entertaining. Gift vouchers. 6x6 Militant Wagon, Discovery, Defender and quads. Refreshments, on-site. Also: clay pigeon, archery.
Other Notes:	Open all year. Endorsed by FORDS.

Company:	**Ronnie Dale Off Road Adventure Driving School**
Address:	Whiteburn Farm, Abbey St. Bathans, Duns, Berwickshire
Tel:	01361 840244 / 0831 122110
Fax:	01361 840239
Price Range:	Half day £100/120; full day £215/250; 2 days £430/500
Payment Methods:	Cash, cheque
Booking Details:	2 weeks
Capacity:	Four 4x4s inc Land Rover, Shogun and Frontera
Insurance:	Fully comprehensive
Facilities:	Corporate entertainment. On-site cottage accommodation, food locally. Caravan park.
Other Notes:	Off-road for children on mini quad bikes. Specialist and instructors' courses available. 2,500-acre site. Also: training available on own vehicles.

PAINTBALL

Time is running out. It is 19:40 hours but inside the wood the temperature is still above 80°. I have been struggling through neck-high undergrowth for what seems like an age, thorns and brambles are tearing holes in my camouflage overalls, and sweat is pouring down inside my goggles. I spot some bloke in a green face-mask crouching in the path. I'm about to decorate his back with white paint when I see he's sporting a purple arm band. He's on my side. Casualties caused by friendly fire are equally frowned upon in the surreal world of paintball.

We make eye contact and start to inch forward. From the clearing below, a hailstorm of paint opens up, spattering the trees above our heads. He motions me back, I crawl along the path, until I reach an open clearing with a ditch on the other side. Now what? I make a dash for it, nobody fires at me, and I slide feet first down into the ditch. Except it's twice as deep as I thought with a muddy puddle at the bottom. Nothing for it, I hit the mud, squelch and turn right ready to fire. Still nothing. Up and over the other side and I'm on the edge of a field. I crawl along on the parched earth, half dazzled by the sunlight. Tactically I'm in a mess. I've lost my fire support and I can only hope that the yellows aren't expecting an assault from the rear.

Wrong. At a gap in the foliage I raise my head a fraction. A barrage of fire greets it. Fortunately it is all much too high, but continues to splatter the trees and grass while I kiss the earth for what seems like an hour but is less than a minute. Time to wait. 'Four minutes left, purples,' booms the game marshal. Most of our team are pinned down in a firefight around two wooden towers 200m deeper in the woods. I wait for the two other members of the 'left flank through the deep undergrowth assault group', to come at the yellows' flag. 'Two minutes left.'

179

The firing is closer. I make a move expecting to be mown down. Through the undergrowth, dive behind a tree. Two yellows open up on me. A pellet hits my knee. Damn. I look down and it hasn't exploded. The enemy closest to me is having a gun problem. Tough. Take them out. Splat. Bye-bye yellow. I've linked up with my two colleagues with 40 seconds left and we've 30m to get to the flag. I take out a guy in a black T-shirt – good he got me in an earlier game – but he doesn't seem aware. No time to call for a check, we've got to get the flag. 'Game over.' Blast. So near, yet so far.

MAYHEM

An hour before, I thought I was on the wrong rave site waiting for something to happen. Sitting behind a large oak tree in a small wood in Essex, with Pulp's *Sorted for Es and Whizz* buzzing around my head, wondering if any of the opposition were ever going to get this close to our base so I could zap them. I made a few jump but they were already dead, holding their weapons in the air with paint marks over various parts of their anatomy. Now that was a boring game and I wondered if the wife had been right all along.

'Paintball?' she had scoffed. 'That's not an adventure sport. It's just an excuse to run around the woods playing soldiers and shooting people with guns.' 'I like running around the woods, shooting people with guns,' interjected my son. 'Can I come?' Unfortunately, I was to be denied his support as children must be at least 12.

There is more to paintball than revisiting the war games of your youth. At its height in the late 1980s, there were some 400 locations around the country where people could go and shoot at each other, although that has now dropped to fewer than 100. In the early days, the pistols were cruder, less accurate, firing only six shots before requiring a new magazine. Now the standard issue guns at Mayhem are pump action with a magazine capable of taking more than 100 pellets while the serious players use weapons that can cost over £300 each, are dead accurate and almost silent. At it's top level, paintball is a serious pursuit. The Mayhem Open, staged every May, sees teams of five, from all over the world, competing for a purse of £60,000. In a 10-minute game, the pros will fire up to 800 rounds – more than I got through in an entire evening when I joined Wave Tech Mobile Communications of Welwyn Garden City in their battle with Rathbone Media of Brentwood.

Paintball is very popular with companies as it encourages teamwork, teaches you to trust your partners, can be played by both sexes and all ages, and most people end up enjoying the adrenaline kick. Strange things can happen on the field of battle. The mousy secretary transforming into the Killer Amazon from Hell. Or the managing director, who always believed he was loved by his employees yet was always the first of his team to be shot during every game. Shot in the back.

——— A MATTER OF HONOUR ———

Mayhem, near Ongar in Essex, is run by Robert Hollings, who has found an alternative use for his farmland. He has created some 10 different game scenarios in both woods and open ground. What looked like a dump full of abandoned cars, buses and tractors is in fact the setting for the urban game. The idea is to play a lot of games quickly so that people who get shot early on don't get fed up waiting for another go. Each game has a safe haven surrounded by netting. When hit, a player hangs his gun outside on the numbered hook and can take his mask off once inside.

On arrival each player is asked to change into overalls – which can be hired if you're not Rambo with his own set of camouflage fatigues – and is issued with a pouch containing three blue tubes full of paintballs, a face mask and goggles. Safety is a constant worry so masks have to be worn at all times when carrying guns. The guns are powered by a gas cylinder which doubles as a butt and are loaded by pulling the pump action on the barrel back then forward, paintballs are fed from a large magazine on top of the gun. It is possible to maintain a fast rate of fire but, if you get it wrong, the gun can jam up, making you very vulnerable. They are fairly accurate up to 20m and a well delivered paintball can sting and leave a bruise mark for days.

A hit is scored on any part of the body or gun. Ricochets off cover are common and are adjudged by the games marshals, who tend to give you the benefit of the doubt. During one game, I was sheltering under a wooden cable drum with balls splattering all around but I was finally called dead because of a direct hit on the front of my magazine that I never saw or felt. It is easy enough to brush off the paint so the game does rely on personal honour, which most people adhere to. Most of the time.

—— TACTICS VERSUS SCRATCHES ——

The objective of each game is to infiltrate enemy territory, capture their flag and return it to your own base. Sound tactics are essential. If you play a lone game no matter how good a shot you are you will end up dead. My first game was on the yellow team (Rathbone Media) who, though outnumbered, operated in groups of three. They would spot an enemy individual, isolate him and then shoot him. In the second game, the purples learnt their lesson and kept moving forward until the yellows were forced back to defend their base and were slowly but surely wiped out. Throughout the evening the yellows had a much sounder grasp of group tactics – which was why they won the games series 4-2 – while purples in times of stress tended to revert to individual action. The women on both sides, though naturally less aggressive and unconcerned when they got hit, were generally better at operating to a plan.

To win, you have to keep moving forward, which naturally exposes you to enemy fire. Sometimes a direct hit can hurt. I caught one cracker on my shoulder and another on the left leg, which was still marked a week later. The other mistake I made in the heat was not to wear an extra layer under my overalls. Long cotton trousers and a T-shirt rather than shorts and singlet would have meant many fewer scratches.

After the frustrations of the third game, when our final assault was denied only by time running out, the purples were determined to redeem their standing in an open field with large round hay bales set up as cover. The tactic is to operate in pairs and go hell for leather to gain a position.

It starts badly as my partner and I head for different bales and I find myself pinned down under fire from two guys, with no support. One shot hits the edge of the bale and ricochets on to the gun barrel. The marshal allows me to stay in but I have to wait stuck behind a bale for 5 minutes until the pair pinning me down are hit.

With 3 minutes left, we have to make the charge. Running across open ground I make cover 20m from the enemy base, three bales forming a defensive position. A figure pops over the top and fires wildly in my direction. There's one purple on my left who is keeping his head down (because he's carrying our flag which has to be planted in the enemy base), another on my right whose gun is jammed. I don't know if there's one or two enemy left so it has to be death or glory.

Surprise is the key. I sprint for the corner, expecting at any moment to be shot. As I pass the corner I dive forward, hitting the ground hard with my right shoulder. In one movement I roll, point the gun under my stomach and fire. The sound of the splat and the defender's scream come simultaneously. The force of the roll has opened the back of my magazine and I am surrounded by dozens of unfired paintballs. The girl I've shot just above the right breast from 1.5m has dropped her gun and is rubbing her chest in pain and shock. The marshal congratulates me on a great move. I feel embarrassed and a bit of a heel.

That feeling doesn't last more than 5 minutes. The next game is due to start. Adrenalin kicks in and I'm all ready to reprise my Rambo role. Unfortunately, there isn't the space in between the wrecked cars and the coach. Asking for cover, I make a 1.5m dash across open ground seeking the safety of a rusty oil tank. I'm only half way when I'm mown down, hit three, four times.

No more glory today, but there will be other nights.

WHO TO CONTACT

The United Kingdom Paintballing Sports Federation (UKPSF)
Write to them if you need information on clubs in your area.
41 Cedar Road
Hutton
Brentwood
Essex CM13 INS

Tel: 01277 262230

▶ **The UKPSF was set up mainly to talk to government bodies, district and local councils about the sport, to unify rules and regulations within paintballing competitions worldwide, and to keep in contact with other paintballing federations around the world.**

——————— WHERE TO GO ———————

Company: Mayhem Paintball Games
Address: Pryors Farm, Ongar Road, Abridge, Essex RM14 1AA
Tel: 01708 688517 / 01708 688424
Price Range: £18 per day. Hire of overalls £2; extra paint 6p per ball. Group discounts available.
Payment Methods: Cash, cheque, Visa, Mastercard
Booking Details: 2-4 weeks in advance
Capacity: 12-40
Facilities: Local hotel. Catering facilities; separate M and F changing rooms, showers and toilets (1 disabled); gift/equipment shop; corporate events and gift vouchers. Free pick-up from Theydon Bois underground station (Central line).
Other Notes: Lots of different sites, very friendly marshals.

Company: National Paintball Games Company
Tel: 01705 499494 (central booking)
Fax: 01705 471168
Price Range: Average £40 per person per day inc equipment, though there are regional variations
Payment Methods: Cash, cheque, all major credit cards, no debit cards
Booking Details: Groups 3 weeks; individuals 4-7 days
Capacity: 50-240
Insurance: PA inc
Facilities: Very strong corporate side. Many sites have on-site facilities for accommodation, conferences etc. Contact particular site for details.
Other Notes: The NPG have a minimum of 32 sites across the country and claim that one of them will be within an hour of where you live. All sites have to come up to basic standards of facilities and game sites – see the Survival Game, Scotland, for an example of specific facilities.

Company: **Skirmish Lasham**
Address: Manor Farm Buildings, Lasham, Alton, Hants GU34 5SL
Tel: 01256 381173
Fax: 01256 381628
Price Range: £17.50 inc 100 paintballs; camouflage fatigues £1, pellets £3.50 per 50
Payment Methods: Cash, cheque, Visa, Access, Delta
Booking Details: Groups, 2 weeks
Capacity: 20-250
Facilities: Full indoor catering facilities, hot showers, toilets. Equipment shop. Corporate entertaining and company days. Gift vouchers.
Other Notes: Open Sat/Sun all year round, weekdays for groups. Europe's longest-running Paintball site, est 1989. Formerly an RAF base, it boasts real air-raid shelters, bunkers, slit trenches and bomb craters which are scattered throughout the whole playing area. Varied game scenarios range from bridges and towers to complete village settings.

Company: **Task Force**
Address: Crowbridge, Cardiff, Vale of Glamorgan, Wales
Tel: 01222 593900
Price Range: £17 for 6 games half day, evenings; £22 full day inc equipment and 100 paintballs. Extra balls £8 per 100; £65 per 1,000.
Payment Methods: Cash, cheque, Visa, Access
Booking Details: Groups 24-48 hours
Capacity: Min 15, max. 90
Facilities: Café, changing rooms and toilets. Corporate events and gift vouchers available.
Other Notes: Open every Sat/Sun, weekdays by arrangement. Also junior games (aged 11-16) from £20 per day.

Company: **The Arena Indoor Paintball**
Address: Unit 5, Granville Mill, Vulcan Street, Oldham
Tel: 0161 628 0028
Price Range: £10 for 3-hour game (£8 under 18) inc 50 shots; £3 per 50 shots
Payment Methods: Cash, cheque
Booking Details: 3 days for open sessions. Always book in advance.

Capacity:	10-100
Facilities:	Café; changing rooms and toilets; shop. Corporate events organised.
Other Notes:	Top floor of an old mill, 45,000 sq ft arena – 'a post urban nuclear game' (ie lots of rubble). Open 7 days a week 10.00-22.00.

Company:	**National Paintball Games**
Address:	Adventure Sports Ltd, Wedgenock Rifle Range, Wedgenock Lane, Warwick, Warwickshire CV35 7PX
Tel:	01926 491948
Fax:	01926 490010
Price Range:	Half day/6 games £25 (inc 250 paintballs); full day £35 (inc 350 paintballs); £2.50 per 50 extra
Payment Methods:	Cash, cheque, Visa, Access
Booking Details:	1 week
Capacity:	20-100
Facilities:	Several good hotels within 5 miles. Lunch, tea, coffee and other refreshments available. Changing facilities with showers and toilets (inc disabled). Disabled access to clubhouse. Corporate multi-activity, team-building events.
Other Notes:	Open 7 days, all weekends, groups in week. Also: clay shooting, archery, off-road 4x4 course, quad bikes, tank driving, assault course; field target, rifle and pistol shooting.

Company:	**The Survival Game Scotland**
Address:	Overton, Kirknewton, Mid Lothian EX27 8DP
Tel:	01506 884088 / 0468 808322
Fax:	01506 884288
E-mail:	steve@maximillion.co.uk
Price Range:	Half day £12.50 (+ equipment hire); Premier full day £30 inc equipment
Payment Methods:	Cash, cheque, Amex, Access, Visa
Booking Details:	One week
Capacity:	10-70
Facilities:	Catering, toilets, equipment sales. Corporate entertaining, gift vouchers available.
Other Notes:	There is a second site at Killearn. Open weekends for individuals; larger groups (min 20) on weekdays. Has 12 game sites and is rated among top 6 in the

country. Also other activities including team-building, off-road driving, quad bikes etc.

Company:	**Wild West Paintball**
Address:	21/28a Seymour Place, London, W1H 5WJ
Tel:	0171 935 6603 / 0956 149 745
E-mail:	101715.3100@compuserve.com
Price Range:	£20 per person inc equipment; paint pellets extra
Payment Methods:	Cash, cheque
Booking Details:	Summer weekends 4 weeks; weekdays 48 hours
Capacity:	100 on outside sites, 40 on indoor (Plumstead)
Facilities:	Local B&B. Full cooked lunch available. Toilets on site. Corporate events organised and gift vouchers available.
Other Notes:	Groups of 15+ can have their own game or be incorporated into existing games. There are novice paintball games on the first Sat of every month. There are 3 sites: Dorking (Henfold Lane, nr Newdigate) site includes a full-size double-decker bus and an old village. Reigate; Grubwood, Surrey (nr Junction 8 of the M25). Plumstead (Nathan Way, London SE28) – an indoor, post-apocalyptic site.

Company:	**Active 8**
Address:	62/63 Worcester St, Wolverhampton, WV2 4LQ
Tel:	01902 8354 43
Price Range:	£35 inc equipment and 400 pellets. Half days at £19.50 (inc 200 pellets); extra at 6p per ball.
Payment Methods:	£5 deposit, cheque, cash, Visa, Access
Booking Details:	1 month
Capacity:	10-200
Facilities:	Corporate entertaining, gift vouchers; on-site catering; local accommodation available; on-site toilet facilities; plenty of parking; gift and equipment shop.
Other Notes:	20 fields over 100 acres around Tong Castle inc villages, bunkers. Two sites in South Birmingham and Coal's Hill, between Birmingham and Coventry. Also: junior days (12-16). Weekends open to individuals, weekdays groups only.

Company:	**Foxwood Skirmish**
Address:	114 Plumstead Road, East Norwich, Norfolk NR7 9NF
Tel:	01603 701539
Price Range:	£12.50; paintballs from 6p per ball
Payment Methods:	Cash, cheque, Access, Visa
Booking Details:	2-3 weeks
Capacity:	14-100
Facilities:	Corporate entertaining – bring in outside caterer; gift vouchers; local accommodation; burger bar; toilet facilities and parking.
Other Notes:	Largest professional site in East Anglia since 1987, with 11 playing fields in 50 acres of woodland. Plus specialist features – Speedball, Maginot Line and Village. Open end Jan to mid-Dec at weekends, mid-week by arrangement.

Company:	**Hot Shots**
Address:	European Strike Command, RAF Greenham Common, Newbury, RG19 6HN
Tel:	01635 41308
Fax:	01635 41310
Price Range:	£20 basic inc equipment, Sterling Bronze pumps and 50 balls. Extra ammo £6 per 100.
Payment Methods:	Cash, cheque, Access, Visa
Booking Details:	Groups 2 weeks; individuals 1 week
Capacity:	20-150
Facilities:	Local hotels and B&B. Licensed bar, catering facilities; toilets; parking. Corporate events organised – conference room available.
Other Notes:	Open 9.15-16.00 at weekends. An urban site with 72 single and 2-storey buildings, it was developed from the former Cruise Missile base (so if irony is your thing!). Comes highly recommended by Mr Jeb Hoge: 'I played there last summer when I was in Oxford and can honestly say it was spectacular. 120 players divided into 2 teams, it's definitely oriented towards new players. It is not cheap but worth every pound.'

Company:	**National Paintball Fields**
Address:	Bassett's Pole, Sutton Coldfield, Birmingham
Tel:	0121 327 3961

Fax:	0121-327 3967
Price Range:	£10 + £4 kit; paintballs £8 per 100, £100 per 2,000
Payment Methods:	Cash, cheque, all credit and debit cards
Booking Details:	2 days to a month
Capacity:	Min 25, up to 400
Facilities:	Hot and cold refreshments served. Portaloos and changing facilities. Corporate games packages designed to suit, possibly combined with karting. Easy access off A38.
Other Notes:	20 arenas over 200 acres make 'the largest site in Europe'. Open 9.30-16.30 every weekend; weekdays for groups (inc stag parties). Juniors (aged 13-16) last Saturday of every month.

Company:	**Paintball London**
Address:	Pondware Farm, Pondware Lane, White Waltham, Nr Maidenhead, Berks
Tel:	01734 320333
Fax:	01734 340012
Price Range:	£40 per day inc equipment (semi-automatic Marlers!)
Payment Methods:	Cash, cheque
Booking Details:	2 weeks' notice
Capacity:	20-160
Facilities:	Corporate entertaining, gift vouchers. Catering van, toilets.
Other Notes:	Open 7 days a week, 200-acre forest and 7 different playing areas allow separate games for beginners, intermediate and experienced paintballers. Play down on the modern village arenas and aim for a great day out rather than catering to the paintball professionals.

PART FOUR
SKY

BUNGEE JUMPING

This is not a good idea.

The thought whirls around my head like one of those infuriating pop songs you hate but can't exorcise from the memory. I announce it out loud to the other occupants of the cage, who nod with the distracted air of veterans who have heard that refrain so many times that it no longer has any meaning. I'd like to run away but I am hobbled like a pony, my ankles encased in velcro, and I cannot move my feet more than 15cm in any direction. There is a large rope attached to the ankle hobble and to the harness around my waist, so even if I did make a break for freedom I could only hop 70m before falling flat on my face.

This is not a good idea and I haven't left the ground yet. Hang on, why am I here? I always said I would never do something this stupid. When I discussed writing this book, I blithely told the publishers 'I'll do everything except bungee jumping'. They, naturally, wanted to know why and my litany of excuses incorporated such gems as, 'I might consider it if I could jump off that suspension bridge in New Zealand, at least it's pretty there'. Or, 'It's not a sport'. Basically, these excuses could be boiled down to, 'Because the idea scares the pants off me, so I'm not going to do it'.

—— AN ANCIENT TRADITION ——

Bungee jumping is an ancient tradition in the Pentecost Islands of the South Pacific. As part of their rituals for attaining manhood, generations of young men have dived off high bamboo towers with vines tied to their ankles. This was also supposed to guarantee an excellent yam harvest. Not a lot's changed. Substitute a 100m crane over the River Thames for the bamboo platform, an elastic rope for the vine, and you will find thousands of young men determined to show off their manhood. Sadly, there has been no recorded upturn in the South London yam harvest to date.

Appropriately, modern bungee jumping began on April Fool's Day 1979, when four jumpers made a simultaneous and illegal leap off the Clifton Suspension Bridge using elasticated rubber ropes. News of this new method of achieving an adrenaline rush soon spread around the world, most notably to Queenstown in South Island, New Zealand, where a suspension bridge over the scenic Skippers Canyon has become an essential stopover for thrill seekers Down Under. There is some confusion over the spelling: Down Under and in the USA it is Bungy; Bungi at Victoria Falls (off the bridge between Zimbabwe and Zambia); and in France it is the ever so poetic 'le saut en élastique'.

In 1989, the UK Bungee Club was formed in Greater Manchester to organise and regulate the sport, under the rules of the British Elastic Rope Sports Association (BERSA). At one point there were eight associated clubs, but this has now shrunk to three. There is only one fixed site in the country – at Chelsea Bridge in London – though there are mobile operations that tour the country. (There is talk of a new fixed site in Tyneside, so if that's your area call BERSA for details.)

── THE MOST EXCITING THING? ──

Despite all my protestations that nothing on this or any other planet was going to get me to jump off that crane, in a moment of bravado I finally booked my first jump. Being a wimp, once I had booked my BJ my entire body was suffused not by a wash of relief but one of sheer terror. Aside from the fact that I always thought there was something intrinsically stupid about diving into mid-air with a rope attached to your feet, I began to work out what could go wrong. After a sleepless night in which I appeared to spend most of it with my head embedded in tarmac like Wile E. Coyote in a *Road Runner* cartoon, I phoned Mark Debenham, the manager of Adrenalin Village for reassurance.

'You're quite right to feel scared,' he said soothingly. 'It is frightening but it will be the most exciting thing you will ever do.' Great. What about safety? The UK Bungee Club has supervised some 250,000 jumps since 1989 and has a 100 per cent safety record. There have been some muscle and ligament injuries but the only serious accidents have occurred with unlicensed operators.

So, anyway, here I am at 1.30 on a Friday afternoon in mid-summer, with my stomach swishing around in my trainers and my heart beating at between two and three times its normal rate. I sit down and watch as the ropes are all laid out on the astroturf. The ropes are colour-coded, depending on the jumper's weight, and are made of unbraided natural latex, composed of hundreds of individual strands to make a rope thicker than my wrist. They can stretch to four times their 70m length. In the office, I fill in a form and happily sign an insurance waiver. Anyone preparing to do a BJ is obviously not sound in mind, so there's no problem there.

I am then asked to step on a pair of scales and my weight in kilos is written on my left hand in very black, very indelible, magic marker. Underneath that is written the letter 'R' indicating that I will be attached to a red rope. Due to the G-forces involved in bungee jumping (the equivalent of car braking heavily at 20mph) it is not a good idea to lie about your weight, not that the staff give you that opportunity. After a few more minutes waiting nervously, I am ushered into the inner corral where I am weighed again and a circle drawn around my hand to show it has been double checked. I then step into a climbing harness which is pulled up tight around my groin. A large red handkerchief is slotted in the front of the harness as a further failsafe. I sit down on the bench of trepidation to await my turn.

——————— NOW IT'S MY TURN ———————

The first jump of the day is a 'staff jump' designed to show the waiting punters that they will survive the experience. For some reason, all the staff are very keen to do this. Up goes the cage, pulled by the crane, and the lad's out toppling backwards, doing somersaults on the rebounds and giving whoops of joy. So why do I not feel like talking? As the cage comes back to earth, Mark fits on the ankle harness, pulls it tight over my bare ankles, fastening the velcro strips so it is secure. Too, too soon, it is my turn.

It's so undignified having to hop 2m, feeling like the prize in a turkey shoot. My photographer Michael Hoppen and one of the staff, clutching a video camera (capture this moment for ever – only £10), are in the rear of the cage and I plop down on the tiny bench, my legs are trembling, my heart is pounding and I just know that this is a bad idea. One of the staff attaches the end of the rope to the bottom of the cage. Then they attach one clip to the ankle harness and the other to the waist harness. Now I have to stand up and the palms of my hands could irrigate the Sahara, and my stomach contains a Black Hole that could swallow the Starship Enterprise.

The operator in charge of the cage is a genial young man with an interesting collection of tattoos and a jolly sense of humour. I want to strangle him. He rechecks both my harnesses, putting an index finger down the ankle straps and announcing, 'good, not too tight'. By this stage I am incapable of any conversation other than repeating 'This is not a good idea'. Suddenly we're off the ground, the giant crane pulling the cage up into the air, swinging out over the River Thames. A river boat passes beneath us and dozens of tourists look upwards, I wonder if they know or care what is going on. The cage operator runs through the instructions once more, tells me what is going to happen and, if I was listening then, I certainly can't remember what he said now.

Oh yes, I can. Michael has convinced me that for the sake of his pictures I should do a back flip for my first jump, rather than the more conventional swallow dive. Mr Cageman tells me his favourite jump. Bungee jumpers seeking an increased thrill put their hands inside the harness and don a blindfold. He then holds them out of the cage and lets go when he feels like it. 'I pull them in and out a couple of times for fun,' he smiles sadistically. 'Your mouth gone dry yet?'

'No,' I lie, but the word comes out parched and arid. He tells Michael, while looking straight at me, that only two people have ever refused to jump and come back down in the cage. I still think they are the bravest of all – prepared to endure ridicule rather than join the lemming brigade. Now we're at the top and, as the cage swings in the wind, he grabs a rigid steel rod and clips it on to the cage. In half a minute we are stationary, 100m above the Thames. I look down through the steel mesh floor, realise that this was a bad idea and stare fixedly in the direction of Big Ben. It's there all right, but I can't focus. Mr Cageman opens the door, he grabs on to the handle on the front of my waist harness and I hobble backwards. The balls of my feet are inside the cage, my heels hanging in mid-air, my hands grasp the bars, stretching out to take all my weight. He lets go and there I am high in the air, waiting to fall backwards into space. No way back. No way out. Only down. 'Three. Two. One. Bungee.'

I let go.

I am going to die.

This is the only certainty in my mind as I fall and I fall, and it seems to go on forever (two seconds actually) and I can't open my eyes because they are clenched so tight that I'd need a jemmy. But I'm not dead yet and they open, and I see the rope and it's taking my weight, it's stretching and I'm still alive and I'm falling, and the fear and the butterflies and the sweaty palms and the dry mouth have all gone because I've just given myself an un-repeatable adrenaline rush. Now I've reached the end of the rope and, twang, I'm catapulted back up in the air. That gives me another rush of fear, followed by another burst of adrenaline, and I'm flying. Back up towards the cage which I don't quite reach and then I'm falling again and bouncing, and falling and bouncing, as the cage is lowered to the ground. And this is fun and I'm quite relaxed and, well, this bungee jumping lark's pretty easy after all. Now the crane's swung around and I'm just above the ground and Mark is grabbing my arms and hauling me in, over to a large bean bag.

———————— DO IT AGAIN! ————————

They unclip the rope, remove the ankle harness, order me to stay lying down for a few seconds. I ignore them, stand up, my legs are wobbly and my head is still flying. This disorientation lasts for a few seconds and I realise I have survived. There are three other men waiting their turn on the bench of Purgatory, not one of them looks at me. The next guy up used to be Asian, now he's grey and he doesn't want to see some idiot grinning maniacally at him.

A radio reporter from the BBC World Service thrusts a mike into my face. He asks a few questions about the jump and I burble because the adrenaline is still coursing through my body like an electric current. Then he asks 'Will you do it again?' Only 10 per cent of people doing their first bungee jump decide to repeat the experience and 1 per cent do more than two. Will I do it again? Maybe. Maybe not.

Some nights when I drive across Chelsea Bridge the crane is lit up, lights running along the arm, 100m above the river. Some nights it is beckoning me, teasing me to come up again. Some nights it is seductive, on others an irritation.

The answer, incidentally, is 'Maybe not'.

——————— WHO TO CONTACT ———————

British Elastic Rope Sports Association (BERSA)
33a Canal Street
Oxford OX2 6BQ

Tel: 01865 311179
Fax: 01865 311189

▶ Bungee jumping is now practised worldwide and BERSA claim approaching a million people have jumped in the UK.

▶ BERSA was formed in 1989 by a group of enthusiasts with the collaboration of the United Kingdom Health and Safety Executive and an independent adviser from the Safety and Reliability Division of the Atomic Energy Authority. They also act as a centre of expertise for the development of other elastic rope activities like Catapulting and the Twin Tower Vertical Launch.

▶ BERSA exists to ensure the highest standards of safety are maintained at all times. Affiliated clubs agree to follow the procedures and safety systems laid down in an extremely comprehensive Code of Safe Practice. In order to ensure that this is upheld, they are also subject to random and un-announced inspections by specially trained safety officers who constantly assess staff, equipment and procedures.

▶ BERSA also offers comprehensive full legal liability insurance covering claims that the jumper or third parties may make against the club, crane company, site owner, Uncle Tom Cobbley and all. There are Bungee clubs that operate outside of BERSA but they do not have this comprehensive cover.

▶ There are currently only three clubs – down from a maximum of eight – that are members of BERSA, though there may be others operating by the summer of 1997. BERSA is also a member of the Royal Society for the Prevention of Accidents and the British Standards Institute.

WHERE TO GO

Company:	**UK Bungee London**
Address:	Adrenalin Village, Chelsea Bridge, London, SW8 4NP
Tel:	0171 720 9496
Fax:	0171 627 8861
Price Range:	£35 + £15 membership fee for first jump, video available for £10
Payment Methods:	Cash, cheque, Visa, Access, Switch, Amex
Booking Details:	Week in advance
Insurance:	Carries employers and public liability insurance up to £1 million. Have to sign indemnity waiver.
Facilities:	Café/clubhouse; bar; souvenir shop. Toilets being installed.
Other Notes:	Open Thurs-Fri, 1pm to dark, weekends 10am to dark. This is currently the only fixed site in the UK but the UK Bungee Club also runs 3 mobile sites which are available for events around the country. Also available is catapulting (a reverse bungee jump) and a Skydive Simulator, while the Club also arranges adventure weekends in France.

Company:	**UK Bungee Ltd**
Address:	57 Newhill Road, Monk Bretton, Barnsley, S. Yorkshire ST1 1XH
Tel:	01226 282 890
Price Range:	£39.50 per jump from 50m crane; £80 from 100m crane; £2,200 for corporate day
Payment Methods:	Cash, cheque
Booking Details:	Call Jon Snape who will advise on times and location – approx 15-20 per year
Capacity:	100-120 per day. The record is 173 jumps in one day!
Insurance:	£2 million PL to cover jumper
Facilities:	Accommodation and catering depend on site. Ring for details.
Other Notes:	UK Bungee Ltd handle the northern mobile sites and are in partnership with Jon Nichols at UK Bungee London. Corporate days are flat fees for as many jumps as you want. Contract days have to guarantee a minimum 40 jumps in a day but Jon Snape will then help with flyers etc.

Company:	**Oxford Stunt Factory**
Address:	27 Latimer Grange, Latimer Road, Oxford, OX3 7PQ
Tel:	01865 750846
Fax:	01865 311189
Price Range:	£40 per jump, or £900 per day + crane hire (prices exc VAT)
Payment Methods:	Cash, cheque
Booking Details:	Call to discover local dates and times
Capacity:	100-120 per day, depending on weather
Insurance:	£2 million PL which covers the jumper
Facilities:	Locations usually chosen to provide comfort facilities for participants and spectators.
Other Notes:	The OSF is primarily a display team and uses a mobile crane to travel around the country doing bungee jumps. An offshoot of the Oxford University Dangerous Sports Club, they have been in operation since 1979 and are involved in arranging stunts like a recent launch for the Renault Espace and the big 700ft jump at the beginning of the James Bond Movie *Goldeneye* (yes, it was dangerous and, no, don't ask). Also: street luging, velcro walls, white-water rafting, fire breathing, surfing, cheese rolling etc.

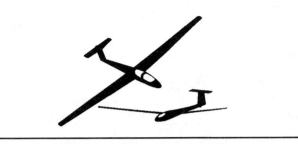

GLIDING

Third time lucky, I hope. Curses on the English weather. In London it's sultry, sunny with wisps of cloud. Down at Lasham the cloud base is low but with a good forecast. 'Come on down but be prepared for a wasted journey,' they say. Sod it, if I don't go this time it'll never happen. Three times in a week the weather has conspired to prevent my even leaving town, let alone the ground. First time I was already feeling post-curry queasy and the report from Hampshire was bumpy. 'If it's your first flight make sure the conditions are right,' the phone reassures, which is great advice as three hours later I am lying on my sofa doubled up with stomach cramps. It would not have been a good day to go flying. Second time, the cloud base is solid and low so nobody is going up unless they have an instrument rating.

Third time lucky it is. I turn down a leafy country road and suddenly there are gliders above me. Set up at 600ft on the Hampshire downs between Basingstoke and Alton, Lasham Aerodrome was built as an RAF base in 1942 and has been a gliding centre since the early 1950s. It is now the biggest gliding centre in the UK – and, according to General Manager Phil Phillips, the world – and launches some 40,000 plus flights every year. Britain has around 10,000 qualified glider pilots with 2,000 gliders in the country (of which 10 per cent are based at Lasham) and a reputation for turning out some of the very best pilots in the world.

That, Phil explains, is because of the unique weather conditions prevalent in the UK. Living on an island means that flying conditions can change rapidly within a short space of time and just a few miles. On the continent, weather patterns tend to be fixed for longer periods. Even so, during the summer they fly two days out of three from Lasham. I've just been unlucky.

Looking at a glider I wonder if this is such a good idea after all. Single seaters are such little things, they appear so flimsy, as if for a joke someone had taken a balsa wood model and made it big enough to put a body in. I decide that what I need before going up in one of those red things – a K13 two-seater trainer – is a stiff drink. Unfortunately this is forbidden, until after I've come down again.

BLUE LEVER, RED KNOB, WHOOPS!

Phil Phillips used to fly jets; nowadays he owns his own small plane but glides for fun. He talks nineteen to the dozen about his sport with an evangelical fervour that is very catching. Even the butterflies in my stomach are impressed. 'Gliding,' he says, 'is not about going up and flying around for 20 minutes, it's about flying 500km triangles, the equivalent of from Lasham to North Wales and back, and staying aloft for up to 6 hours.' It is a very safe sport, on a par with driving a car, there is only one mid-air collision every two years, and this invariably occurs when there are too many gliders spiralling up the same thermal. Usually, the worst that can happen is having to make a landing in a field where concealed rocks or unseen barbed-wire fences can damage the glider, not the pilot. 'But to be on the safe side we always wear these,' he says handing me a parachute. 'I've never had to use one yet.'

After clipping on my 'chute, Phil shows me the controls. The cockpit of the K13 has a reassuring Heath Robinson feel to it, all coloured levers, large, wooden floor pedals and a joystick. The student sits in the front, the instructor behind, both with identical controls. He runs through them quickly, pushing the stick forward and back, while the fore and aft elevators on the wings respond happily. Move it right and left to bank in the direction you want to go and the ailerons on the tail flap. 'Don't worry about the rudders,' he says pointing at the foot pedals, 'they're for balance and I'll do them.'

Then he points out the trimmer, a green lever on the right hand side of the cockpit, which appears to act as a sort of cruise control; a giant yellow bead on the left which is the cable release and the air brake, a blue lever which pushes blocks up from the wings and brings the speed of the glider right down, enabling us to land very quickly. 'Whatever you do,' he jokes, 'don't pull the red knob, that releases the canopy.' On both of my flights I have this overriding urge to pull the red knob.

The instruments are pretty simple: the air speed indicator (ASI), which measures your speed in knots; the vario, which tells you whether you are climbing or descending; the altimeter, which gives your height in feet; and a compass.

WE'RE GLIDING

At Lasham, trial flights are generally towed up by a light plane to around 2,500ft, enabling one to get a proper flight. Phil assures me that in the event of an emergency, or if I feel ill, he can get me back on the ground in 90 seconds. Oh good. The take-off is uneventful, the glider rising in the air before the light plane takes off. After 5 minutes we are up at 2,500ft and heading for a grey cloud which might give us a thermal. 'You have control,' says Phil generously during the tow. This is tricky and we start flying out to one side like a water-skier on a slalom course. 'No I haven't,' I retort. He tells me to release the cable tow and suddenly the speed drops to around 45 knots and it is wonderfully quiet. We're gliding.

No, I'm gliding, staring out of the nose, keeping the ground equally visible on both sides. It takes only the lightest of touches on the stick to change direction; push it forward and we gain speed; pull it up and we slow down. It isn't difficult though it's hot under the canopy and I am starting to wish I wasn't wearing my cool photo-journalist's waistcoat. It would also be nice to relax my grip on the stick before cramp sets in. Phil has spotted another glider who has found a thermal and wants to head for it.

The technique is simplicity itself. To bank left, first look out the side, then look forward, then move the stick until you have reached the right angle of bank, then check the stick back to the centre. I do all these and we do indeed bank left, my stomach banks right and my whole body goes taut, if my right hand was not superglued to the stick it would now be scrabbling at the cockpit release button. Even horses do not sweat this much. Phil tells me we're going up, orders me to look at the vario. So we are.

—— IN SEARCH OF THERMALS ——

A glider stays aloft as a result of the aerodynamic forces acting upon it. They may resemble ordinary aeroplanes, but they are extremely light in weight, have a low wing load (the ratio of weight to wing area), and have a high aspect ratio (the ratio of the wingspan to the wing width). Glider wings are much longer and narrower than those of powered aircraft. So when flying level in still air, it sinks at a rate less than 90cm per second, and therefore is able to climb in an air current that is rising at the rate of about 2mph. To get extra height, a glider pilot is looking for either ridge currents or thermal currents. Ridge currents are formed when a steady wind blows against the side of a ridge or a range of hills. Thermal currents are formed by heat rising from the ground. Such currents occur over a bare field on a hot day. Thermal currents are always present under cumulus clouds, so the perfect day for gliding is warm with lots of fluffy clouds about.

Once in the air, the pilot directs the glider in search of up-currents. If making a cross-country flight, the pilot flies by 'cloud chasing' or 'thermal sniffing' – searching for thermal currents that will give the glider lift. When such a current is found, the pilot will spiral the craft to remain within the current while gaining altitude. After reaching the maximum altitude to which the current will lift the glider, the pilot glides away to find another current. Well, that is the theory, but the first time I start spiralling up a thermal I feel very sick.

Due to my ineptitude, we lose the updraft. By now there is one glider above us, another below and a couple more heading in our direction like dogs after the only lamppost in town. This time we try a bank right. The advantage is that I can't grab the red button but my left hand is clenched on the air brake cable. 'Keep an eye out for the other gliders,' says Phil. 'Make sure you keep in the thermal, watch the vario, see we're getting big updraft.' The vario jumps to 4 as my lunch makes a leap for my gorge. I am frying in the sunshine, sitting in a pool of sweat, my mind overloading under all this unaccustomed information. My right arm is still rigid but at least we're still banking right.

'You have control,' I groan, and as soon as the acknowledgement is received I let go of the stick, slide open the vent in the cockpit and scoop cool air in. God, that feels good. After a couple of minutes I recover sufficiently to do a bit more level flying but the attractions of another thermal are lost on my guts. The next five minutes I spend cursing myself in between bouts of nausea. Phil brings us down right in the queue for the winch tow. He banks left, pulls on the air brakes and we land with the slightest bump.

A FLYING START

Canopy raised, 'chute off and fresh air inhaled, I start to feel human again. This, Phil reassures me, is very common on a first flight. 'You were doing really well to begin with so I tried to get you to take in too much new information at one go. Take 10 minutes and then maybe do another flight on the winch.' I've always held to the philosophy that you should do everything twice, once to see what it was like, and the second to see whether you actually enjoyed it the first time. At Lasham they have a similar thesis and offer the Flying Start, three flights which include two tows and one winch, that way you get to settle the collywobbles and enjoy it.

I am not convinced and when the winch pulls up at a sharp angle it's like my worst nightmare big dipper. I close my eyes and wonder whether my stomach can take it again. But as the cable is dropped at 1,600ft, I feel a similar sense of release. My touch is lighter, defter on the stick, the banking is easier, my whole body position is relaxed, and my stomach does not heave but rumble with hunger. We're high up in the sky, in the distance I can see Basingstoke. From the air it actually looks quite pleasant. This flight is only for 10 minutes but I love it, we find a thermal and do a quick spiral to prove the point and, though my attempts to use the trimmer both end up with us plunging in a dive, I feel secure. I even pilot the glider to within 200ft of landing when Phil takes over as the grass is a bit crowded.

Yes. I have a sense of triumph. I could do this. And next time I'll ride the thermals like a pro.

──── WHO TO CONTACT ────

The British Gliding Association (BGA)
Kimberley House
Vaughan Way
Leicester
LE1 4SE

Tel: 0116 253 1051

▶ **Gliding in the UK is not controlled by the Civil Aviation Authority but by the BGA.**

▶ **Most clubs in the country are affiliated to the BGA so if you require more information about local clubs write to the BGA.**

▶ **In addition to a club listing, the BGA provides informative booklets about the history of gliding (did you know that the first man-carrying glider in history was built by Sir George Cayley on his estate at Brompton near Scarborough in 1853? It was flown across a small valley on the estate by his coachman) and reassuringly simple explanations about 'how gliders stay up'. The BGA is helpful and charming in a very old-fashioned way.**

──── WHERE TO GO ────

Company:	**Lasham**
Address:	Lasham Aerodrome, Alton, Hants GU34 5S
Tel:	01256 381322
E-mail:	office@lasham.org.uk
Fax:	01256 381415
Price Range:	Trial flight £45; Flying Start (3 flights) £99; fixed price to solo £750
Payment Methods:	Cash, cheque, Switch, Delta, Visa, Mastercard
Booking Details:	2-3 months in advance for courses, 1 week for trial flights. Always call on day to check conditions.
Facilities:	Basic accommodation on site; list of local B&Bs

can be provided. Good restaurant, changing rooms, showers and toilets. Limited disabled access.

Other Notes: Endorsed by BGA. The biggest club in the UK, with an international reputation.

Company: **Deeside Gliding Club**
Address: Aboyne Airfield, Dinnet, Aboyne, Aberdeenshire AB34 5LB
Tel: 013398 85339
Fax: 013398 85339
Price Range: Air Experience Flights £33, cost refunded if you join club within a month. No instruction fees.
Payment Methods: Cash, cheque
Booking Details: Bookings required for Sept and Oct; can normally book on day
Capacity: Two 2-seater gliders
Facilities: Bunkroom, camping, toilets. Gift vouchers.

Company: **Enstone Eagles Gliding Club**
Address: Old Control Tower, Enstone Airfield, Enstone, Oxfordshire OX7 4NP
Tel: 01698 677461
Price Range: Trial lesson £20; 3-flight mini-course £45; 5-day course £195-255
Payment Methods: Cash, cheque
Booking Details: Course bookings at least a month in advance
Capacity: Two 2-seater trainers
Facilities: Camping facilities on site; local B&B; showers, toilets; café on airfield (Club has no catering); bar (after flying!); gift vouchers.
Other Notes: Most launches are by winch, though aerotows are available on request.

Company: **Herefordshire Gliding Club**
Address: Shobdon Airfield, Herefordshire HR6 9NR
Tel: 01568 708908
E-mail: lessjkaye@aol.com
Price Range: £35 trial lesson
Payment Methods: Cash, cheque
Booking Details: 1 day but not essential
Facilities: Local B&Bs, canteen and bar. Changing facilities

with showers and toilets. Corporate events organised and gift vouchers available.

Other Notes: BGA endorsed.

Company: **London Gliding Club**
Address: Dunstable Downs, Tring Road, Bedfordshire LU6 2JP
Tel: 01582 663419
Fax: 01582 665744
E-mail: info@gliding.powernet.co.uk
Price Range: Trial lesson 1000 £30; trial lesson 2000 £50; gliding day £120; 5-day courses start at £179
Payment Methods: Cash, cheque, all major credit cards
Booking Details: 1 week to 1 month, depending on type of course
Capacity: 400 members. Standard courses have 4 students per glider and a guaranteed 25 flights, or equivalent time in the air, on a 5-day course.
Facilities: 5 twin rooms, restaurant, showers and toilets; equipment shop; corporate events organised.
Other Notes: Endorsed by BGA. The Club is open 364 days a year from 08.30. British gliding started here in 1930 and the Bedfordshire Downs provide year-round soaring and the quick-warming, thermal-producing countryside allows the club to run courses starting in late March through until late October. Youngsters can fly at any age provided they are tall enough to reach the pedals (5ft) but cannot fly solo until they are 16 – and they need parental permission until they are 18.

Company: **South Wales Gliding Club**
Address: Gwernesney, Usk, Gwent
Tel: 01291 690536
Fax: 01495 785499 (chief flying instructor)
Price Range: Trial lessons £38 (aerotow); £16 (2 winch launches)
Payment Methods: Cash, cheque
Booking Details: 1 month for course, just turn up at weekends for trial lessons
Capacity: Two 2-seat training gliders
Facilities: Locally available accommodation. Hot and cold drinks but no food on site. Showers and toilets. Training literature, sweaters and badges can be bought. Disabled sessions by arrangement. Group

Other Notes:	bookings for trial lessons. Gift vouchers. Open weekends throughout the year and 7 days a week during summer courses, and summer evenings for groups.

Company:	**Stratford-on-Avon Gliding Club**
Address:	Snitterfield Airfield, Bearley Road, Snitterfield, Warwickshire CV37 OEX
Tel:	01789 731095
Price Range:	Trial Lessons (winch) £20; second flight £7.50; 5-day courses £215
Payment Methods:	Cash, cheque
Booking Details:	Courses 2-4 weeks in advance; trial flights 1 week
Capacity:	Five 2-seater gliders
Facilities:	Camping, local B&Bs. Toilets, changing facilities; hot and cold snacks.
Other Notes:	Gift vouchers from Harry Williams on 01926 53985.

Company:	**Vale of White Horse Gliding Centre**
Address:	Sandhill Farm, Shrivenham, Swindon, Wilts
Tel:	01793 783685
Price Range:	Air experience flights £20 winch launch (inc 1 month membership); aerotow launch £33
Payment Methods:	Cash, cheque
Booking Details:	Week in advance
Capacity:	2 twin seat training gliders
Facilities:	Kettle for tea-making. Toilets. Corporate events and gift vouchers available.
Other Notes:	A training lesson is 3 winch launches or one aero-tow, giving at least 15 mins instruction time. It is a voluntary club and instructors give their time free.

Company:	**Wolds Gliding Club**
Address:	The Airfield, Pocklington, East Yorkshire YO4 2NR
Tel:	01759 303579
E-mail:	101774,1573@compuserve.uk
Price Range:	£20 first winch launch, £5 each subsequent launch; aerotow £30 first launch, then £15 per 2,000ft; 1-week course £235 low season, £335 high season
Payment Methods:	Cash, cheque

Booking Details: For single flights no advance booking necessary. Book in advance for holiday courses.

Capacity: Five 2-seater trainers

Insurance: Members are already covered so no extra insurance necessary

Facilities: Café, changing rooms, showers and toilets on-site. Local hotel. Gift vouchers available.

Other Notes: The Wolds is one of the 5 biggest gliding clubs in the UK with over 200 members.

Company: **Yorkshire Gliding Club**

Address: Sutton Bank, Thirsk, North Yorkshire YO7 2EY

Tel: 01845 597237

Fax: 01845 597307

E-mail: http:\\www.webmarketing.co.uk\ygc

Price Range: Air experience flights: aerotow, £40; winch £25

Payment Methods: Cash, cheque

Booking Details: In advance for courses; 2 weeks for air experience flights

Capacity: 2 full-time instructors, three 2-seater training gliders

Facilities: Catering facilities and changing rooms, showers, toilets on-site. Accommodation available.

Other Notes: BGA authorised instructors. The Club was established in 1932 and is set in the North Yorkshire Moors National Park, in an area of the UK geared to tourists seeking outdoor pursuits. The scenery is breathtaking and there are plenty of other things to do, such as visit Rievaulx and Byland Abbeys, Helmsley Castle and Lightwater Valley, while the famous White Horse at Sutton Bank can be seen both on foot and from the air.

Company: **Black Mountains Gliding Club**

Address: Troed yr Harn, Talgarth, Powys LD3 0EF

Tel: 01874 711463 (airfield) / 01874 711254 (farm, evenings)

Fax: 01558 823681

Price Range: Introductory lesson £40

Payment Methods: Cash, cheque

Booking Details: Introductory flight can be available on day, courses at least 2 weeks in advance

Facilities: Local B&B and hotels. Showers and toilets available for club members. Disabled toilet. Corporate events organised.

Other Notes: The Black Mountains generate lift so the club has impressive flight time statistics, the highest in England and Wales. Week-long gliding courses are available in June, July, August.

Company:	**Booker Gliding Club**
Address:	Wycombe Air Park, Marlow, Bucks SL7 3DR
Tel:	01494 442501 / 01494 529263
Fax:	01494 438262
Price Range:	Trial flight £40; £70 for 2 flights on same day; 5-day courses from £355-£450 depending on season; 1-day courses £115 weekends, £105 weekdays
Payment Methods:	Cash, cheque, credit cards
Booking Details:	2-3 weeks for trial lessons, at least a month for courses
Capacity:	Six 2-seaters, 4 tug planes
Facilities:	Corporate entertaining and gift vouchers; local accommodation; club house and toilet facilities; aviation shop and restaurant.
Other Notes:	Open 7 days a week. Member of BGA.

Company:	**Buckminster Gliding Club**
Address:	Saltby Airfield, Sproxton Rd, Skillington, Grantham, Lincs NG33 SHL
Tel/Fax:	01476 860385
Price Range:	Aerotows £13-15; winch launch £4 plus glider hire at 20p per min
Payment Methods:	Cash, cheque
Booking Details:	One week plus in advance
Capacity:	Three 2-seater training gliders
Facilities:	Corporate entertaining, gift vouchers; local accommodation; limited catering facilities; shower and toilet facilities.
Other Notes:	Open 7 days a week

Company:	**Cornish Gliding (& Flying) Club**
Address:	Perranporth Airfield, Trevellas, Nr Perranporth, Cornwall TR6 9QB
Tel/Fax:	01209 216583

Price Range: Air Experience Flight £28; 5-day course £275
Payment Methods: Cash, cheque, major credit cards
Booking Details: Week in advance for trial flights, a month for courses
Capacity: 2+ instructors in summer
Facilities: Gift vouchers; local accommodation; limited catering facilities; toilets (suitable for disabled) in clubhouse; also small shop.
Other Notes: Summer season open every day. Winter season (end Sept-Apr) open weekends and Wednesdays only. Training for Private Pilot's Licence also available in Super-Falke motor glider.

Company: **Norfolk Gliding Club**
Address: 3 Mackenzie Road, Thetford, Norfolk IP24 3NQ
Price Range: Trial lessons from £16.50 (winch) and £30 (aerotow)
Payment Methods: Cash, cheque
Booking Details: One week in advance
Capacity: Five 2-seater training gliders
Facilities: Facilities at Tibenham Airfield include toilets, café and changing room. Disabled facilities including flying lessons.
Other Notes: Open Wed, Thurs, Sat, Sun all year round.

HELICOPTERS

I can't go up in that thing, its smaller than my car. I haven't even got as far as the Heli Air offices at Denham Aerodrome before I find myself having second thoughts. Parked right outside the door is this little red object which I assume has to be a helicopter because it has rotor blades. It's just a little bubble, smaller than the front seats of a Mini with a long thin tail. And I'm supposed to go 2,000ft straight up in the air in that!

Glenda Wild, my pilot/instructor, senses my feelings instantly and takes me off on a guided tour of the hangar. Her first stop is at a Bell 47, a machine familiar to anyone who has ever seen the TV series *MASH*. It can seat three in a huge bubble and perhaps because of its familiarity looks comfortable. When I learn that it is very noisy with a top speed of only 65mph, and its 6-cylinder engine guzzles fuel, I am less impressed. This leads neatly on to extolling the virtues of the Robinson R22, which we will be flying.

The R22 is the culmination of Frank Robinson's dream to design a helicopter that could park in a family's back garden. An engineer who worked at both Bell and Sikorsky, Robinson could find no corporate backing to realise his dream, so in true pioneer style made the first R22 in his garage. He has since sold over 3,000 round the world, which Glenda tells me is remarkable for any small aircraft. The R22 (which costs around £80,000) has a range of 350 miles, a top speed of around 100 knots and is highly manoeuvrable, which makes it a great favourite with the police and the American forces who train their helicopter pilots on it. Its major drawback is its size; any man over 6ft 4in tall is going to be very cramped and it has virtually no luggage space, except for under the seat, which is a bit difficult to access when you're flying. Glenda then shows me the 4-seater R44 (mine for a mere £200,000) and a 5-seater Bell Jet Ranger (a snip at £490,000).

——— ONE THING AT A TIME ———

Sitting in the right-hand seat of the R22 is not as cramped as I imagined it might be. However, the sight of dozens of dials, switches, knobs and pedals causes instant brain overload. 'We're only going to concentrate on one thing at a time,' says Glenda. 'First there is the collective lever.' To the left of both of our seats lies what looks like a giant hand brake, except that the handle revolves. The handle is the throttle and in some helicopters this has to be constantly controlled with the wrist. The R22 has a little switch that keeps the throttle going so I don't have to worry about that. Basically, the collective lever raises and lowers the vertical height of the helicopter.

Next is the cyclic stick. This is a T-shaped stick that rises from the instrument panel with a handle that can be grasped by both occupants. The handle is then placed on the right thigh and small movements to right and left, or forward and back, control the helicopter's movement though the air. Pushing the handle forward pushes the nose down and increases speed, pulling back slows it down, move to the right and the machine turns right. 'Be relaxed,' says Glenda. 'You'll find you only have to make very small movements to get a tremendous response. It's like driving a high-performance sports car.'

Finally we come to the pedals – or anti-torque pedals to give them their full title – which are used to control sideways movement during a hover, through the tail rotor. If a helicopter did not have the tail rotors (the small propeller on the tail) the movement of the rotor blades would cause the whole machine to spin in the opposite direction at high speed. During a hover, the torque causes a perpetual, if slight, drag to the right, so while it only requires a touch on the right pedal it needs more pressure on the left.

Glenda goes through a series of checks and fail-safes, turning on the engine, watching the tachometer to make sure that the Rotor and Engine RPMs are equal, various yellow choke lights go on and off but by now I'm in a daze from trying to take in so much information. We put on headphones and can at least converse without shouting. Let's get flying. I've been up in helicopters a few times, once as a passenger in a Jet Ranger and several times in a giant Russian MI8 over the ever-changing ice of the Bering Straits, but nothing had prepared me for this.

We hover about 10ft off the ground for a few seconds and then Glenda sets off, moving forward and up in a smooth movement that leaves my stomach back where we started. It is simultaneously exhilarating and disconcerting. Soon we are 1,000ft up, smugly watching the traffic jam on the M25, the fields unfold like a patchwork quilt and I feel rather sick. I am in a glass bubble in the sky and because there is glass at my feet as well as on all sides I am disoriented. When Glenda goes into a right turn, for a second I feel as if the door has sprung open that I have fallen out of the machine. Nobody, she informs me, likes that bit to begin with.

—— 1,000FT OVER AMERSHAM ——

Now its my turn. At 1,000ft over Amersham she tells me to pull the collective lever up and to watch the manifold pressure gauge power up to 25. The machine rises to 2,000ft, when she tells me to lower the lever until the gauge reads 20, where we will maintain our hover; then I drop it down to 15 and we follow. Were it not for the altimeter, I wouldn't know if we've gone up or down.

That all seemed pretty easy but now I've got to handle the cyclic stick. My right palm is all sweaty as I pull it over and rest the handle on top of my thigh. I am gripping it so hard that I feel it might break off in my hand. I feel sick. 'Level flying,' says Glenda, and I stare out towards the horizon, my arm rigid. 'Push it forward,' she commands. I do so gingerly and the nose tilts forward and we're zipping along. Immediately, to compensate, I pull back and we slow up. It doesn't take much lateral movement to get an instant response. 'Now make a turn to the left,' she grins. 'I won't make you do a right yet.' I creak the cyclic stick to the left a fraction and the machine responds slowly, it seems to take forever but eventually the turn's complete and Glenda takes back control while I massage some life back into my right hand. I look down and realise I don't feel sick any more.

As we fly towards Watford, Glenda explains some of the conventions of flying a helicopter in the UK. Only the police can fly as low as 200ft. Private pilots are supposed to keep over 500ft. Below that they can spook horses and we mustn't have that. She is going to land in the back garden of a friend but we approach his place by flying over as few houses as possible, for the R22 is a noisy beast. She drops into a hover between a wall and some trees, feet tip-tapping on the pedals, left hand on the lever, right on the stick. I have difficulty patting my head and rubbing my stomach at the same time.

MAKING IT DANCE

Heading back to the airport, I ask if I can attempt a right turn, my tummy complains as I ask, but sod that. This time I grip the stick gently and as we make the turn my mind stays inside the helicopter. Turning it back again I feel very smug – except for the sweat dripping off my forehead.

Although in many ways a helicopter is a safer machine to fly in than a small fixed-wing plane – any problem and you can put down almost anywhere there is a small field – there is the residual belief that if there is a problem you will plummet from the sky like Icarus with singed wings. I mention this to Glenda who promptly suggests she show me what happens when you lose power. Against my better judgement I agree. The result is that we come into the ground fast and then, at the last moment, Glenda pulls the stick and the nose rises and we land with a slight bump. 'We might bounce a bit if there was wind,' she says. 'Now let's try hovering and using the pedals.'

She holds us straight 12ft above the deck while I use first the left then the right pedal. The right needs only the slightest touch while the left requires much more. It's tricky and my shins hurt from the weekend's cricket, so I don't feel at ease. Glenda takes the R22 for a dance, skipping forwards and back from side to side, pirouetting over the grass, still 12ft above the ground, seemingly close enough to touch. It's wonderful. I want to do it like that, but unfortunately I have not logged 3,000 hours on a helicopter.

Back on terra firma the reality takes hold. My £95 intro-ductory half hour, which seemed to last both for ever and no time at all, is very popular as a present and some of the best fun I've had legally. However, to qualify for a licence would take a minimum of 40 hours flying time – the average is 50 – which at £229 an hour does not leave much change from ten grand. If money is not the problem, there is very little else to stop you. Glenda has taught teenagers as young as 15 ('as long as you can reach the pedals that's OK') and men of 73. You do not have to get a fixed-wing licence first. After 12 hours' flying you have to get a medical certificate from a CAA certified doctor to make sure your blood pressure and breathing are okay. You are not allowed to do the medical if you are pregnant. Eyesight does not have to be perfect as long as you wear glasses, or contacts like Glenda. Most of the rest of it is down to common sense.

'Don't fly if you are too tired or hungover,' she says. 'People do get very nervous so we approach it very gently, by the third hour most people are relaxed, they have got over their fear of falling and they are holding the stick gently. The most dangerous thing is people's attitude. An over-confident city type, who takes it fast and furious like his business dealings, can be a danger to himself. It is difficult to change people's personality, though I have trained timid individuals and watched them flower. It teaches you about geography, engineering, physics, and you even get to speak a new language – radio telephony.

'I can tell how people will do in the first half hour. You're about average,' she says, 'you have good balance and you're not too taut. The question is, can you afford it?'

Driving home, I made a mental note to buy some extra lottery tickets.

——— WHO TO CONTACT ———

British Helicopter Advisory Board (BHAB)
Graham Suite, Fairoaks Airport
Chobham
Woking
Surrey GU24 8HX

Tel: 01276 856100
Fax: 01276 856126

▶ The BHAB is the trade association for the civil helicopter industry throughout the UK. They will not recommend specific clubs but will provide a full list of training schools if none of the following list is satisfactory.

▶ Helicopter pilots are required to be licensed by the CAA before they can fly in command of any form of powered aircraft away from a recognised training course. A Private Pilot's Licence (PPL(H)) costs around £10,000, while the basic Commercial Pilot's Licence will set you back around £40,000.

▶ The CAA approved flying course stipulates a minimum number of flying hours, gained under instruction and solo. Ground exams in related subjects and an aviation medical must be taken.

Helicopter Club of Great Britain
Ryelands House
Aynho
Croughton
Northants OX17 3AT

Tel: 01869 810646
Fax: 01869 810755

▶ A club for helicopter owners and pilots which organises events in the summer. If you are stuck, and very polite, they will help with recommendations based on personal experience.

——————— WHERE TO GO ———————

Company:	**Heli Air Ltd**
Address:	Warkworth Grange, Warkworth, Nr Banbury, Oxfordshire OX17 2AG
Tel:	01295 712500 / 0836 358270
Fax:	01295 712555
Price Range:	Trial Lesson £95; flying lessons £190 + VAT per

flying hour; 1-day introductory course with 2½ hours' flying £475 + VAT

Payment Methods:	Cash, cheque, major credit cards
Booking Details:	Minimum 2 weeks in advance
Capacity:	9 Robinson R22s; 4 Robinson R44s; 4 Bell Jet Rangers; a Hughes H269 and a Hughes 369
Facilities:	Denham has parking, toilets, kitchen area, lecture rooms. Corporate entertaining and flights, gift vouchers.
Other Notes:	Heli Air operate from four airfields:

Wellesbourne Airfield, Nr Warwick (Tel: 01789 470476, Fax: 01789 470466)

Denham Airfield, Nr Uxbridge, Middlesex (Tel/Fax: 01895 835899)

Nottingham Airfield, Tollerton, Notts (Tel/Fax: 01159 819922)

Cardiff Airport, White Building, Rhoose (Tel/Fax: 01446 711191)

Their sister company Skyline 2000 is an approved Service centre which specialises in the maintenance of small helicopters.

Company:	**Grampian Helicopter Charter Ltd**
Address:	Cairnhall, Kintore, Aberdeen, AB51 0YQ
Tel:	01467 633040
Fax:	01467 633030
Price Range:	£100 inc VAT for 30-min trial lesson; £185 + VAT per hour
Payment Methods:	Cash, cheque, Access, Visa
Booking Details:	24 hours' notice required
Capacity:	1 student at a time
Facilities:	Toilets. Disabled access arrangements. Gift vouchers.

Company:	**Helicopter Centre**
Address:	General Aviation Building, Belfast International Airport, Belfast, Northern Ireland BT29 4JT
Tel:	01849 453663
Fax:	01849 423233
Price Range:	£50 per 30 min sightseeing tour; £170 + VAT per hour for lessons
Payment Methods:	Cash, cheque
Booking Details:	1-2 weeks in advance

Capacity: 3 instructors, 4 helicopters

Facilities: Accommodation at Aldergrove Airport Hotel; catering facilities at Aldergrove Airport. Changing rooms with showers and toilets. Disabled access arrangements. Corporate events organised.

Other Notes: CAA approved with AOC, ATOL member of British Helicopter Advisory Board.

Company: **Lomas Helicopters**

Address: Lake Heliport, Abbotsham, Bideford, N. Devon EX39 5BQ

Tel: 01237 421054 (Bideford), 01392 446636 (Exeter)

Fax: 01237 424060

Price Range: 12-min trial lesson £75; 30-min trial £120; 1-hour trial/flying lesson £235

Payment Methods: Cash, cheque, major credit cards

Booking Details: 1 week in advance or less, depending on availability

Capacity: Robinson R22, Schweizer 300C

Facilities: Local B&B and hotels, tea and coffee available, toilets at Bideford but not Exeter (no wheelchair access), gift vouchers and occasional corporate events.

Other Notes: Endorsed by BHAB, CAA. Flights from both Bideford and Exeter airports.

Company: **Southern Air Ltd**

Address: Flight Centre, Shoreham Airport, Shoreham-by-Sea, West Sussex BN45 5FF

Tel: 01273 461661

Fax: 01273 454020

Price Range: Trial Lesson £125 for 30 minutes; £225 per hour for flying lessons

Payment Methods: Cash, cheque, major credit cards

Booking Details: 4-5 days in advance

Capacity: Enstrom F28 A

Facilities: Disabled catered for, depending on disability. Corporate activities can be arranged.

Other Notes: Also fixed-wing flying courses. Taster lessons from £55.

Company: **Stephenson Aviation Ltd**

Address: Hangar 3, Goodwood Aerodrome, Goodwood,

	Chichester, West Sussex PO18 0PH
Tel:	01243 530165
Fax:	01243 539921
Price Range:	30 min pleasure flights: 2 passengers £145, 4 passengers £240; 30 min trial lesson £125; flying lesson £200 + VAT per hour
Payment Methods:	Cash, cheque, Visa, Mastercard
Booking Details:	Summer: weekends, 2 months; weekdays, 1 month: Winter: weekends, 1 month; weekdays, 2 weeks
Capacity:	N/A. Training on Enstrom 28A or Hughes 500
Facilities:	Local hotels and B&Bs. Catering facilities available on airfield, toilets. Merchandise available from reception. Disabled access.
Other Notes:	Endorsed by BHAB, CAA.

Company:	**Sterling Helicopters**
Address:	Hangar E, Gambling Close, Norwich Airport, Norwich, NR6 6EG
Tel:	01603 417156
Fax:	01603 410791
Price Range:	£150 for 90-min lesson includes 30 mins flying; pleasure flights from £110 for 20 mins (2 passengers), £215 (4 passengers); flying lessons £210 per hour + airport fees + VAT
Payment Methods:	Cash, cheque, Visa, Mastercard
Booking Details:	One week plus in advance
Capacity:	Sterling operate Hughes/Schweizer 300, Bell Jet Rangers, Single Squirrel, Double Squirrel, Bolkow Bo105
Facilities:	Corporate entertaining; gift vouchers; toilets; catering facilities at Norwich Airport.
Other Notes:	Also based at Silverstone race circuit. Operates to CAA AOC standards.

Company:	**Yorkshire Helicopter Centre**
Address:	6 Swinton Meadows, Swinton, Mexborough, South Yorkshire S64 8AB
Tel:	01709 571720
Fax:	01709 571721
Price Range:	£100 for 20 mins, £150 for 40 mins; £200 for 60 mins
Payment Methods:	Cash, cheque, major credit cards

Booking Details: One week in advance
Capacity: 2 Robinson R22 helicopters
Facilities: Accommodation available locally, from camp sites to 4 star hotel. On-site coffee bar, changing room and toilets. Disabled access. Gift/equipment shop. Corporate events organised.
Other Notes: CAA endorsed.

Company: **Biggin Hill Helicopters**
Address: Building 158a, Biggin Hill Airport, Kent TN16 3BN
Tel: 01959 540803
Fax: 01959 571176
Price Range: Trial lesson £125; pleasure flights from £99 per person
Payment Methods: Cash, cheque, major credit cards
Booking Details: 2-4 weeks in advance
Facilities: Corporate entertaining; gift vouchers; local accommodation; on-site catering and toilet facilities; parking; gift shop.
Other Notes: CAA licensed Public Transport Company. They also offer the 10 min Hover Challenge for only £59.

Company: **Burman Aviation Ltd**
Address: Hangar 1, Cranfield Airport, Cranfield, Beds MK43 OJR
Tel: 01234 752220
Fax: 01234 752221
Price Range: £94 for trial lesson in Robinson R22 – 30 mins flying; £200 per hour flying lessons
Payment Methods: Cash, cheque, major credit cards
Booking Details: One week's notice
Capacity: 6 Robinson R22s, 3 Bell Jet Rangers
Facilities: Corporate entertaining; gift vouchers; local B&B; pub-restaurant; toilet facilities suitable for disabled; parking and souvenir shop.
Other Notes: Endorsed by AOPA, BHAB. Burman also has bases in Cambridge, Gloucester and Newcastle.

Company: **Coventry Helicopter Centre**
Address: Coventry Airport, Rowley Road, Coventry, CV3 4FR

Tel:	01203 639206
Fax:	01203 301304
Price Range:	Topgun trial lesson £117.50; Skyrider (15-min flight) £75; flying lessons £170 + VAT (Robinson R22); £193.5 + VAT (Enstrom F28A)
Payment Methods:	Cash, cheque, credit cards
Booking Details:	2-4 weeks in advance
Facilities:	Corporate facilities; gift vouchers; local accommodation; on-site catering and toilet facilities, downstairs disabled toilet; parking; T-shirts, badges, caps etc for sale.

Company:	**East Midlands Helicopters**
Address:	Oaklands, Loughborough Rd, Costock, Loughborough, Leics LE12 6RQ
Tel:	01509 856464
Fax:	01509 856444
Price Range:	£99 20-min flight; £140 30-min flight in Robinson R22. Jet Ranger £425 + VAT per flying hour
Payment Methods:	Cash, cheques, all major credit cards
Booking Details:	2 weeks in advance
Capacity:	3 Robinson R22s, 1 Bell Jet Ranger
Insurance:	TPL
Facilities:	Toilets, shop, parking. Corporate events organised.
Other Notes:	CAA approved.

Company:	**Fast Helicopters Ltd**
Address:	Thruxton Airfield, Andover, Hants SP11 8PW
Tel:	01264 772508
E-mail:	Ianmac@pavilion.com.uk
Fax:	01264 773824
Price Range:	Pleasure flights from £39 (4 people sharing a Jet Ranger); trial lessons from £75
Payment Methods:	Cash, cheque, all major credit cards
Booking Details:	2 days' notice mid-week; 1 week for weekends
Capacity:	3 full-time instructors, 3 part-time. 2 Robinson R22s, 5 Jet Rangers
Facilities:	Corporate entertaining; gift vouchers; local B&B; on-site catering facilities; ground floor toilets suitable for disabled; parking.
Other Notes:	Fast also based at: Shoreham Airport, Shoreham-by-Sea, Sussex BN43 5FF, Tel: 01273 465389

MICROLIGHT FLYING

Partaking in too many adventurous activities may do something to the brain. It makes me see ghosts.

Perhaps it was caused by the frustration of trying to find Davidstow Aerodrome on a hot summer day, perhaps it was from the heat haze rising off the crumbling runway, flickering between the disused buildings, but when I finally located the Moorland Flying Club I could have sworn that sitting outside there was a figure taking his ease in a deck chair. A Coastal Command pilot, sheepskin-lined flying jacket thrown on the grass, black Labrador at his side, waiting for the command to scramble again. So I blinked, opened my eyes again and there, instead, was a sheep, summer shorn, munching contentedly on the grass. It was still 1996, not 1940.

But inside the clubhouse that feeling of stepping back into a different time was further magnified. It's a boys' room, reeking of musty, comfortable male smells, a place which does not reject the female touch, it just doesn't want it. The walls are lined with the paraphernalia of flight, the counter covered with cups of tea and roll-your-owns; flying suits casually strewn over ancient chairs; dogs slurping down water from an old casserole pan. It is a place that exists to serve those who fly close to the sun.

Fancies and fantasies aside, microlight pilots do encourage the ghosts of the past. They have more in common with the early pioneers of flight than with modern-day fixed-wing or glider pilots. Microlights are open to the skies, vulnerable to the elements, incapable of flying long distances or attaining great speeds, yet those drawbacks are the essential part of their existence. When flying a microlight, you come closest to understanding what Bleriot felt, to realising man's perpetual dream of emulating birds.

── THE FLYING LAWNMOWER ──

There are two distinct types of microlight aircraft: the 'three axis' which may have an enclosed cockpit and which you fly like a conventional aircraft, using a joystick, rudder and ailerons; and 'the weight shift' in which by manually moving the angle of the wing you control the direction of flight. The three-axis microlights are much closer to conventional fixed-wing flying so I have placed myself in the weight-shifting hands of Ian Callaghan, a transplanted Geordie.

While early weight-shift microlights were little more than a deckchair powered by a two-stroke lawnmower engine hanging from a hang-glider wing, the latest generation are a compelling mixture of low and high technology. The actual wing was developed from discarded NASA technology and the cables that run from the wing to the tricycle beneath may resemble the criss-crossing wires on an old biplane but owe more to modern sailing technology. Microlights did suffer from a bad press, mainly dating from the late 1970s and early 1980s when they were deregulated, home-made machines – some of which displayed heavier-than-air, and consequently fatal, characteristics.

Nowadays, microlights have to be built to Section S standard, which requires them to be able to withstand stresses greater than those on a Jumbo jet – up to 6G positive and 4G negative. The combined weight of the passengers should not exceed 28 stone and the total weight of the tricycle engine and passengers is not allowed to exceed 390kg (approx 61 stone). Today, the majority of accidents are minor scrapes occurring on the ground, generally when taxiing to and from take-off and landing. To get a full licence, you need 25 hours flying, of which 10 hours must be solo flights, and to pass four written and one oral examinations. There are roughly 3,000 qualified pilots in the UK, the majority of whom own their own machine. A new microlight costs £8-20,000 but a good second-hand model can be picked up for £3-4,000. Every year a pilot has to pay £55 for his permit renewal and his machine has to be taken up for a test flight by an inspector.

— INTELLIGENT FLYING MACHINE —

'It's safer than driving a car,' insists Ian. Now this is a comparison offered by nearly every practitioner of an adventure sport I've ever spoken to and, considering the way most people drive their cars, does not fill me with an excess of confidence. Nor, I have to admit, does my first sight of a microlight Man Air 582 Blade. The passenger has to sit in the rear, slightly raised above the pilot, legs apart as if he or she had just given birth to an intelligent flying machine. While I gawp and try not to appear concerned, Ian goes through a set of very methodical checks. Every wire, every connection, every strut is checked, a small segment of each wing is unzipped and he puts his head in, looks down the length of the wing to check that everything is how it should be. Then he fills the engine with two-stroke fuel and double checks that all the engine components are securely fastened. 'What you don't want,' explains one helpful local, 'is for the propeller to fly off and go up into the wing. Then you would be in trouble.' Has that ever happened? 'Not recently,' comes the enigmatic answer.

Before preparing to go aloft, Ian and I each put on a lined flying suit, a pair of headphones with attached mike and a crash helmet with visor. We are connected by a communication umbilical cord and can converse with each other while oblivious to the rest of the world. I hop in first and secure my seat belt, then Ian gets in, does a visual check all around him, including the fuel tank, and starts the engine. We taxi towards the runway, weaving our way between sheep, their droppings and rubble, Ian using foot pedals to drive the microlight and his hands to keep the wing in balance. We have another check around before going on to the runway. 'We could use the grass but we've got the runway,' says Ian. Take-offs and landings are always done into the wind and we're airborne almost before I've cleared my throat, climbing at 500ft a minute into the Cornish skies.

It's not a millpond day, the winds are gusting off Bodmin Moor and it's a bit turbulent up to 3,000ft. I enjoy the initial climb to about 700ft, the sensation of wind and flight are exhilarating, but when we make a gentle right bank my heart starts to race. Perched up here above the pilot without a clear field of vision, I feel most exposed and vulnerable, and when we bank my body is telling my mind I'm going to fall out. Of course I'm not, as I'm strapped in very securely, but part of me refuses to believe this self-evident truth. I also feel more uncomfortable the higher we get, which is again illogical. The higher we are, the more time we have to react if something were to go wrong.

——— WEIGHT SHIFTING ———

As we head out towards the coast, Ian starts to explain the techniques. His hands are seldom still, constantly making small movements to maintain a level course. Once we have established the right height and setting, he cuts back the throttle. The wing maintains a level flight and it is we underneath who determine by shifting weight where it goes. Unlike a conventional aircraft, where to turn right you shift the joystick to the right, in a microlight you do the opposite. Later, when I'm attempting to fly in a straight line back towards the aerodrome, I find the machine wants to bank left and to prevent this I have to push towards the left, which initially seems unnatural and surprisingly hard work. As a good pilot like Ian is forever anticipating and correcting, he only makes small movements.

By the time we are 2,000ft above the ruins of Tintagel Castle I am enjoying myself, musing what the shades of King Arthur and Merlin make of this strange dragon circling above their heads. The sea is an inviting blue, the coastline stunning and the ants below inhabit a different world. Then we hit a succession of bumps, I remember where I am and the blood drains into my boots. Ian goes into a bank, it's only about 25° but I am convinced that this time I will fall out and the sea is no longer so inviting. 'We can bank up to 60°,' say Ian, ' which pulls about 2G. If you remember, we're tested up to 6G. Would you like to do one?' No, thank you.

Before returning, Ian climbs to 3,000ft above the clouds where the air will be smoother. We skim through the top of one fluffy cotton-wool cumulus. I've flown through many clouds but I've never inhaled one before. In the calmer air, I am allowed to take the controls. Because I am in the rear seat, I have to stretch my arms wide and grasp two handles. That first stint at the controls was not relaxing, and sometimes pushing the bar appeared to take all my strength (probably because my brain believed that if I pushed too far I'd fall out of the cockpit!). After a few minutes I started to get the hang of it, trying to feel the movement before it happened, then pushing into it, correcting the angle of flight, then checking back in the opposite direction. When Ian suggested I make a turn, I thought I'd faint but in fact it was much easier actually doing something than being a mere passenger. A couple of times I overcompensated and the nose swung round sharply to the right, following my instinct I then continued to push in the opposite direction. The result was a steeper bank and a pang of panic soon calmed down by Ian. By the time we reached the runway I was shattered.

Ian circled the aerodrome a couple of times and once again, as we dropped to about 500ft, my fears evaporated. The landing was smooth, effortless and with a great sense of relief I entered the club ops room for a cup of tea and to listen to the war stories and general flying chit-chat. Although Ian was the only person actually flying, there were four other men chin-wagging away. One of them was George Cooke, a sprightly seventy-six, an RAF ground staff veteran who had always yearned to fly. He took up hang-gliding in 1979, bought an engine to fit under his wing, and by 1989 he was skilled enough to help an over 60s team fly a two-seater around the British Isles. He has also survived a broken back after a crash landing caused primarily by the sudden downdraft from a military Chinook helicopter. Moorland pilots are a tough breed and George certainly wasn't going to stop flying (another pilot based there who is confined to a wheelchair has modified his controls so he can fly his own microlight) or indeed talking about it.

DREAMS OF FLIGHT

The next day, after dreams of flying, I returned to Moorland – nominally for Ian to take some photographs with his wing-mounted camera. Attempts to go surfing had been prevented by zero waves, yet the winds off the moor were even more blustery. During the summer, Ian reckons to fly twenty days a month; very low clouds and heavy rain can prevent flying and, while experienced pilots can land in force 6 gales, they prefer not to. Usually on a second training flight Ian would sit in the rear allowing me fuller access to the controls but the conditions – and a returning sense of dread – determined otherwise.

Second time around, everything was smoother – except the conditions which were turbulent and choppy, requiring Ian to be forever making tiny adjustments. 'There's a lot of similarity between the air and the sea,' he said, 'conditions are always changing. The only difference is that you can't see the air. You can only feel it.' We were doing 50° banks over Tintagel and I was sweaty-palmed rather than dripping all over. Flying back, I felt more relaxed but the wind conditions still made it hard work. Above the airfield, Ian took control and decided to demonstrate a landing without power.

Before I could venture an objection, he switched the engine off and took us into a downward spiral. We levelled out 700ft above the ground to slow our rate of descent to the minimum of 450ft a minute. A passing seagull stopped to admire this big and now silent bird and began to imitate our flight patterns, turning and swooping, chattering away until we touched down as smooth as glass.

A perfect case of life imitating art, or was it the other way round? I watched the gull wheel and effortlessly flapping his wings head for the coast, to the sea and Merlin's lair and I wondered whether he could be the reincarnation of a Coastal Command pilot. I already knew their ghosts still lurked here.

Enough fanciful rubbish I decided. So I went inside to drink tea, to hear real tales from men who find their solace not in the pleasures of the earth but in the vastness of the sky.

——— WHO TO CONTACT ———

The British Microlight Aircraft Association (BMAA)
Head Office BMAA
Bullring
Deddington
Banbury
Oxon OX15 0TT

Tel: 01869 338888
Fax: 01869 337116

▶ The BMAA was originally formed as a forum where pilots could interchange ideas on aeroplanes, their capabilities and their safety together with flying and training techniques.

▶ Initially microlighting was a sport with no rules, and no licence was needed to fly, but in 1981 CAA legislation set control and safety standards which rapidly changed the role of the BMAA. It is now a CAA approved organisation that makes recommendations for the issue of Private Pilot's Licences Microlight and the appointment of examiners and instructors. It is a member of the Royal Aero Club and the Federation Aeronautique Internationale, and supported by the Sports Council.

▶ Other benefits of BMAA membership are access to third party and personal accident insurance 'at favourable rates' and various other facilities. Contact them for a directory of clubs and schools, of which there are approximately 125. Also available is a video, *The Dream*, for £6.50.

▶ Be warned, however, that if you are looking for instruction the majority are one-pilot shows and the BMAA are not actually very helpful in recommending particular places. Microlight flying is still a very individual sport, so if that appeals you will have to work for it!

——— WHERE TO GO ———

Company:	Kemble Flying Club
Address:	The Control Tower, Kemble Airfield, Kemble, Cirencester, Glos, GL7 6BA
Tel:	01285 770077 / 0836 591596
Fax:	01285 770888
Facilities:	All types of accommodation available locally. Briefing rooms, kitchen, hot drinks, toilets, payphone. Local B&Bs, cafés, pubs. Corporate entertaining enquiries welcome; gift vouchers. Good disabled access, but ring to discuss beforehand.

Price Range: Air Experience £50 for 30 mins; £76 per hour instruction
Payment Methods: Cash, cheque
Booking Details: 3-4 weeks in advance
Capacity: 1 full-time instructor, 2 regular part-time
Insurance: Passenger/co-pilot must arrange own insurance
Other Notes: David Young has been a flying instructor for 12 years and offers lessons either in a 3 Axis AX3 fixed wing, or a Pegasus Quantum 582 Flex Wing, plus PPG flying lessons (powered paragliders) – prices on application.

Company: **Mercury Flying School**
Address: 7 Bury Lane, Brinscall, Withnell, Lancs PR6 8RX
Tel: 01254 831345 / 03788 862616
Price Range: Taster £30; £60 per hour; £795 for 15 hours
Payment Methods: Cash, cheque
Booking Details: 24 hours
Capacity: Taster flights, groups of 6-12
Facilities: Caravan on-site available; local café; toilets; disabled access; corporate events and gift vouchers.
Other Notes: Fly from Cockerham – a farm strip, both tri-axial and weight-shift. Tony Wells has been flying for 14 years.

Company: **Skylight Aviation School**
Address: 715 Hucknall Road, Nottingham, NG5 1NX
Tel: 01159 626279 / 0850 634624
Price Range: Trial flight £30 for 30 mins; £54 per hour
Payment Methods: Cash, cheque
Booking Details: Day before
Capacity: 1 instructor
Facilities: Portacabin café. Changing rooms/toilets coming soon. T-shirts, badges, gloves etc. on sale. Corporate events organised and gift vouchers available.
Other Notes: Open every day except Mon.

Company: **Somerset Microlights**
Address: 4 Gravelands Lane, Henlade, Taunton, Somerset TA36 5DC
Tel: 01823 442391 / 0836 613544 (airfield)
Price Range: Taster £35 per 30 mins; £64 per hour

Payment Methods: Cash, cheque
Booking Details: Summer weekends 3-4 days, 2 days in week
Capacity: 2 instructors in summer
Facilities: Camping available and local B&Bs. Café, bar and toilets. Corporate events organised using rest of airfield facilities – parachuting, biplanes and conventional aircraft. Gift vouchers.
Other Notes: Also available at Dunkeswell: Devon and Somerset Parachute School and Dawn Patrol, vintage biplane and aerobatic rides.

Company: **Airbourne Aviation**
Address: Popham Airfield, Nr Basingstoke, Hants SO21 3BH
Tel/Fax: 01202 822486
Price Range: Taster £30 for 20 mins flying; £69 per hour
Payment Methods: Cash, cheque, all credit cards
Booking Details: Always check day before for flying conditions
Capacity: 4 instructors with 6 at weekends
Insurance: PA available at £7.50 per day
Facilities: Corporate entertaining; café; toilets; bar; BBQ; light aircraft and helicopter landing site.
Other Notes: Airbourne is the biggest and oldest microlight centre in Britain. It has been in operation for 16 years – Mac Smith bought the second microlight in the country and the BMAA was born at Popham. They fly over 1,000 training flights a year, depending on conditions, and are open from 08.00 until dark every day except Christmas Day. 90 per cent of students are now flying 3-axis microlights, as they will only require a further 17 hours to get a fixed-wing licence. Birthday, wedding and stag party vouchers are available as gifts. They also have autogiros and paramotors (engines strapped on back of paraglider).

Company: **Dragon Aviation**
Address: 3 School Lane, St Martins, Shropshire SY11 3BX
Tel: 01691 774137 / 01691 772659 (airfield)
Price Range: Taster £35 per 35 mins; £55 per hour
Payment Methods: Cash, cheque
Booking Details: Day before
Capacity: 1 instructor

Facilities: Chirk Airfield has café, toilets and car parking.
Other Notes: Ray Everitt flies a 3 Axis Thruster, 7 days a week, all year.

Company: **Flylight Airsports Ltd**
Address: Sywell Aerodrome, Sywell, Northants NN6 0BT
Tel: 01604 494459
Price Range: Trial £35 per half hour; £65 per hour; lessons £60 per hour + club fees
Payment Methods: Cash, cheque
Booking Details: Weekends, one week in advance; weekdays, a few days
Capacity: 3 instructors, 4 school aircraft
Facilities: Hotel, restaurant, toilets, car parking on aerodrome
Other Notes: Open 7 days a week all year. Tuition on both 3 Axis and weight-shift. 70 per cent of students are flying weight-shift machines. Flylight has been in operation for 2 years and flies 1,500-2,000 training hours a year.

Company: **Moorland Flying Club**
Address: Davidstow Aerodrome, Nr Camelford, Cornwall PL32 9YE
Tel: 01840 261517
Fax: 01840 213844
Price Range: £35 for 30-min trial flight; £25 for 20; tuition for licence £59-75 per hour
Payment Methods: Cash, cheque
Booking Details: One week in advance, more in summer
Capacity: 1-3 instructors
Facilities: Basic clubroom; hangarage
Other Notes: Tuition available for both 3-axis and weight-shift microlights.

Company: **Northern Microlight School**
Address: 2 Ashlea Cottage, St Michael's Road, Bilsborrow, Preston, Lancs PR3 ORT
Tel: 01995 640713
Price Range: Taster £27 for 20 mins; £60 per hour lessons
Payment Methods: Cash, cheque
Booking Details: Weekends 7-14 days in advance; midweek 24 hours

Capacity:	1 instructor
Facilities:	St Michaelson Wyre Airfield has toilets.
Other Notes:	Closed Sat and Tues, but flying all year, weather permitting.

Company:	**Old Sarum Microlight Club**
Address:	Hangar 3, Portway, Salisbury, Wiltshire SP4 6BJ
Tel:	01722 322525
Fax:	01722 323702
E-mail:	sarum.flying@dial.pipex.com
Price Range:	£25 taster sessions; £60 per hour
Payment Methods:	Cash, cheques, Visa, Mastercard
Booking Details:	Cancellation fees for bookings cancelled less than 24 hours in advance
Capacity:	On application
Facilities:	Fully-licensed bar and restaurant, disabled access and toilets.
Other Notes:	Also: fixed wing, helicopter training, gift certificates.

Company:	**Pegasus Flight Training**
Address:	Sutton Meadows Airfield, Sutton, Ely, Cambs CB6 2BJ
Tel:	01487 842360 / 0585 173877
Price Range:	Trial lesson £55, 25 mins on the ground, 45 mins flying; £65 per hour flying
Payment Methods:	Cash, cheques
Booking Details:	Minimum of a week
Capacity:	2 instructors
Insurance:	TPL; not PA
Facilities:	Toilets, car parking.
Other Notes:	Pegasus is a franchise, loosely connected to other two centres in Oxfordshire and Gloucestershire.

Company:	**Ulster Microlight Centre**
Address:	16 Cherryhill Gardens, Dundonald, Northern Ireland BT16 0JF
Tel:	01232 481843 / 01247 813327
Price Range:	£25 per half-hour taster; £50 per hour for lessons
Payment Methods:	Cash, cheque
Booking Details:	Week in advance
Capacity:	Solo instructor on weight-shift machine

Facilities:	Ulster Flying Club at Newtonards Airfield has a restaurant, toilets and car parking.
Other Notes:	Summer: 7 days a week; winter all day Sat and Sun, some evenings in daylight.

Company:	**Windsports Training**
Address:	The Control Tower, Wombleton Aerodrome, Kirbymoorside, N. Yorks YO6 5RY
Tel:	01751 433358
Price Range:	£30 for half-hour trial, £60 per hour; lessons £55 per hour; £445 basic course
Payment Methods:	Cash, cheque
Booking Details:	Weekends and evenings a week in advance. Beginners courses run Tues-Fri.
Capacity:	1-3 instructors, depending on demand
Facilities:	Car Parking, clubroom, toilets.
Other Notes:	Open Tues-Sun all year. June-Sept busy period. The oldest microlight training school in the north-east of England.

Company:	**Wright Flight**
Address:	Little Gratton, Stoodleigh, Tiverton, Devon EX16 9PQ
Tel:	01398 351568
Price Range:	Taster £25 for 20 mins; £60 per hour
Payment Methods:	Cash, cheque
Booking Details:	By arrangement
Capacity:	1 instructor, 2 at weekends
Facilities:	Clubhouse at Westonzoyland Airfield
Other Notes:	Open Mon-Sat all year. Flights are weather-dependent.

SKYDIVING

Time is standing still. The only sound in the world is that of a cold wind streaming past my face. Above is a primary blue sky, below a Lincoln green earth, slashed with brown and black. There is no sensation of speed. I am falling towards the ground at 120 miles per hour and I don't care.

Back on the ground, written on paper the very concept of doing a first parachute jump as a free fall from 12,500ft appeared as just a drill, another step towards the conquest of all fear. Fear was the key, expressed by that gnawing void in the pit of the stomach, watching life flash before the eyes, an everlasting bundle of clichés. Or, alternatively, was this free-falling lark just an exercise in machismo from a man in his late thirties raging against the dying of the light, a desperate attempt to recapture being adventurous by scaring myself out of my jumpsuit?

Falling 1,000ft every 5 seconds is exhilarating. Terror is cast away, three 'chutes into the wind. So I go through the practice routines, three times I put my hand on to the rip-cord handle, three times my right hand goes back out in my feeble attempt at the skydiver's arched star. I go into my second 'Circle of Awareness'. I glance below me at this speckled carpet that purports to be the ground, my altimeter reads 7,500ft, I mouth this to my secondary instructor Dave Spencer, glance at Pete Allum on my right. He indicates I should straighten my legs.

I relax. I feel at perfect peace. My head is miles away from reality, when someone rudely starts to tug at my shoulder. Deep in the recesses of my dinosaur brain I know this should mean something. Something about pulling a rip cord. It doesn't matter, I'm enjoying myself, it'll come back to me in another 10 or 15 seconds. Except that in another 15 seconds I will be only 1,500ft above the ground and in serious danger.

Accelerated Free Fall (AFF) Training was introduced to Britain by Headcorn Parachute Club back in January 1985. Until AFF, skydivers could only progress through a series of static line jumps. They would start by jumping out of a plane – or a tethered balloon – at 2,000ft with a line attached that opens the chute automatically and progress towards free fall over a period of 50-100 jumps. That has changed now and a Free Fall Level 8 parachutist is able to jump alone but has to be supervised by an instructor, both in the plane and on the ground, until he has successfully completed 10 consolidation jumps (£33 each).

The state-of-the-art equipment – each trainee rig costs £3,000 – is thankfully packed full of fail safes. On the first jump, the student is flanked by two instructors who can each pull the rip cord if the student cannot – or will not. If everything goes wrong, the pack is equipped with a barometric pressure gauge that will automatically deploy the reserve chute at 2,000ft.

My plummeting reverie is rudely interrupted by Pete Allum, thrusting my head into my chest. My altimeter reads 4,500ft. My brain freezes, both hands fall to my sides in a gesture of supplication. My balance gone, instantly I start to flip over in a back loop. I hear what might be a curse, feel a rip at my side, look down to see two bodies hundreds of feet below me. I look up not into blue sky but a huge blue canopy.

I feel an idiot. I have forgotten the essential part of my training. Pulling the rip cord.

DIRT DIVING

It had all seemed so easy during 'dirt diving' – the intensive 6 hours of ground training Pete Allum puts all students through before their first free fall. Again and again he would pump questions, different danger scenarios at us.

'You look above your head and all you see is a bag of washing,' he snaps. This means that my main chute has not opened properly. Unless I do something about it, when I deploy my small reserve chute it too will get tangled up and send me hurtling on a one-way rendezvous with Mother Earth. 'What do you do?'

With my right hand I peel the yellow cut away grip from the velcro. Simultaneously, my left hand and thumb have hooked on to the reserve chute handle. My right hand pushes, the left punches. In an emergency this would 'cut away' the main parachute and release the reserve. Two days later my wife is rudely awakened by me ripping off the duvet cover and punching her in the side.

Pete Allum is a bouncy man with piercing, bright blue eyes and the jaunty confidence that is the mark of the adventure instructor. The secondary jump master is Dave Spencer, a former HALO (High Altitude/Low Opening) instructor in the army. He has jumped from 47,000ft wearing oxygen and free fallen for 4 minutes before opening the chute at about 1,500ft. When it's for real, the HALO boys do it at night.

————— WAITING TO FALL —————

The waiting is the hardest part. Training complete, we have to wait for a large enough gap in the clouds. Naturally, the English summer reverts to type. We wait for an endless afternoon, the next morning, then a couple more hours. Skydivers have to learn infinite patience, to wait without seeming to wait.

The weekend before my jump there had been two parachute accidents. A charity jumper had been killed in rather strange circumstances after getting tangled up in a helicopter's rotors and a skydiver was seriously injured. For some reason this does not worry me, maybe it's because I've bought into the statistics that say parachuting is one of the very safest adventure sports. More likely it's that I have absolute confidence in the two jump masters who will be in control of my life. Without that trust, wild mustangs would not drag me onto a plane.

Suddenly the infinite waiting is over. My name is called. Within 2 minutes I'm in a jumpsuit, radio strapped to my waist. I'm crammed into the back of a small plane with my two instructors and five other jumpers. As it climbs slowly towards the right altitude, my stomach tenses. It is cold sitting there with the door open. The other jumpers drop first at 10,000ft. We continue to climb. Then we're 2½ miles above the ground and my time has come.

I move to the door, held by both instructors. The wind is buffeting me, telling me it is time to fall into the void. I don't want to go, I can't go, my hands are holding on to the sides of the door. 'Oh shit,' I say, or think, or scream and I just let go, tumble out, forgetting all those training dummy runs. I fall and roll and I open my eyes, somehow straighten myself out, look down and see the ground. But at that height it is meaningless, there is no definition, no visual clues to alert myself to the pull of gravity. Once Pete and Dave have flown in and attached themselves to me, we free fall together but because we are all travelling at the same speed there is no sensation of falling. Which is why 60 per cent of first-time free fallers simply forget to pull their rip cord.

Floating down under the canopy is a relative anticlimax after the adrenaline rush of the free fall. It is all over so quickly, maybe 50 seconds in the air, followed by 4 minutes under the wing, talked down by the instructors who have already landed. It's easy enough to control direction and air speed and while I come into the ground a little fast, a couple of feet too high, I still do not fall over. The impact is no worse than jumping off a table. I'm cross about losing it, about failing to open the 'chute but that niggle is lost inside the whole experience.

My body may be subject to the laws of gravity but my head is somewhere else entirely, still up in the clouds. I'm as high as a kite – for the next two days. Driving back to London hours later, I have visual flashbacks, accompanied by physical memories, every few minutes. My stomach balls up, my palms get sweaty, I keep seeing the ground coming up before my eyes. It's like a powerful addictive drug, one that I have to take again. If only to see whether I actually enjoyed it or not.

Somehow I never have. I made that jump several years ago. I wish I'd gone back down that summer and completed the AFF course. Headcorn is still there and flourishing but Pete Allum now lives in the States where he trains four-way competition teams. Parachute technology has advanced and static line jumpers now use identical equipment to AFF students – the square wing chutes which give more control and make for softer landings. Those who just want the free fall experience are encouraged to opt for a tandem jump where they are physically attached to the instructor – it may be cheaper for the schools that way but I think it also cheapens the sensation.

All summer while I partook in new adventure sports, I promised I would go back down and do another free fall. This time I would get it right. And somehow I always found an excuse not to go. The idea both attracts and repels, exhilarates and terrifies me. That first jump still ranks as the greatest, most intense, sensory experience of my life. Even years later, there are summer days with a clear blue sky when I look up and my palms go all sweaty. I look up and feel myself up there again – not falling, but flying.

WHO TO CONTACT

The British Parachute Association (BPA)
Wharf Way
Glen Parva
Leicester LE2 9TF

Tel: 0116 2785271
Fax: 0116 277662

▶ **The BPA was founded in 1962 to organise, govern and further the advancement of Sport Parachuting in the United Kingdom. Its aim today is to encourage participation and promote excellence at all levels of skydiving.**

▶ **There are currently 35 affiliated parachute clubs throughout the country with over 25,000 members.**

▶ **The BPA represents the majority of British skydivers. It is funded by subscriptions, shop sales and Sports Council Grants and has an annually elected council of 15 full members who control all aspects of skydiving on behalf of the CAA (Civil Aviation Authority).**

▶ **Clubs vary from full-time professional centres to weekend clubs run on a part-time basis, offering standard courses for students. Courses are all taught by approved BPA instructors and follow specific BPA procedures.**

———— WHERE TO GO ————

Company: **Headcorn Parachute Centre**
Address: Headcorn Aerodrome, Headcorn, Kent TN27 9HX
Tel: 01622 890862
Fax: 01622 890641
Price Range: Static line round £105 (Tues); £120 (Sat); static line square £185 (midweek); £195 (weekends); tandem jump £180; AFF £1,250
Payment Methods: Cash, cheque, major credit cards
Booking Details: 1 month in advance
Capacity: Depends on course
Facilities: Accommodation available both on-site and locally. On-site canteen. Changing facilities and toilets available but basic. Gift/equipment shop. Limited disabled access. Corporate events organised.
Other Notes: Open weekdays 09.00-dusk; weekends 08.30-dusk. Slipstream Adventures (Tel: 01622 890862) also offer one-on-one AFF training.

Company: **Cornwall Parachute Club**
Address: Fran's Ranch, Old Naval Airfield, St Ervan, Nr Wadebridge, Cornwall PL27 7RT
Tel: 01841 540691
Price Range: Static line square £125; tandem £145
Payment Methods: Cash, cheque
Booking Details: 1 month in advance
Capacity: 12 students per instructor, 18 for 2 instructors
Facilities: Local B&Bs and camping; coffee bar and snacks; toilets. Corporate events. Gift vouchers.
Other Notes: Open weekends 08.00-sunset; Wed and Fri 13.00-sunset.

Company: **North West Parachute Centre**
Address: Cark Airfield, Flookburgh, Nr Grange-over-Sands, Cumbria
Tel: 015395 58672 / 01772 336337 (weekdays)
Price Range: Static line round £100; static line square £150 (£25 per additional jump). Group discounts.
Payment Methods: Cash, cheque
Booking Details: 1 month in advance
Insurance: PA available at extra cost, sign medical form
Facilities: Local B&B; café, toilets and showers on-site.

Gift/equipment shop. Corporate events organised occasionally.

Other Notes: Open weekends and Bank Holidays; midweek by arrangement.

Company: **Skydive Scotland**
Address: The Parachute Centre, Errol Airfield, Grange Errol, PH2 7TB
Tel: 01821 642673
Fax: 01821 642004
Price Range: Static round £99; static square £140; tandem £16; AFF negotiable
Payment Methods: Cash, cheque
Booking Details: 1 month in advance
Facilities: Bunkhouse with showers. Canteen and sitting rooms; toilets; gift shop. Disabled access. Corporate activities up to 250. Gift vouchers.
Other Notes: Open Fri-Sun.

Company: **Stirling Parachute Centre**
Address: Thornhill, Nr Stirling, Scotland FK8 3QT
Tel: 01786 870788
Fax: 01786 870748
Price Range: Weekend course static line £105; midweek £85; apply for tandem price and group discounts
Payment Methods: Cash, cheque
Booking Details: Call centre
Facilities: Catering, changing, shower, toilet facilities available.
Other Notes: Open weekends and some midweeks.

Company: **The Black Knights Parachute Centre**
Address: Patty's Farm, Hillam Lane, Cockerham, Lancashire LA2 0DY
Tel: 0151 924 5560 / 01524 791820 (weekends)
Price Range: Tandem jump (price on application); static line round jump £100 (additional jumps £20); static line square £150 (additional £28)
Payment Methods: Cash, cheque
Booking Details: 2-4 weeks
Capacity: 25-30 students
Insurance: Extra personal protection can be arranged
Facilities: On-site bunkhouse. Also B&B. Canteen, shower

Other Notes: and toilets. Groups by arrangement. Gift vouchers. Open weekends and Bank Holidays only.

Company: **Wild Geese Skydive Centre**
Address: Movenis Airfield, 116 Carrowreagh Road, Garvagh, Coleraine, Co Londonderry BT51 5LQ
Tel: 012665 58609
Fax: 012665 57050
Price Range: Tandem £125; static line round £80; static line square £120; 6-jump square course £200
Payment Methods: Cash, cheque
Booking Details: At least 2 weeks in advance
Facilities: Bunk-bed accommodation (36). On-site catering; changing; showers; toilets. Corporate events.
Other Notes: Courses run weekends, although other days may be arranged if numbers justify.

Company: **Border Parachute Centre**
Address: Brunton Airfield, Chathill, Northumberland NE67 5ER
Tel: 01665 589000
Price Range: Static line round £99; static line square £135; tandem £200; AFF (8 jumps) on application.
Payment Methods: Cash, cheque, major credit cards, postal orders
Booking Details: As much advance booking as possible but will take late bookings.
Facilities: Local B&B/bunkhouse facilities. Toilets (suitable for disabled). Parking. Corporate events organised.
Other Notes: BPA Advanced and Approved Instructors. The Centre, 40 miles north of Newcastle, has been in operation for 25 years, and is situated on Brunton Airfield, an old RAF base (which they still use as a target area for trainee pilots to attack). It has 3 runways, which means parachuting can take place regardless of wind direction. The Northumberland coastline is very beautiful with plenty of other activities available locally including scuba diving and hill walking.

Company: **British Parachute Schools**
Address: The Control Tower, Langar Airfield, Langar, Nottingham, NG13 9HY

Tel: 01949 860878
Fax: 01949 860878
Price Range: Tandem skydive £150; static line round jump £115; static line square jump £165; AFF Course (8 jumps) £1,350
Payment Methods: Cash, cheque, credit cards
Booking Details: Up to 4 weeks
Capacity: Different courses have different restrictions – phone to check
Insurance: You will have to sign a declaration of fitness
Facilities: Gift vouchers; local accommodation; canteen and bar facilities; toilets (suitable disabled) and shower facilities; specialist parachute shop plus T-shirts etc.
Other Notes: You have to be a member of the BPA. The BPS is based in the scenic Vale of Belvoir, 12 miles east of Nottingham. Originally built as a bomber base in World War Two, Langar Airfield – which covers some 1,750,000 sq.m. – is now one of the largest civilian drop zones in the UK. The school has been in operation since 1977 and makes around 17,000 jumps a year. It is a full-time school, open 7 days a week every day of the year – except for Christmas Day – as even jumpers believe in Santa Claus. Jumpers should be careful to check that their weight is within the guidelines given in the brochure.

Company: **British Skysports Paracentre**
Address: East Leys Farm, Grindale, Bridlington, East Yorkshire YO16 4YB
Tel: 01262 677367 / 0836 276188
Price Range: Static line square £159; tandem £140; AFF £1,340
Payment Methods: Cash, cheque
Booking Details: Month in advance
Facilities: Corporate entertaining; gift vouchers; camping and local B&B; canteen; toilet and shower facilities on-site – access for disabled under review. Shop with T-shirts etc.
Other Notes: Open 7 days a week 08.00-dusk.

Company: **Devon and Somerset Parachute School**
Address: 30 Tower Way, Dunkeswell, Nr Honiton Devon EX14 0XR

Tel/Fax:	01404 891690
Price Range:	Tandem jump £145; square static line £135; AFF £1,145
Payment Methods:	Cash, cheque, major credit cards
Booking Details:	Best 2 months in advance, but can do with 3 days' notice
Capacity:	Static line, 12; tandem, 10; AFF, 3
Insurance:	BPA, TPL; sign fitness declaration
Facilities:	Local B&B. Airfield café, bar, showers and toilet. Will accommodate any groups.
Other Notes:	Check opening times with club. Founded in 1992, the six instructors have an average of over 2,600 jumps each, while chief instructor Andy Guest has logged 3,750 jumps while participating in seven world record and 17 British record events.

Company:	**Oxon and Northants Parachute Centre**
Address:	Hinton-in-the-Hedges Airfield, Steane, Nr Brackley, Northants NN13 5NS
Tel:	01384 393373 / 0850 762349
Price Range:	Tandem jump £160; static line square £155; static line round £115
Payment Methods:	Cash, cheque
Booking Details:	2-4 weeks in advance
Facilities:	Training based in local village hall. Food provided on courses. Some corporate courses.
Other Notes:	Open weekends and midweek by arrangement during summer.

Company:	**Peterborough Parachute Centre**
Address:	Sibson Airfield, Wansford, Peterborough, PE8 6NE
Tel:	01832 280490
Fax:	01832 280409
Price Range:	Static line round £105 (midweek); £120 (weekend); tandem £160
Payment Methods:	Cash, cheque, Visa, Mastercard (not Amex)
Booking Details:	Tandem week in advance, more for courses
Capacity:	30 students per course with 4 instructors
Insurance:	BPA TPL; arrange own PA
Facilities:	Sibson Airfield has café and bar; loos; showers and on-site bunkhouse accommodation/camping. Local B&Bs.
Other Notes:	Open Tues-Sun all year except Christmas. The club

should be running RAPS (square chutes) courses by 1997. Contact for details. For accelerated free fall contact The Free-Fall Company, Tel: 01832 280055, Fax: 01832 280409) which is run by Pete Allum and Kevin McCarthy who offer various packages. Pete is an excellent teacher who took me for my first jump.

PART 5
EXTREME

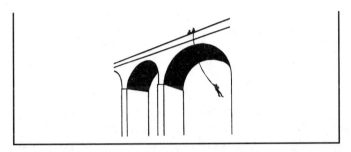

BRIDGESWINGING
AND ZIP WIRE

Yes, I have finally found something I am not going to do. An activity that does not send a surge of adrenaline coursing through my body. Instead it sends a surge of such terror that I cannot move my feet. My brain says 'go'. My feet reply something uncouth along the lines of sex and travel. My toes curl up inside my boots as if they were preparing to take root, turn me into another tree along the cliff edge. All it takes is a leap of faith.

I was all right last time. Then I had something to clutch on to, a peg upon which to hang my fears, a strap between my face and the drop. This time there is nothing. 'Take your hands off the rope. Now!' commands Mad Jeff. 'The pulley will take your fingers off. Just walk over the edge. Two steps. Go!' I can't. My legs won't obey me. I stand frozen, an eternity passes, galaxies are born and die until a small boy behind me asks 'Mum is he ever going to go? It's my turn next.'

Once you are clipped on to the zip wire pulley there is no turning back, only a step forward into the chasm. The water 60m below is azure blue, a Mediterranean colour but an arctic temperature. It might be 30 metres deep at the central point but if you fall that far you are a dead man – perhaps that's why this is no longer called the Death Slide, reverse psychology at play here. The finish is 100m away, another clifftop with crumbling slates underfoot and a reassuringly large tree to embed myself in. I know it's safe, I know the brake works. I've done it once already and I've seen dozens try it. My brain knows that I am attached to a climbing harness by a carabiner at the small of my back. I can't see it, but I know it's there. So why won't my bloody legs move?

Here goes nothing. I don't know how or why but my legs suddenly worked. I might even have started to run. Two paces and there's nothing, no ground, just air, followed by a drop that might be 10ft, might be less, might be more, but it's enough to drive the pit of my stomach into my gullet and make me start breathing again. My eyes are open wide, probably because I want to see my last moments on this planet. Whap, the slack is taken up, my arms click out to the side, my legs out behind me. I am flying at 45mph. Straight at a tree.

For how long? I have no idea – 2,3,4,5 seconds? – just eternity trapped in no time at all. I see the water, memorise every crack on the cliff face. I must scream but I cannot find my mouth. My jaw has locked it open. The tree is coming towards me I can see the brake. I break all the rules and grab it. 'No, no,' yells Alec Greening, 'that's dangerous.' I don't care. I don't want to attain some reverse momentum and catapult back over the water. I'm alive and I'm staying that way. I've been Superman for a few seconds and nobody is getting me on that thing dangling upside-down from an ankle strap. No one.

A CURE FOR VERTIGO

Alec Greening specialises in leaps of faith. In 1984, when drinking at the Wheatsheaf Inn in Brigsteer, Cumbria, one of his mates, William Branchini, confessed to suffering from terrible vertigo – which somewhat limited his earning capacity as a builder. Alec, a former teacher and qualified climber and potholer, set out to develop something that would help Branchini overcome his fear of heights and provide everybody else with an adrenaline surge. He came up with bridgeswinging, and so the Brigsteer Bridgeswingers Club was born.

Twelve years and 4,000 different swingers later, I am standing on a disused railway bridge just outside Sedbergh. The waters are bubbling past 65ft beneath me – and I can see it clearly because most of the bridge flooring has rotted away. It is 7pm on August Bank Holiday Saturday. Naturally enough it is pissing with rain. Because it is raining – and has been for days – the water level is rising so I am going to have to clamber through the railings and rest my feet on a ledge 4ft below the parapet. On the count of three, I will push myself out backwards as hard as I can. I will fall and then the rope threaded underneath the bridge and anchored by Alec on the far side will swing me through and high in the air on the other side. If I choose to go upside-down and stretch my hands above my head, they will be about 2ft above the water and I will be travelling at over 30mph.

Milliseconds, and a half-screamed, half-strangled but very audible obscenity later, and I am swinging high at the apex of my first arc. I don't know how I got there but it's fun, playing Tarzan as a grown up, brushing the trees, shrieking with delight, swinging back and forth until it is time for Alec to let out some slack and deposit me in the arms of the waiting catchers.

'The second time is tougher,' Dave tells me. Dave is a local Cumbrian with a shaved head, a body that wins tattoo competitions, the sort of guy who knows no fear. 'My first jump was off a higher bridge. I got ready for the second jump and I simply couldn't go. I had to climb off the railing.' Thanks, Dave, I really appreciate that.

In fact, the worst part of my second swing was waiting on top of the bridge while the heavens opened and soaked me to the skin. It was, Alec confided later over several pints of bitter, one of the worst evening's swinging ever. Sometimes when the sun is shining, as many as a hundred people will turn up to take part or just to gawp or maybe set up a barbecue. They use other, higher bridges too, which require a much more positive jump out; if you don't take up all the slack with your first leap it will jar the back and is not recommended for those with any form of back problem. The higher the bridge, the more time you have to fall and the higher the swing.

SCREAMS OF VIRGINS

There is no membership fee to join the Brigsteer Bridgeswingers Club. Swing once, zip wire once, and you are a lifetime member. You don't need skills, just faith and courage. If you are going to play with the Bridgeswingers, you have to have absolute faith in the system. Just because it is an amateur operation – Alec charges nothing for bridgeswinging, a nominal £1 a go on the zip wire and consistently refuses to cash in on his activities – does not mean that the approach is amateur. The angles of the swings have all been worked out mathematically and the first guinea pigs were bags of potatoes, while the ropes are only used a few times to make sure they maintain elasticity. The pulley used in the zip wire is tested up to 9,500kg, enough to support a baby elephant (though he would make a mess of the tree at the other side). Each of the two static ropes is tested to 5,500kg and will only be used six times. Both have been given to Alec by the RAF Mountain Rescue Service. In addition to the brake rope at the far side of the quarry, there is also a trailing back rope that can be used as an emergency brake.

The setting for the zip wire is stunning. Hodge Close near Tiberthwaite is a dead end, a 2-mile drive off the Windermere-Coniston road, down a small tarmac track through beautiful woodland where the moss and mushrooms flourish. The site takes the breath away, a simultaneous punch in the gut and an admiring wow! For 200 years, until the late 1950s, it was a slate quarry but now nature is fast reclaiming it, as the trees grow and the undergrowth creeps down the shallower inclines. Cut sheer by generations, the cliffs plunge into the water, which can be reached by a walk down through another quarry, ending in a spectacular arch through which you can hear the screams of the zip wire virgins as they hurtle across the abyss 200ft up in the air.

A FAMILY DAY OUT

On Bank Holidays, people from all walks of life, all classes and religions make their pilgrimages to Hodge Close from all over the country, even the World. Reactions do vary. Diane comes regularly from Newcastle by way of Blackpool with her mum, husband and four children. She loves it and quite happily brings her four-year-old son, Daniel, attached in his own harness, across with her, while her older son comes across on his own displaying far more sang-froid than I ever did. Alec and Tina hail from Zimbabwe and are quite happy to hang from an ankle strap. Clare and Len, who have twin four-year-old boys, have come up from Essex as a surprise treat for Len. Len, who really wants to learn to free fall, knows no fear, throwing himself off bridges one evening and zip wiring upside-down the next day. Clare gamely has one go on the wire, her screams bounce off the walls, and her knees are still shaking half an hour later. 'Once is enough,' she says. Katya, a mediaeval art expert from Bulgaria, thinks it's wonderful; her husband, photographer Matthew Ford, goes pale green and very quiet.

EVEN MORE EXTREME

Dave, the living work of tattoo art, prefers zip wiring to bridgeswinging but he loves rap diving most of all. 'It's the best,' he enthuses, after a zip wire descent that saw him running off the cliff face-first, hooking his feet around the cord and flying upside down, posing like a man possessed. 'You'll love rap diving,' he tells me. As I am still speechless from my face-first descent, he takes the strangled gulp as affirmative. I'm wondering whether fainting would be an acceptable option. Is there no limit to this insanity?

It appears not. Weather permitting, once the zip wire is up and running, Alec, Mad Jeff and other bridgeswinging climbers will rig up some more exotic forms of thrill seeking – bicycle abseiling, rap diving and Tyrolean traversing – to stimulate even the most jaded adrenaline glands. Tyrolean traversing is sometimes known as a monkey crawl and involves two ropes about a metre apart and straight across the quarry. One arm and one leg are hooked around each rope and you inch forward in a crawling motion. (One year a couple of ten-year-old boys had managed to tangle the back brake rope in a root, got stuck half-way across the zip wire and did not have enough weight to get any more forward momentum. Alec had to crawl up and rescue them.)

Bicycle abseiling looks spectacular. Using the petzl stop, a variable friction device, a mountain cyclist can ride down a sheer cliff face in control of his rate of descent. The petzl stop is attached to the abseil rope, which is attached to both man and machine. Rap diving (short for rapid diving) is also a variant on abseiling, except you run down cliffs face forward, going as fast as possible. The adrenaline rush is reportedly extra extreme because you, the rap diver, are completely dependent on the second man standing at the bottom in charge of the ropes. He controls both speed and braking, so if you don't trust the brake man, don't do it. Last year Dave did his rap dive so fast and the friction it created was so extreme that Alec, the brake man, burnt his hand on the metal clips.

Alas for Dave, Len and all the other fearless adrenaline seekers, today there will be no further games. There have been showers all day and now the heavens are threatening a deluge that will make the sides of the quarry wet, slick and lethal. Regretfully, Alec decides to call it a day just after 4pm. Personally I am not unhappy at this news, my courage bottle is nearly empty and needs extra alcohol to fill up again.

'Last one,' he shouts over the quarry as the rain starts. Alec from Zimbabwe whizzes over, grinning from ear to ear. 'Hold on,' he says, 'There's a bunch of Indians just turned up.' This is not a figure of speech, a group of Asians from Birmingham have just appeared and one wants to have a bash. His screams should have been recorded as performance art. He wants all his friends to have a go.

'This is how it goes on,' grins Alec, 'They'll tell all their mates and next Bank Holiday someone new will turn up. I don't need to advertise, the word just keeps on spreading. It might be a couple of years but you'll be back up here again.'

———— WHO TO CONTACT ————

▶ The Brigsteer Bridgeswingers Club was formed by Alec Greening in 1984. It is still based at the Wheatsheaf Inn in Brigsteer, Cumbria.

▶ There are over 1,000 members. It is a club only in the loosest sense of the word as it has no rules, membership fees or hierarchy. If you have bridgeswung, zip wired, or done any of the other 'activities', you are a member.

▶ Events are chosen by requests from members, or suggestions from Alec. Alec is also a qualified mountain guide who will take groups climbing, caving or set up other adventurous pursuits to your own specifications.

———— WHERE TO GO ————

Company:	**Brigsteer Bridgeswingers Club**
Address:	Holeslack Cottage, Helsington, Kendal, Cumbria LA8 8AQ
Tel:	01539 561214
Price Range:	£1 per zip wire
Payment Methods:	Cash
Booking Details:	Contact Alec Greening
Insurance:	Own risk
Facilities:	Local B&B; parking. Corporate events organised.
Other Notes:	Bridgeswinging takes place from various bridges at different times, depending on demand and weather conditions. The zip wire is set up at Hedge Close from 11.00 on the Sunday of every May and August Bank Holiday and on an unspecified day between Christmas and New Year. Rap diving and bicycle abseiling also take place depending on the weather. Climbing harnesses are provided. If you have your own, bring it and plenty of courage.

Company:	**Oxford Stunt Factory**
Address:	27 Latimer Grange, Latimer Road, Oxford, OX3 7PQ
Tel:	01865 750846
Fax:	01865 311189

See page 198 (bungee jumping) for details

MULTI-ACTIVITY LISTINGS

A great many of the centres listed in this book also offer other activities. Watersports centres may offer dinghy sailing, canoeing, windsurfing and water-skiing, while the multi-activity weekend is particularly popular at centres like Rock Lea. If you wish to try any activity beyond a quick taster session, do make sure that the body is recognised by the relevant national organisation.

Companies already listed in this book:

The Outdoor Trust See page 21 (windsurfing)
Ardclinis Activity Centre See page 23 (windsurfing)
Calshot Activities Centre See page 24 (windsurfing)
Clywid Outdoors See page 114 (white water rafting)
Croft-Na-Caber See page 114 (white water rafting)
Current Trends See page 115 (white water rafting)
Edale YHA Activity Centre See page 125 (caving)
Open Door Outdoor Activities Centre See page 136 (climbing)
Outdoor Adventure See page 26 (windsurfing)
Outer Limits See page 137 (climbing)
Rock Lea Activity Centre See page 126 (caving)
St George's House Christian Outdoor Centre See page 92 (surfing)
Twr-y-Felin Outdoor Centre See page 93 (surfing)

Also:

Company:	**Skern Lodge**
Address:	Appledore, Bideford, Devon EX39 1NG
Tel:	01237 475 992
Price Range:	Weekend: £100 inc accommodation and insurance; Activity Days £20; half-days £12
Payment Methods:	Cash, cheque, Visa, Access, Amex
Booking Details:	As much as possible (groups); 2-4 weeks (individs)
Capacity:	150
Facilities:	Accommodation and catering available. Changing rooms, showers, toilets.
Other Notes:	Multi-activities include: surfing, canoeing, archery, climbing, abseiling, assault courses.

Reader's Report Form

Future editions of this book will be improved if you write with your comments, letting us know of any experiences, good or bad, that you have with any of the companies listed in the book, or any other company offering similar services. We'd be glad to know of any other recommendations for activities, or companies to include in the guide, too.

Send your comments to:

Metro Publishing Ltd
19 Gerrard Street
London W1V 7LA

Daring Days Out Report Form

To the author

From my own experience, I would like to make the following comments/recommendations:

Activity: ....

Company Name: ....

Company address: ....

....

Comments: ....

....

....

....

Your Name: ....

Your Address: ....

....

....

The UK Bungee Club
Adrenalin Village, Chelsea Bridge, London
2 BUNGEE JUMPS FOR THE PRICE OF 1
on presentation of this voucher.

For full details, call 0171 720 9496.

Terms and conditions: This offer is valid until 1 October 1997 and applies to a maximum of 2 people. Fulfilment of this offer is the sole responsibility of the supplier. Subject to availability.

Outer Limits
Pwll-y-Garth, Penmachno, Gwynedd, North Wales
10% DISCOUNT on any choice of activity
on presentation of this voucher.

For full details, contact Chris Butler on 01690 760 248.

Terms and conditions: This offer is valid until 1 October 1998. Fulfilment of this offer is the sole responsibility of the supplier. Subject to availability.

Virgin Balloon Flights
54, Linhope Street, London
10% DISCOUNT on pleasure flights; 20% DISCOUNT on City Skyline flights on presentation of this voucher. Free club membership included upon booking.

For full details, contact Virgin Balloon Flights on 0171 706 1021.

Terms and conditions: This offer is valid until December 1998 and applies to a maximum of 2 people. Fulfilment of this offer is the sole responsibility of the supplier. Subject to availability.

Jet Ski UK Limited
Lake 11, Cotswold Water Park, Near Cirencester, Gloucestershire
10% DISCOUNT on a half-hour jet ski session (including full tuition, wetsuit, buoyancy aid and helmet) on presentation of this voucher.

For full details, contact Andy Archer on 01285 861 345.

Terms and conditions: This offer is valid until 30 September 1998 and applies to a maximum of 2 people. Fulfilment of this offer is the sole responsibility of the supplier. Subject to availability.

Outdoor Adventure
Widemouth Bay, Nr Bude, Cornwall
10% DISCOUNT on any surfing or windsurfing weekend, 3 day break or full week on presentation of this voucher.

For full details, call Lisa Gregory on 01288 361 312.

Terms and conditions: This offer is valid until 10 November 1997 and applies to a maximum of 2 people. Fulfilment of this offer is the sole responsibility of the supplier. Subject to availability.

Reader's Report Form

Future editions of this book will be improved if you write with your comments, letting us know of any experiences, good or bad, that you have with any of the companies listed in the book, or any other company offering similar services. We'd be glad to know of any other recommendations for activities, or companies to include in the guide, too.

Send your comments to:

Metro Publishing Ltd
19 Gerrard Street
London W1V 7LA

Daring Days Out Report Form

To the author

From my own experience, I would like to make the following comments/recommendations:

Activity: ....

Company Name: ....

Company address: ....

....

Comments: ....

....

....

....

Your Name: ....

Your Address: ....

....

....